THE TEN COMMANDMENTS OF MAXIMALISM

1 Curate Curate Curate
There, you see, by adding two more 'curates'
I've curated that commandment perfectly.

2 Do what thou wilt
Do do that voodoo that you do so well.
Trust in thee, just in thee...

3 A chatty room is a happy room
Keep the conversation going with your shizzle – if it
starts to bore or refuses to speak, it's time to move on.

4 Balancing act
Symmetry is symmetry but asymmetry is Jedi.

5 Don't be at home to cat lady
Never use 'within easy reach' as a
reason to have stuff in your space.

6 Screw the neighbours
...And I leave it to you to decide how.

7 Avoid half-cooked at all costs
Maximalism lives for total commitment.

8 Sin is in
It's up to you to decide what's naughty and what's nice.

9 Let the gin begin
Never be too sobre.

10 Comfort is king
We all love a cushion for the pushin'.

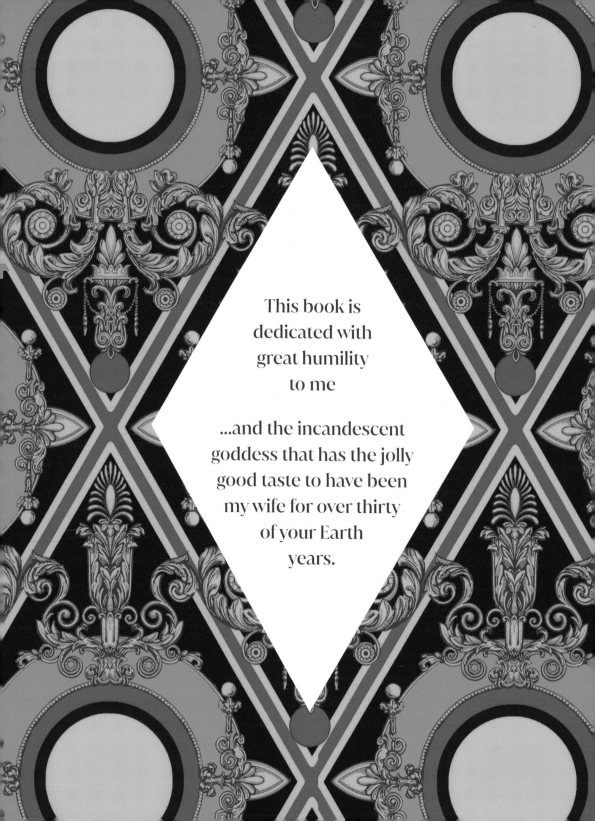

This book is
dedicated with
great humility
to me

...and the incandescent
goddess that has the jolly
good taste to have been
my wife for over thirty
of your Earth
years.

Laurence Llewelyn-Bowen

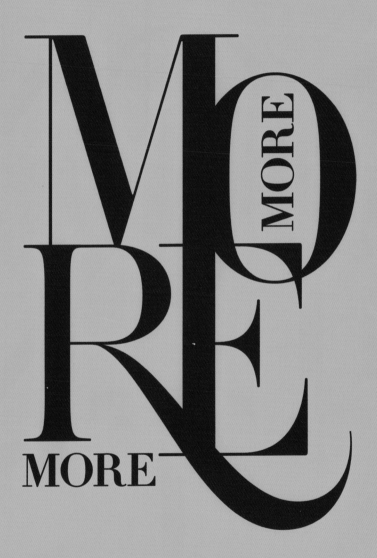

Making Maximalism work in your home and life

CONTENTS

A Manifesto for Maximalism

I need you all to
understand something
from the get-go, and that is...

ABANDON TAUPE ALL YE WHO ENTER HERE...

I want you to see this book as a safe place. A place where what John Betjeman called 'ghastly good taste' finds no succour. There'll be no judgement and no awkwardness about trends, fashions or fads. Instead, a gorgeous, glorious celebration of the known world's most magnificent, munificent design philosophy... Maximalism.

Exactly what the jinkies is Maximalism?

Maximalism gets its name, rather simplistically, from the fact it's the heroic antithesis of Minimalism. In superhero terms, Captain Maximal is locked in perpetual conflict with his arch-nemesis, the evil and malodorous Dr. Minimalisto.

Although simply defining this extraordinarily wonderful way of living as a mere opposite to something ugly doesn't come close to expressing Maximalism's beatific glory. *More More More* is so very much more more more than that.

Now be brave, it's time to meet the enemy. If Maximalism is anti-Minimalism, what's Minimalism and how does one avoid it?

Minimalism was a curious refinement of twentieth-century Modernism, where interiors were starved by force until they damn near expired of glamorexia. The point was to prove to yourself, and your poor battered home, that you were the boss. All those crazy byproducts of existence, like mess, fuss, clutter and love, were to be sacrificed on the altar of clean lines and "less is more".

Now here's something hilarious. Less is more, which was the fridge-magnet slogan of Modernism, doesn't actually mean less is more. In fact, it means more is more. We first meet it as a phrase in the 1855 poem *Andrea Del Sarto*, which was penned by the floppy-locked poet Robert Browning. In it, he uses the term 'less is more' to convey the fact that those fabulously talented yet super show-offy Venetian painters used minimal effort for maximal effect. Literally the opposite of Minimalism, where maximal effort is used for minimal effect.

In Italy today, *sprezzatura* means maximum impact with minimal (seeming) effort. It may as well mean Maximalism.

Five paragraphs in and I've already whooped the opposition's bony ass.

Less is more, albeit a misquote and an accidental antiphrasis, becomes one of the most over-used slogans of the twentieth century and is nearly always erroneously attributed to mid-century Modernist Mies van der Rohe. Young and impressionable master Mies fell in with a group of ranty young designers who together formed the Bauhaus. The Bauhaus is very much the villain of this piece and as such shall be forever pronounced as *boo hiss*.

Under their robot-eyed leader, Walter Gropius, the (*boo hiss*) Bauhaus was the Germanic iteration of a very European obsession with re-making society as some kind of mega-modern factory, where everything worked perfectly, but in a very grey way.

They, like so many creative revolutionaries knocking around the 1920s, had been radicalized by the cloying sentimentality and emotional over-ornamentation of sensible, hard-working, middle-class society. The Bauhaus, in particular, hated curtains, carpets, cushions, paintings that weren't horrid, lampshades and anything else that made living in your living room cozy or comfortable.

The bourgeoisie were apparently to be seen as the beasts of the piece. The Bauhaus held a particular place in hell for what they saw as the corny, stultifying femininities that the ladykind of the bourgeoisie brought into the home to make it a lovely, loving place. Modernists, it seems, didn't like their mothers.

Like a bad smell (cabbage, a bit of sick and a lot of wet newspaper would do it), Modernism clung to the twentieth century right to the bitter end. Looking back at books and magazines of the period, you'd be forgiven for thinking that the world became a place of unflinching, shiny Minimalism. Acreages of white kitchen, tundras of pale ash floors and cliff faces of plate glass seemed to be what civilization on the cusp of the twenty-first century claimed it wanted to look like.

Despite its near-total dominance of glossy magazine covers and its ubiquity in TV advertising, did anyone you know really live as a Minimalist? I'm sure there were plenty that said how much they wanted to… but did they ever actually consummate the pact with nothing but skinny blinds at the window and three green apples in a designer glass bowl? I thought not.

What happened instead was a mushy, euphemistic, high-street soft Modernism in shades of wet cardboard that far too many people bought because they thought they had to.

Maximalism has no style file to sell. No fashion colours or trend forecasts. Pundits have started to try listing off Maximalist must-haves like crochet, rattan, plates on the wall, pineapples on the ceiling… But it's all rather hollow because actually Maximalism is about you. Have a home in which crochet features heavily, by all means, if crochet happens to be your thing. But it's simply not Maximalist to go scurrying off to a charity shop or thrift store in search of dank nylon twine contorted by hooks into crochet just because somebody has told you so.

If Minimalism is control, Maximalism is letting go. Rowing upstream vs surfing with the glorious wind in your fabulous hair.

Existence is hardwired to be Maximalist. All that grows does so to the best and most maximal of its abilities. Plants don't stop halfway up the trellis and say 'Now that's quite enough of that, any more would be too much.' Every carbon-based life form has a cellular duty to expand and flourish. Maximalism celebrates the state of total and utter fuckulence that happens when anything (animal, vegetable, mineral or human) achieves its glorious potential.

Let's meet Jenny From The Rock, our shared, (un)common ancestress. Back in the good old/bad old (delete as applicable) cave days, *womo sapien* Jenny was the matriarch of the kind of pterodactyl-shit-crazy, hairy pelt-wearing family group we'd recognize today. Jenny was the thinker. She was all about working out why that big shiny sun thing rose every morning and set every evening. She considered why things died, why things lived and why the cave looked sooooo much more homey after she'd cunningly created a feature wall using the whole tribe's stencilled hand prints. Nearly all the other caves on the rock block were into a Minimalist vibe. Shelters, really – just a few discarded animal bones. When they saw what Jenny had done with hers, they went crazy for this new and super-now 'decorated' look. It was luxe, lush and terribly boujee.

Decorating something shows you love it. Embellishing anything carries with it an immediate association that it's something special.

Decorating something shows you love it. Embellishing anything carries with it an immediate association that it's something special. Because no one will make decorative marks in the exact same way as anyone else, decoration makes it personal. But to decorate something, you need time. Since that's an activity not essential to the whole sordid business of staying alive, you need leisure. Food, water, shelter, fire. If you've ticked all the above, you've bossed existence. You've reached the elite. What better way of showing off than by ornamenting what you've got? Let's face it, it's a celebration of the conspicuous consumption of the time that lesser creatures are compelled to expend on basic survival. Ornamentation is a unique symbol of humanity's ability to square off the circle of life.

For Jenny, there was no 'less is more' bollocks. No, for Jenny, the more she could do to her cave, the more she could celebrate her magnificent pre-eminence. *Ta-dah* – Maximalism is humanity's factory setting. By the way, we have no clear understanding of what OG Jenny's sexing partner thought about all of this because he spent most of his time away from the cave. Anyway, if it made Jenny happy, it made him happy.

So the basic principle of *fancy = powerful* starts gathering a real head of steam as evolution evolves. The more carved something was, the more human effort had been consumed in its creation.

The first really legible illustration of this is the early obsession with building things with straight lines. Nature grows in curls and circles. In a curly, natural landscape, when something's all straight lines and angles, it will stand out. It looks super man-made (back then, men did most of the building).

But even as early as the ancient Romans, anti-fancy feeling starts to ferment. Before the gorgeous explosion of glorious Romanity that the Emperors unleashed on the ancient world, Republican Romans were super-sneery about ostentatious schmancy-ing. They dismissed it as effete (even back then, anti-Maxers were misogynists) and symbolic of an absolute power that could capriciously command the twiddlying-up of something that could do its job perfectly well without any twiddles at all.

Up until about 300 years ago, there was no question: 'If you've got it, flaunt it' was the universal war whoop of a world that used stuff to show off where everyone sat in the social pecking order.

In certain corners of the globe, straightforward have vs have-not societies started to transmogrify into a more complicated system of have-as-much-as-possible vs have-quite-a-lot vs still-have-not.

This opened up a whole new world for aesthetics. Suddenly, it wasn't just about a few pieces of catwalk couture but a full range of *pret à porter* ready-to-wear as well. Meanwhile, the good old have-nots settled for a life of muddy turnip tops and a hovel made of twigs.

Back then, Minimalism wasn't a style choice – it was poverty. It still is for millions of people today.

But the have-quite-a-lots, or the middle class (or the bourgeoisie, as urban continentals called them) couldn't help feeling all at sea when it came to picking the right sort of stuff. Aristocratic have-as-much-as-possibles had hundreds of years to practise choosing tchotchkes that said 'have' in the right sort of way.

So this is the moment when the absurd concept of taste gets invented. Taste was supposed to guide those with the small change to buy things towards things that been certified as being the right sort of thing for them to buy. Too simple and it looked way too have-not, darling. Too glitzy and you ran the risk of toppling the social order because you had the temerity to own an object posher than you were.

The bourgeois middle classes weren't actually appalled at that idea. In fact, there was often a rather defiant, devilish voice in their ear that wanted the posh stuff… the glittery things… the patterned walls and big draped curtains… They'd worked hard to achieve all they'd got. What better way to celebrate that sweaty labour than by treating themselves to all the fancy fripperies their bourgeois gold could buy? What aesthetic anarchy.

So this is when Britain, America and, to a lesser extent, France create the newly minted title of tastemaker. A bloke (of course) with side whiskers like mud flaps who decides what's appropriate and what's not appropriate for you to buy. Good taste, which they made as empirical and scientific as possible, became defined for all to see. It was an encouragement for those without a clue not to fall into the dark siren clutches of that arch-nemesis of all that's holy on the high street: bad taste. Heaven forfend.

If you're not keen on opinions with a side order of whiskered patriarchal condescension, look away now. Any possible opportunity to express anything other than total interior obedience was denied the householder. All of this tastemaker stuff came from a place of genuine concern for making people's lives better, but it kickstarted a tradition of interior pronouncements that ended up bedevilling the twentieth century.

Modernism wouldn't be Modernism without its clucking chorus of opinionated villains. There's nothing live-and-let-live about Minimalism. You're either in the right or distinctly in the shite with these rule-bound aesthetic schools of the twentieth century. Added to which, there's the Hydra-headed monster of property value. Realtors and estate agents, perfectly straightforward homely people before the dawn of the 1990s housing boom, transformed overnight into ravenous Furbies of empowered opinion. So as if it wasn't already bad enough that your home was in thrall to the tutting of tastemakers, suddenly there's a new force on the block who want to ensure your home is as easy to sell as possible. Homogenized, pasteurized cookie-cutter boxes with pre-agreed price tags. The expression of personal style could not be countenanced.

So, the high-street Modernism that surrounds us is not popular because people like it. Oh no. People have made the decision to embrace the Greynaissance out of duty. They are told – and they believe – that one step outside the beige canon of drone decorating will knock noughts off the price of their home.

Luckily, style is a vigorous force of nature that will forever grow towards the light.

There always were plenty of people with the chutzpah do their own thing. Prevailing fashions or must-have fads would be dismissed with a snort and a comely wrinkle of the nose. Enlightened ones have known all along that a home without personality is a home without heart. These perfecti saw Modernism for the emperor's new clothes of interiors that it was, and maintained their own Illuminati-sense of style, despite the prevailing storms of conformity. For them, the delusions of blandeur that beset twentieth-century living were but a phase. They were so right.

And now, friends, it's time for you lunatics to take over the asylum. To be fair on the twentieth century, it changed more of its inhabitants' lives for the better than any century ever before. It's just someone, somewhere, made the decision that this immense social revolution had to be achieved at the expense of lovely.

We live in a time of great change. Tectonic plates of style grind and flash together, but I can see, through the still-steaming magma, a new continent forming. One of the big things that's happened is the death of taste.

Or at least the end of the rule of taste. The world has recognized that it doesn't need to be told what to like. Working out what you like, and why you like it, is great fun. There's no such thing as good taste or bad taste, just your taste and my taste. (Mine is obviously much better than yours, BTW.)

Which is a good thing, because for the last few decades, it's obvious that people have been constructing taste-free cocoons. Protective spaces in which they cower from the judgement of others. Believing themselves incapable of good taste and fearing they may be found to have bad taste, they've burrowed deep beneath the tarpaulin of shop-bought soft Modernism.

> *There's no such thing as good taste or bad taste, just your taste and my taste.*

Maximalism is a popular and deeply democratic thing to do with your knick-knacks. But a pandemic knocked that for six. Confined for months in bunkers of our own devising, the sensible majority have worked out that where we live needs more us in it. If only there was an interior philosophy that encouraged self-expression, individuality and the dense display of all the bits and pieces that you know make you special…

The veritable influenza of influencers that clutter up the neurotrash of social media have actually been very beneficial for Maximalism. There, I bet you weren't expecting me to say that. There's no space for the Boomer attitude on this one because the digi-chatter that Millennials, post-Millennials, pre-Millennials and perennial Millennials furnish their headspace with has solidified just how subjective Maximalism is. The *raisin d'être* of these sultanas of social media is their ordinariness. Influencers aren't trained lifestyle-ateers, but simple souls who've worked out their own way of doing something. Thus the Modern Maximalism we see all over Instaland has an in-built, home-grown accessibility that wouldn't be there if it was exquisitely lit, shot and printed in a glossy magazine.

Meanwhile, there's a new kid on the style block, who is actually rather old. Nostalgia. It's a truth universally acknowledged that when the going gets tough, the tough get poke bonnets and a bustle. A few years ago we'd all be hiding from the present in the future, but at the moment you'll find us hiding from the now in the then. Occasionally, when you discover the lid on the peanut butter jar is too tight, you have to screw it backwards to move it forwards. A philosophy feared beyond measure by Modernists, but a philosophy that gave the world the Renaissance, which didn't end up so badly.

Does our current nostalgia actually count as nostalgia? Taking direct inspiration from the moment in time before time went wrong could feel more like a reboot. Meanwhile, hopping off the merry-go-round of must-have-newness feels like a very responsible thing to be doing right now. The Modernist obsession with the Minimalist perfection of an object allies it to a philosophy of designer consumerism. Maximalism as a style is, let's face it, an anti-style that's happy to embrace anything, be it old, bald, baggy or dog-eared. If you love it, Maximalism loves it.

But in a style with no rules, what are the rules? Let's have a musical interlude to help…

- *Enjoy Yourself (It's Later Than You Think),* Guy Lombardo and His Royal Canadians (and Socrates a few centuries earlier)

- *Express Yourself,* Madonna

- *Don't Dream It, Be It, The Rocky Horror Picture Show*

- *I Am What I Am,* Gloria Gaynor (and Yahweh, while temporarily identifying as a burning bush)

You see, Maximalism is an expression of the loveliness of you, and the loveliness of you is expressed through the things you happen to own. Although it's not a pop lyric, let's meet the tee-shirt slogan of Maximalism. The pithy summation of all that makes Maximalism Maximalism comes from the swivel-eyed mid-century Satanist Aleister Crowley. 'Do what thou wilt' is perfect for our purposes, although I do feel I should encourage you not take it as far as our Al used to, unless you're prepared for an enormous amount of mopping-up afterwards.

What Maximalism is *not* is a charter to clutter. Celebrating the ownership of something is a gazillion miles away from just leaving it where it is, because it's handy to have the cats' ointment by the armchair.

Anti-Maxers love it when they prove to themselves that Maximalism is Cat Lady Clutter without thought or intellect. Without properly engaging with each and every object, Maximalism does lose its love. Being utterly clutterly isn't Maximalism, it's just plain lazy. Or, worse, it's being practical. Living life around how to make things work better for you isn't living, it's just surviving.

More More More is here to show mortalkind how important it is to express how much objects are loved and valued through the way they are presented. Museum-quality shizzle under a pile of pizza boxes and back copies of the *National Enquirer* is not doing anyone any favours.

Whereas the loving display of even the most everyday objects (yes, I do mean your cats' ointment) shows a loving acceptance of life's simple abundance. Owning ordinary is top-level Maximalism.

So how will *More More More* work? Along with hench hints and terrific tips, we'll meet some icons of Maximalism. It's always helpful hearing how others have lived inspirational and Maximalist lives. Plus there'll be some of my own post-prandial musings on why we should never take some elements of Maximalism for granted.

I've decided to not illustrate *More More More* with tiresome pictures of people's living rooms. This isn't a school textbook. Instead, I'd love you to treat this book as a launchpad to propel you and your Maximalism into a glamoursphere of loveliness. It's my intention to embellish it, to ornament it, like *The Book of Kells* or *Les Très Riches Heures du Duc de Larry,* with a tchotcke-ism of mine own clutter. And a few of those swirly patterns that keep drip, drip, dripping off the end of my pen.

Let's get started. There's going to be no judgements from me, so don't fear on behalf of your brand of Maximalism. In fact, deliberately loving something because others say it's ugly is one of those things that gets me up in the morning. This book will help you unpack why you love something, which is exactly what you're going to need to empower you to start erecting your own Maximalist museum of you.

So as I draw a fabulously tasselled curtain open, behold the bonny, bright horizon of Maximalism revealed in all its celestial glory…

Ooooh, do pour the gin.

Imhotep

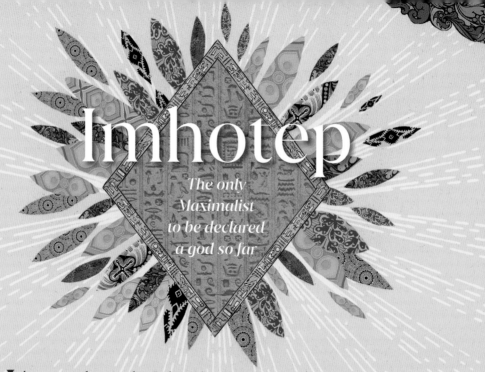

*The only
Maximalist
to be declared
a god so far*

It's a struggle to take Imhotep's dates seriously. The idea that he built the Step Pyramid for the pharaoh Djoser, in the Saqqara necropolis in Egypt, around the year 2700 BC, seems inconceivable – it's an *astonishingly* long time ago. And what's even *more* astonishing is that we still know his name, after all this time.

Imhotep wasn't a king or a pharaoh, but an administrator. An administrator illustrious enough to have his name cartouched on the base of his client Djoser's statues. From there, add the odd millennia or two, and Imhotep ends up elevated to godhood as a protector of the cunning. Never-ending fame.

But that's the Egyptians for you. They went big on eternity.

Speaking of eternity, Imhotep has built up an impressive post-mortem CV in the 3,000 years since he was alive. After the Romans take over Egypt, following the whole Cleopatra-killing-herself-with-an-asp episode, Imhotep even starts to crop up amongst Roman deities, rubbing shoulders with Jupiter and the like – Emperor Claudius had a particular fondness for him, apparently. For the bonkers post-Renaissance alchemical community, Imhotep was up there with Hermes Trismegistus, or Thoth, (claimed by some to be Imhotep's dad) as guardians of the arcane and concealed path to knowledge.

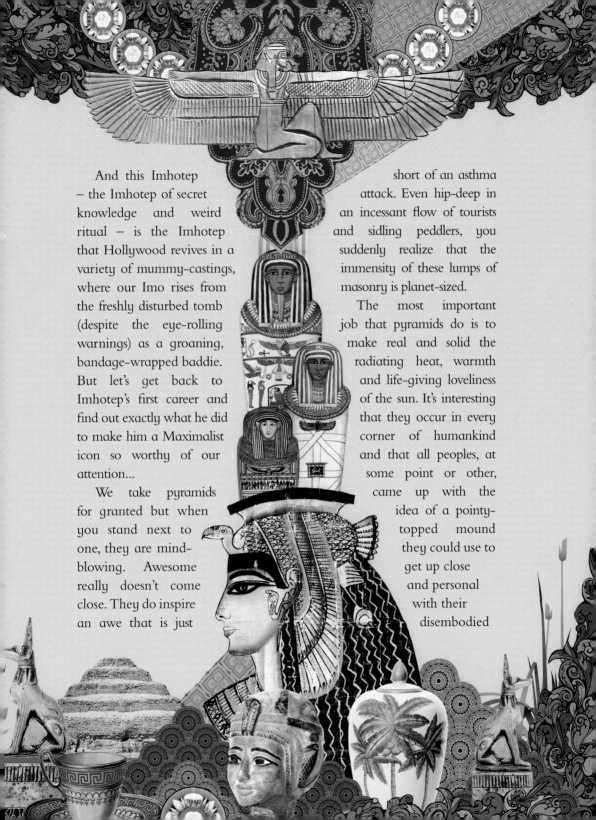

And this Imhotep – the Imhotep of secret knowledge and weird ritual – is the Imhotep that Hollywood revives in a variety of mummy-castings, where our Imo rises from the freshly disturbed tomb (despite the eye-rolling warnings) as a groaning, bandage-wrapped baddie. But let's get back to Imhotep's first career and find out exactly what he did to make him a Maximalist icon so worthy of our attention...

We take pyramids for granted but when you stand next to one, they are mind-blowing. Awesome really doesn't come close. They do inspire an awe that is just short of an asthma attack. Even hip-deep in an incessant flow of tourists and sidling peddlers, you suddenly realize that the immensity of these lumps of masonry is planet-sized.

The most important job that pyramids do is to make real and solid the radiating heat, warmth and life-giving loveliness of the sun. It's interesting that they occur in every corner of humankind and that all peoples, at some point or other, came up with the idea of a pointy-topped mound they could use to get up close and personal with their disembodied deities. Or the other way around. A *deus ex machina* (literally), down which his or her holy moly-ness could descend like Fred and Ginger down a Hollywood staircase.

I love Egypt. I love its art, its architecture and its culture, but I am happy to stick my neck out and admit that I don't see the Egyptians as Maximalists. In their world, scale is maxed and size is supered, but for a questor after every element of Maximal, what goes onto those humungous, architectural cliff faces is a bit meh. Loads and loads of wig-wearers and the odd zoo-faced god all to add heft to the mind-numbingly detailed lists of stuff carved onto the sides of the pyramids, which the ancient Egyptians hoped would make the pharaoh, cartouched in the corner, sound cooler than the one before. Although, this particular pharaoh actually looked exactly like the one before (and probably had the same name).

But that was it – it was meant to convey timelessness. The Egyptians being focused on continuity meant that the civilization did virtually nothing to change the winning formula they'd hit on for over two thousand years. There was a cosmic point being made about the eternity of Egypt and the eternal nature of its pharaohs. Which means you get some shocking missed opportunities in Egyptian art.

At Dandarah, on the wall of one of the most resplendent temples the Nile has to offer, there's a Bollywood-poster-sized carving of a woman. It's typical ancient Egyptian style standardization. Life-size for a superhuman, the head in profile, eyes full, body front on but feet to the side, looking somewhat like Picasso's sweepings. Just like all the other figures on the walls of that particular temple… and all the other temples you'll see in Egypt. But this is no cookie-cutter cutie…

We take pyramids for granted but when you stand next to one, they are seriously mind-blowing. Awesome doesn't come close.

This is last-ever pharaoh Cleopatra VII (yes, *that* Cleopatra). At her side is the son she had with Julius Caesar (yes, *that* Julius Caesar). What a phenomenally missed opportunity. The most fascinating woman in the ancient world and here is a carving not from life, but from her lifetime. If only the Egyptians had paparazzi. Had the artist been in the Roman or Greek tradition, we'd be confronted by a depiction that could be used on a passport.

Pyramids had been around for a while before Imhotep got his hands on the plans. But at that stage they were really more like big lumpen piles of rough-ass baked-mud bricks. These are called mastabas rather than pyramids as they don't have the right pyramidical geometry. They also rise from rectangular bases. The first thing Imhotep does is make the base square. Next? He reduces the infinite number of ramshackle steps that make up the profile of the mastaba to a few elegant platforms. *Ta-dah*: the step pyramid is born.

Inside, it's even more innovative. Instead of using vertical courses of baked-mud bricks, Imhotep lays them horizontally, cambering them slightly towards the centre for an incomparably stronger and far more permanent bond. But the big change

is what this pyramid is built *from*. Eschewing the traditional and highly crumbly baked-mud bricks, Imhotep uses hewn blocks of limestone instead. This is one of the first moments in history where dressed stone, rather than found boulders, is used to make a structure. It's almost certainly the first time that deliberately fashioned stone columns are used for support, too. I'm sure it will come as no surprise that these stone columns look familiar. With their gently swelling papyrus head tops and bound-reed shafts, they will live on to define the look of columns until the point when ancient Egypt stops being ancient Egypt.

Imhotep also takes the traditional decorative elements that had been used to enliven and ornament sanctuary walls and mortuary temples and reflects their traditional forms and patterns in carved stone. Again, these architectural elements, once fixed in immortal stone, remain unchanging for centuries to come.

This is the genius of Imhotep. He got it so right in one building that an entire civilization decides to press the architectural 'copy' button. The only shame is that, thanks to all those subsequent pyramids, temples and palaces, it's easy to get a bit style-blind and lulled into warm boredom by its eternal repetition.

A Maximalist History of the World

Part the First... Original sin is in

It starts with nature. Existence is the ultimate paradigm of successful Maximalism. All growing things are, without exception, hardwired to grow… to increase… to get flouncier, fuller and more lovely. Then they die.

But in dying they provide nourishment for the next growing thing, which will do the same, possibly to even more success and excess.

Existence ain't easy and thriving takes work, particularly for the human race. But once the basic needs (shelter, sustenance, warmth) were nailed, humanity found it had enough time on its hands to start doing things just because. Like painting bison on their cave walls or basking in the dull glow of the 'fire' they'd just invented.

However, caves have their limitations. Believe me, there's a long list of yabba-dabba-don'ts when it comes to getting the cave look right. Consider the location, location, location: your location has to be where there are caves, regardless of whether it's convenient for local amenities or a tad too close to less evolved hostiles.

Instead, it's far better to construct a shelter from bits and bobs you find lying around. Follow the lead of the other carbon-based dwellers of the veldt and build like the ants, the beavers, the birds and sabre-toothed fauna as yet unnamed by your *homo erectus* homies.

I'm going to pin my colours to the old-school view that actively choosing to do buildings dictated by style, rather than practicality was something the ancient Greeks kicked off first. They looked at the natural world with all its curvy lines and rambling vegetative shapes and perversely decided to invent the right angle.

The ancient Greek civilization was bent on making its mark, and nothing says mark of mankind more than a load of straight edges slicing through the natural environment. But here we part company with Greek style because they didn't really do Maximalism. Everything was too timeless, too serene, too symmetrical.

Onto the Egyptians who followed the same basic ancient Greek building tenets: all upright columns and spanning horizontals. Obviously the pyramids were a moment of pure aesthetic *ta-dah* and they did create architecture on a humungous scale. But Maximalist? Nah. Acres of bas relief wall decoration: all too samey.

Actually, when you think about it, Egyptian decoration relies far too heavily on lists, lists and endless lists of gods, titles, pharaohs and sheaves of wheat. This was ancient bureaucracy rather than real red-blooded Maximalism.

Unlike the Assyrians.

Despite using the same architecture as their sworn enemies, the Egyptians, and despite getting architecturally hooked on the same sorts of lists of vanquished foes, the Assyrians were out-and-proud Maximalists who knocked the Egyptians into a cocked hat of lushness.

Egyptians took pride in cookie-cutter repetition, while the Assyrians wallowed in the minutiae of aesthetic ingenuity. Confronted with an Assyrian frieze, you're overwhelmed by a swathe of exquisitely infinitesimal detail. Every warrior's beard has a slightly different twist to their eddying curls. Every tassel edging every genie's toga expresses an unalike grace. Every human-headed bull has an original twinkle in his almond eye and a distinctive dangle to his bullishness.

You'll find thousands of these sculpted reliefs marching round the palace walls, up the columns and through the dados. Yes, it's all there to show off the mighty might of the ancient Babylonian Empire, but it's all done with a huge commitment to make it all as lovely as possible. How very, very Maximalist.

Now come the Romans. The Roman Empire was, architecturally speaking, a game of two halves. Before half-time, blocky and blokey; after half-time, a veritable Vegas of ostentation.

Republican Rome took pride in its humble domesticity. Most of their lifestyle was an import from the much more evolved Greeks, although the dark complexity of indigenous Etruscan culture clung on in some of their gloomy corners.

Republican Romans were fiercely republican (naturally) and embraced an almost hysterical belief that citizens shouldn't get above themselves or do fancy things or live in fancy ways. So imagine their feather-spitting fury when one of their number installed big paired columns with a triangular pediment above his front door. This front door belonged to a certain J. Caesar Esq. and he knew very well that this particular bit of architectural enrichment was specifically used on only one type of Republican Roman building: the temple.

Yes, *that* Julius Caesar, with his fast-growing god complex, obviously needed cutting down to size. Which he was, twenty or more times with a variety of daggers, paper knives and a vegetable parer or two.

What came next was a mixed salad of Caesars.

Rome's second half – Imperial Rome – is a very different and much more Maximalist kettle of fish. Emperor *numero uno*, Caesar Augustus, always boasted that he found Rome a city of brick and left it a city of marble. Rome went from homespun Minimalist Republic to epic, sword-and-sandal super-power in one Maximalist generation.

But more than that, those Romans suddenly became very good at building, engineering and organizing. Which meant they could erect structures every bit as big as the Egyptians and just as ornately decorated as the giddily spectacular Hanging Gardens of Babylon.

On top of their building skills, they pioneered new and genuinely modern materials like concrete, which saved time and allowed Rome's classical columns to cover most of the known world pretty damn quickly. Those Romans used their Maximalism as propaganda. Their architecture was an enormous and magnificent branding exercise that they rolled from country to conquered country.

They did such a good job of it that today, 2,000 years later, we are still building in their style shadow, and Roman architecture has become forever known as the architecture of civilization.

Yet civilization ebbs and flows. Eventually the ordered cities that the Romans created from the disorder of the wild world ended up crumbling. Often getting themselves thoroughly crushed under a hoarde of uncivilized insurgents bent on being as violently uncivilized as possible.

Part the Second... **New beginnings in a grave new world**

While the remains of Western European civilization huddled under a flat stone, further east, Romanity carried on flourishing more or less unchecked, thanks to the jolly brightness of the sun and all that nourishing olive oil. And Romanity had thoroughly impressed a new and vigorous society…

Islam was looking to decamp from its nomadic, tenty lifestyle and start putting down architectural roots. It welcomed large chunks of both the Bible's Old and New Testaments into its core teachings and would eventually prove to be crucial to the survival of a lot of classical culture as well. In the embittered and fundamentally Christian West, classical civilization and classical learning (particularly science, medicine, philosophy and engineering) were so vehemently feared they were literally demonized. Islam, however, believed that knowledge was yet another lovely thing created by Allah to make life all-the-more wonderful.

The architecture of Islam took Roman innovations like the arch and the dome and raised them to new heights of artistry and elegance. A lot of the decorative flounces that defined Roman Maximalism survived and got re-mixed to an Arabic beat. The philosophy of Judaism inspired this newly emerging society to mistrust the graven image (commandment lucky number seven) but this constraint would evolve into some of the planet's most beautiful, most Maximalist pattern making.

Like all civilizations, Rome saw itself as the centre of the world, and they were blissfully unaware that in Central America the Maya believed they were the society around which existence revolved. The Maya were the Romans of America – super-good at organizing, impressively warlike and effortless masters of Maximalism.

Even today the most brainiac experts are at a loss to thoroughly explain Mayan design or interpret exactly what's going on within their brilliantly exciting, almost cubist, carvings. No surprise when you've got imagery that looks uncannily like a spinning cat toy with some Shrek hands emerging at odd angles of a gurning human face in the middle. Or some such.

We may never know what they were saying through all of this fabulously stylish detail (which was also originally richly coloured) but it's obvious that the Maya had a near-Assyrian commitment to making it all look wonderful. Having begun at around the same time as the Greeks built the Parthenon, Mayan civilization's fall from grace happens quickly and cataclysmically in the 1500s, when the Roman Catholic Church arrives to plunder the riches of El Dorado and spread the common cold.

But let's return to Europe.

Forget the evolved elegance of Islam and the powerful panache of the Maya, back in the EU it's all gone knobbly, lumpy and a little bit askew. In Western Europe, during what we now refer to as the Middle Ages, it seemed as if everyone had forgotten how to create beauty and started building, carving and behaving very badly indeed.

It didn't help that these frightened, badly dressed and scrofulous people believed that the crumbled ruins of ancient Rome and the highly informative classical literature on how to build lovely buildings were almost certainly personally directed by the devil.

So they started from scratch, building in the hope it would stay up. Which it often didn't. But they had time – more or less 900 years of time, from the 400s till the 1300s in which to trial-and-error what they were doing until something did actually stay upright. It's as if the Greeks and Romans had never existed because these buildings used the tensile strength of natural forms to span spaces, with branch-like supports springing from tree-trunk-like uprights.

The artisans of this period never called themselves Gothic (that was a term invented after the event by the smooth prince of Renaissance painters, Raphael). But Gothic had a real power to it. The lines did the job of focussing you – and your soul – decisively upwards, to the throne of God, as efficiently as a super-Crockett sky rocket. *Goin' on up to the spirit in the sky…*

Was it Maximalism? Certainly there was more ornamentation and storytelling per architectural inch than ever before. There was colour, painted glass, gilded metal furbelows and some fabulously frocked priests. But, at its heart, this era felt too fearful and spiritually transactional to be Maximal.

Textbook Maximalism needs self-confidence, self-belief and a lot of *sprezzatura*.

And thus, let us venture into the era of *sprezzatura*…

Part the Third... Refinement; Rooms for improvement

The Chinese culture of the marvellous Ming dynasty kicked off at about the same time as the Renaissance in Europe and used maximum effort to maximum effect. Minimalist it wasn't. But thoughtful, elegant, delicate and respectful it was.

Two unbelievably luxe Chinese exports had the West in a giddy fog of rapacious jealousy: slinky silk and thin-as-skin porcelain (that did indeed go *Ming* when you flicked its rim).

Thoughtful, elegant, delicate and respectful also describe an architectural philosophy that sought to establish a mutually fulfilling long-term relationship with the natural world from the outset. Horizontality was considered the ultimate in tact. Only prayer pagodas were allowed to be an eye-catching exclamation mark in the landscape. Buildings were deliberately super-straight and super-symmetrical, so that these man-made architectural conceits presented a creative visual opposite to the blousy asymmetry of the rolling views thoughtfully framed by doors, windows and gates.

By Ming time, Chinese decoration had reached its apogee. Objects depicted with great intricacy sit alongside planes of subtle void. From a distance, roof brackets or column ornaments have a majestic emphatic silhouette, but close up they undulate with delicate embroidery-esque detail.

The subtleties of feng shui (these days used with great un-subtlety to inflict wind chimes on spas and New Age break-out rooms) draw you in. And just wait 'til it goes Qing in the next dynasty.

Now here's a big thing to process. Pour a stiff one and loosen tight clothing because, architecturally speaking, the Renaissance was essentially a moment of Minimalism... Yes, I know.

The careful, repetitive geometry, the symmetry, the flat-faced facades and the minimal shallow ornamentation were all deliberately conceived as counterpoint to the opulent encrustation of the pre-Renaissance Gothic movement.

And pre-Renaissance Gothic had actually started to become something wonderful. In France, Flamboyant Gothic (literally translated as 'arches aflame') flickered enthrallingly while England's Perpendicular late-Gothic style actually achieved an almost rational decorum.

But the Renaissance is here because it's a package. Those severe Classical revival structures, textbook-correct with perfect semi-circular arches and deep overhanging cornices were the best possible Armani Casa background to all the rock 'n' roll rollicking, stabbing, feasting, fornicating and poetry-reading that life in an Italian city state of the mid-1450s made *de rigueur*. Never before had sleeves been so stupendous and tights so tight. And don't for one minute think that those days were spent in gentle lute-plucking.

War was an obsession and in Italy it was conducted with the greatest extravagance, wearing costumes of unparalleled opulence and using weapons of the most exquisitely dangerous spikiness. The aftermath of a battle would have been like the remnants bin in Harrods' furnishing fabric department, but with a lot of blood, detached limbs and still-steaming innards.

The Renaissance is when spending, lending, saving and making money really gets going. And a surfeit of wealth leads quickly to the evolution of lifestyle. In this case, banking, warring and whoring. But in a terribly clever twist, rather than risk life and limb themselves, Renaissance princes paid phantasmagorically outfitted freelance (literally) armies to do it for them. Rather like computer gaming today, then, the grunt work is done by fantasy avatars in fancy outfits.

The Renaissance is the first time in the West (more on the East momentarily) where commissioning culture becomes a bona fide example of conspicuous consumption. Sure your horse was Arab, your castle was turret-y, your wife was a princess, your mistress a duchess, but it was who you employed as court painter or poet-in-residence that really defined how oli your garch was.

It was the dawn of celebrity culture. No one knew or cared who in the generations before had carved the cherubs in Milan cathedral. But now, as the 1400s become the 1500s, it started to be all about the brand. Brand Botticelli, Donatello, Leonardo, Michelangelo or – the king of painted skin – Raphael. It's a very interesting, very modern moment, where rich people start using money to buy shiny fripperies from international designer names. It's also when art and culture break away from the Medieval obsession with looking fearfully upwards to a grumpy, vengeful God and start celebrating how surprisingly cool it is to be human. That was a concept the Renaissance remixed from the ancient Roman cultural detritus they found abandoned in Italian hedgerows.

As Italy and, bit by bit, Europe started to burgeon into the flower-like embroidered verdure of a Renaissance tapestry, India was under new management.

OK, we really should have checked in on India earlier. It's so dang Maximalist. I've saved it until now simply because of the Mughals, the poster boys of Maximalism who, escaping from being rather ordinary in Persia, take over running India in the 1520s, bringing a hyper-refined take on Islamic culture with them.

In India, they fall in love with the lush, learned civilization (as we all do, let's face it) that had grown as big and beautiful and as essentially improbable as a mighty Indian baobab tree.

And together this naturalistic, almost Gothic, culture of Hindu India fuses beautifully with the cool, classically derived and exquisitely synthetic Mughal aesthetic. The result? Some show-stopping Maximalist moments: the Taj Mahal, the Red Fort, the mosques, the tombs, the temples… But also the paintings, the poetry, the haute cuisine, the gardens, the jewellery, and then there's the (now-dismantled) Peacock Throne with the Koh-i-Noor diamond throbbing at its centre. Lip-smacking.

Back in Renaissance Europe, two of its greatest celebrities are at war. Leonardo, recently released from jail after an unfortunate incident involving luridly striped tights and sodomy, had declared sartorial war on scruff-bucket Michelangelo. For the silky velvet-bereted Leonardo, Michelangelo represented all that was wrong with being a sculptor… smelly, dusty and broken-nosed.

To be fair, Michelangelo was indeed a frightful under-groomer and once took the skin off his calves when he ripped off the dog-leather boots he'd been wearing non-stop for most of a year. Yuck. And dogskin: discuss.

But Michelangelo was worth it. His sculpture is, let's face it, consistently sublime – and that's nothing compared to his buildings. Michelangelo does jazz to buildings. Like a classically trained musician who knows his scales back to front, he takes all the classical components the Renaissance had decided were beautiful and he skats with them.

His confidence, his bravura, is boundless. He makes columns rise to the full height of a building (surprisingly, the first person ever to do so successfully). He superimposes small triangular pedimented arches on round ones… He puts blank windows like empty eye sockets above a rusticated gateway that looks like a skull mouth. He carves reclining goddesses that are, in fact, penis-less men with breasts like pert macarons on muscle-bound barrel chests just because he can.

This is called Mannerism, which is derived from the Italian word *manieri*, which kinda means 'signature style' although it should really be called Michelangeloism.

 *Not since Imperial Rome has style been so aggressively magnificent.*

This was happening at a time when the Roman Catholic Church was under attack from predominantly Northern Christians angry at its cultural excess. Welcome, Protestantism. Interestingly, at the same time back in India, calls to reform Hinduism (a religion even older than Roman Catholicism) resound from what would one day become the Sikh community. Something in the air, obviously…

Rather than reform, apologize, have cutbacks and prune the excess, the Roman Catholic papacy instead take Mannerism and super-size it, weaponize it and trebuchet it into the midst of a turbulent world. And in those days, that world included the New World of the Maya, Aztec and Inca. Not since Imperial Rome has style been so aggressively magnificent.

Like the unstoppable juggernaut of a carnival float, Mannerism rolls into every Catholic town with a slick slipstream of lachrymose cherubs, chunky, eye-rolling Madonnas and carnivorous curlicues. It's so big, it's so all-encompassing, so weird, but also so passionate, so dramatic and so bloody theatrical, the term Mannerism just didn't seem Maximalist enough to describe it.

Instead, someone somewhere starts calling it 'Baroque', which really means nothing. The word was formerly used to describe those highly prized, surreally shaped imperfect pearls that were costing the super fashionable royals of the time a king's ransom.

It's now the 1650s and Baroque is lolloping through the corridors of power like a giant gold octopus with uncontrollable, over-ornamented tentacles. But suddenly, in France, it stops in its tracks.

Louis XIV reaches for an elegantly carved chair and an equally decorative whip and has that OTT cephalopod sitting nicely, offering its maw and rolling over for the king in no time. He takes Baroque, with its vertiginous energy, unsettling perspectives and coral-reef irregularity, and drills it into a massy magnificence that radiates uncompromising power. Like Louis, it's frightfully sexy. It's taut and muscular but also grandiloquent and borderline Oriental, and it's such a worldwide hit it outsells Adele more or less overnight. It's Louis-mania.

But under the next Louis, this architecture of power, parade and might becomes genetically modified into a style of much smaller, more intimate personality. Inspired by the elegant asymmetry of the decoration on imported Chinese knick-knacks, and conceived as an antidote to Baroque's ponderousness, this style was light, airy and super-girly.

We call it Rococo, which is just as unhelpful as the term Baroque. It's definitely as Maximalist as Baroque but, poor Rococo, often very difficult for us to take terribly seriously. All those suspiciously smooth-cheeked shepherds, under-age goddesses with cellulite-dimpled bottoms, foamy clouds, acres of claustrophobic satin, unashamedly gynaecological roses and shells. *Everywhere*, shells.

The colours too… Neapolitan ice cream melting into pastel mushes. Oriental yellow, jade green and gold like it was going outta fashion. (It actually was; smart Rococo tastemakers like Frederick the Great used silver leaf instead).

To us, it feels excessive and doomed. Most people imagine Marie Antoinette getting guillotined in a Rococo room. Actually, Rococo peaked in 1750 and Marie Antoinette parts company with her head in 1790, by which time Louis's style was in fact quite classical and, by Louis-style standards, almost Minimalist.

Rococo is constantly revived and consistently reviled. It was the aesthetic response to a seismic stylistic change that saw culture turn emphatically towards the natural world for the first time since the Renaissance. Everything was getting simpler and more real. This was, after all, the Age of Enlightenment.

We are very impatient about Rococo. In an ideal world, to reflect celebrity philosopher Jean-Jacques Rousseau's New Simplicity lifestyle, taste would have skipped straight from ponderous artificial Baroque to the thoughtful back-to-basics style of Georgian country gentlemen.

Instead, in between, there's a peculiar outbreak of whimsically asymmetrical twigs and framing panels of broccoli trees painted in shades of shiny pink.

Part the Forth... New world hoarder order

Now the sharp of thinking will have noticed an omission from our romp through Maximalist design history. Where, you may well be saying, is the United Kingdom of Britainity?

It's actually only round about now, in the mid-1700s, that British style makes an impact.

There had been plenty of interesting stand-out personalities – aristos, kings and queens, mostly (not least of which was the Ginger Swinger: Queen Elizabeth I, with her well-known taste for a bit of ruff…). But now is the moment that taste in the UK explodes… and it's detonated from a very unusual place.

Up until this point, taste had always come from the top – from the court, from the monarch – and it would spread like ripples on a pond downward through society.

But 1700s Britain is where taste started to come from the street. Well not quite the street. Not even the high street. It was more like the chi-chi shopping district of Mayfair, but the point was that nobody in their right mind wanted to take aesthetic inspiration from the then lumpen and super-dowdy royals.

Maximalism drives a tractor through twentieth-century design's obsession with practicality.

In fact, British high society was like no other. French nobles felt faint, got nosebleeds and generally panicked if they found themselves more than a mile or so from the court at royal ground zero. Spending time in their own houses, nestled in their own country estates, constituted the ultimate naughty step.

In contrast, the Brits loved hangin' out at home, surrounded by doting peasantry, a pipe and slippers and farting spaniels by the fire. They actually resented any time spent at court.

Brand Britain's economy was firing on all cylinders for a variety of reasons, not least because being an island meant there were no hugely expensive border wars to be fought. Unlike the more or less perpetual arms race that the rest of Europe had locked itself into.

This meant that the peasants who would have otherwise been blown to bits because of a neighbouring nation's land grab were, instead, industriously employed in newfangled factories or tilling the earth. And it was in their interests to work as hard as possible because, unlike their European cousins, Britain's labouring classes weren't indentured or en-serfed. Not only were they free, they paid tax – the ultimate symbol of freedom.

Once tax was paid, they'd make sure there was a little bit left for the batch-produced fripperies that Mr. Wedgwood, Mr. Fortnum or Mr. Mason would be happy to sell them. And thus, middle-class consumerism was born in a blaze of tissue paper and gift wrapping.

Brits being Brits, they had a strong sense of what they wanted. They quickly started calling the aesthetic shots and their taste was for the elegant, dignified, rather Jane Austen-tatious look that launched a thousand TV costume dramas. Maximalist it wasn't.

But in a way, that's what made British style the sensation of the age. Suddenly Maximalism – with all its attendant splendour and ostentation – felt like a particularly itchy symptom of the pathogen that was rampaging through Europe's pyramidically imbalanced societies.

But in the UK shires, roses grew around gaily painted cottage doors, there was beef on the Sunday lunch table and simply stamped decorative borders on the lime plaster walls. An idyll.

Instinctively, the Brits had been emotionally and intellectually drawn to the serenity and balance of Republican Rome.

The very column-fronted porch that got Julius Caesar into such trouble quickly became the must-have entrance flourish for tens of thousands of gentlemen's des res new-builds the length of the UK. And beyond, to America, where they proliferated in their millions, over to India, Australia, Malaysia and wheresoever the union flag fluttered. In an almost exact mirror image of its original stylistic evolution, by the end of the century humble(ish) Republican Romanity starts auto-inflating, until it reaches a pneumatic crescendo of over-blown Imperial Roman Maximalism.

And all because of two *terribly* over-excited tastemakers. Both Napoleon and Prince Regent get their own side bars later (for different reasons), but the Regency or Empire look is, let's face it, catnip for Maximalists. To be rich, to be opulent, to be magnificent, to be elegant, to be big, to be bouncy, but to never cross the line into camp… Maximalism's sucker punch floored any Minimalist opposition.

Richly ornamented Classicism had grown girthy on the fruits of global empire. Mass production swelled as terribly clever machines learned how to sew and carve and besmear objects with icing-sugar-intricate ornamentation which came to define the aesthetic of the first 50 years of the 1800s. Dear old Brits, so earnest, so conflicted and so desperate to make everyone else in their own image. So bloody judgey.

Maximalist consumerism was anti-matter for those with a deep-down strain of snobbish Presbyterianism. They saw mid-Victorian aesthetics as society-imperilling pastiche. There were those who saw the tides of twiddly ersatz as the detritus of a fatally compromised social order. They watched in horror as cities and factories swelled like engorged ticks on the drained blood of formerly healthy, happy, country folk who had been lured into a new and scary, dark, satanic mill-enabled way of life. The brakes had to be put on Maximalism before it careened over the cliff edge.

A new tide of fundamentalist tastemakers saw the antidote in a fresh and simplified aesthetic that celebrated a rosy nostalgia for a completely fictional pre-industrial past. Initially, this had a deliberately Gothic swagger, which chimed perfectly with the swelling back-to-basics Christian congregations that were beginning to piously replace their more morally *laissez-faire* Georgian predecessors.

Gothic was great for public architecture like town halls and libraries, but its fiddly crockets and cheeky gargoyles quickly became too much of an ornamental temptation. In the blink of an eye, the naughty middle classes had let their homes slide back into a mire of machine-made shizzle, although this time it had a Gothic twang to it.

No, what was needed was a tough-love commitment to integrity and craftsmanship. This found focus in the creation of a merry-England arty-crafty style that, after its inception in the 1860s, managed to become nation-defining design for the following 150 years.

It's a style that is unashamedly middle-class at heart.

So, for true blue-blood Maximalism, we have to go to the New World. America had become adept at reworking prevailing European taste for its own needs. As its power, influence and economy exploded, wealthy Americans sprung forth with an aesthetic confidence that left the Old World rather stunned.

Taste in Britain had always been slightly constrained by history and space, while Europe often lacked the resources and the manpower, thanks to all that perpetual heavily armed squabbling.

No such checks on American architectural ambition.

From Britain they took Gothic, they took the newfangled Arts and Crafts, and they took the technology to bend and shape glass and steel into Crystal Palaces. From France, they developed a taste for high-cholesterol Louis style that came over in the same shipment as the Statue of Liberty – a nation-warming gift from the French people only 100 years late.

East Coast cities spread like ink blots, with suburbs that boasted just about every aesthetic style to be borrowed from the dressing-up box of Europe. All on a scale and to a level of magnificently unashamed ornamentation that astonished everyone. Even when there wasn't access to European materials like marble or sandstone, American builders used local brownstone or wood.

One of the most defining icons of American nineteenth-century Maximalism is the Scooby-Doo haunted house… the tall, turreted Addams family home, with its malevolent mansard roof and bats-in-the-belfry ironwork. All of those spooky tropes derive predominantly from European Maximalist architectural style, but were delivered by

American craftsmen with great ingenuity – and a lot of lathe time – in local painted wood. America's gilded age enshrined the stylistic confidence that only money could buy.

Back in Europe, as Britain settles into a cozy middle-class domesticity surrounded by a lot of comforting wooden beams and bold earthy patterns, France plays a dangerous game of thrones.

French politics had become a revolving door of revolutions since the first revolution divorced the last Louis from his rather gammon-y head. By the 1850s, France was being ruled by a president who had made himself an emperor, who knocked down Paris and rebuilt it in the kingly taste of a Louis (despite the fact he was actually a Napoleon).

Napoleon III's 20-year reign gave the world an impossibly seductive Disney/Louis style that left its mark on buildings from Bangkok to Ballarat. Basically indescribable (although Beaux Arts is used to cover it), one of this movement's best known jewel boxes is the *Phantom of the Opera* Opera House in Paris. There's a sort of Mannerist Baroque bone structure at work but it's difficult to see underneath the lavish application of stone-carved flounces, floozies and floristry.

It all ends badly for Napoleon, with a bloody war fought against a German invading force and, in a besieged Paris, the upper crust found themselves forced to eat the animals from Paris zoo. Albeit with some truly wonderful sauces.

There's just time for one last huzzah before the advent of the twentieth century closes the door on Maximalism with a resounding, dreaded slam.

Now, we haven't heard much from Japan. Such a big player in the game of taste in the modern age, Japan kept its own counsel and its borders firmly closed right up until the 1870s.

Then suddenly, Japonism explodes in Europe and America with a cultural firework display as the Japanese notion of taste thunders through drawing rooms everywhere.

But it's not the Japan that we are used to. It's not the Japan of simplicity, bonsai, monochromatic Minimalism and so-called Zen gardens. This is Japanese aesthetics, Gangnam-style.

It's the Japan of the fabulous embellished kimono, the glister and lustre of satsuma-ware ceramics, the Japan of complex geometrical lacquerwork and, above all, the Japan of pattern on pattern on pattern. It's a Japan that encourages a new, taut attitude to Maximalism, which is difficult not to lust after. Sure, there's rich opulent indulgence, but it's displayed with great authority and curated with a muscular confidence.

Just as Chinese-imported style inspired, via Chinoiserie, the home-grown taste-quake that was Rococo, so the novelties of Japan's knick-knacks, thanks to Japonism, lead directly to the

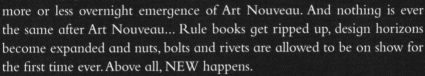

more or less overnight emergence of Art Nouveau. And nothing is ever the same after Art Nouveau... Rule books get ripped up, design horizons become expanded and nuts, bolts and rivets are allowed to be on show for the first time ever. Above all, NEW happens.

The cult of change for change's sake begins. 'Original', 'contemporary' and 'modern' become the words the twentieth century chooses to use about the design it creates to help define its age.

And Maximalism sleeps an enchanted sleep, waiting for a handsome Prince to wake it with true love's first kiss.

TASTE

vs

STYLE

Before rolling up
our sleeves and getting
super-involved in the marvels of
Maximalism, let's do a bit of linguistic
housekeeping. The terms 'taste' and 'style'
need a bit of serious unpacking, which is
something nobody's really been bothered to do
for you ever before. So pay attention – this is useful.

'Taste' is a very specific term that expresses the concept
of an aesthetic judgement formed by a committee. Basically,
taste is what you get from a group of people deciding what's nice
and what's not nice. All very undemocratic and, let's face it, antithetical
to the glorious, self-propelled decision-making of Maximalism.

So, as far as possible, it's a good idea not to use the term 'taste' if
you can possibly help it. It'll make you sound really rather
old-fashioned, if nothing else.

Style, on the other hand, is totally different.
The term comes from the Latin *stylus*, as in an
instrument to write with. Immediately you get
the idea. Style is something you write for
yourself, about yourself. Style is auto-
biographical and subjective and
can be as mad as a box of
frogs if you like.

There, glad we've
sorted that.

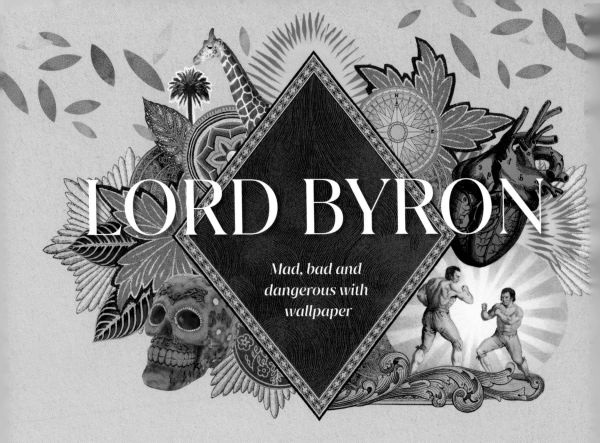

LORD BYRON

*Mad, bad and
dangerous with
wallpaper*

What you need to remember about Lord Byron is that he actually grew up ever so 'umble, if not actually bourgeois. The title, Baron Byron, was filed away in the dark recesses of his distant family during George Gordon's quite straightforward Georgian childhood… Straightforward in that he was raised by an overbearing, overwrought and over-upholstered mother – his father, mad Jack Gordon, had callously squandered what was left of his wife's fortune, then died young. Straightforward costume drama.

Thanks to the strange rules of primogeniture, our George finds himself 6th Baron Byron, after a great uncle quite literally pops from high blood pressure. Self-assured and highly sexed (thanks to a kindly nanny who made sure that from a young age every bedtime story had a happy ending), Byron inherited a fabulously dilapidated Gothic extravaganza of a house at Newstead Abbey.

Meanwhile, the Grand Tour, which was when young posh Brits trailed around the high spots of Classical culture (and the sin-spots of Europe's capitals) had been cancelled until further notice due to the gross inconvenience of the French Revolution. People were forced to discover the staycation. So instead of sighing over the serenity of the Florentine Renaissance or being moved to tears by Roman Baroque, society found itself on a quest to rediscover Britain's sublime landscapes and ruinous Medieval history. Inspired by the newly trending Gothic, as 1800 dawned, passionate Romanticism became the new black (literally). The cry went out for an appropriate poster boy for this freshly-minted, elegantly emo era.

Byron wasn't tall and he had inherited his mother's fleshy predisposition. But he did have a fine Classical profile, and he *truly* believed that he was the star of the show. His show, their show, your show... he instinctively knew how to steal the scene, which he did, decisively and very, very sexily. He used sex to sell himself as the very first rock 'n' roll celebrity poet. And he did the job so well that 'the Byron look' remains the seminal pose for teen studs in the dark, disaffected

corners of high school common rooms around the world to this very day. He's so terribly quotable, and is responsible for the *bon mot*: 'a celebrity is one known to many persons he's glad he doesn't know'.

Brand Byron was synonymous with everything that the middle classes feared their daughters might bring home for tea (we'll talk about the sons later). *Épater la bourgeoisie* could have been invented for Byron and his punky anti-social camp. Polite society saw before them an extravagantly voracious poly-sexual aristocrat who questioned God, the king and all that's right, good, decent and fair. He was vampire-pale when ruddy complexions were to be expected of a gentleman. He wore his hair long and straight (when he took the curling papers out) and his collar was floppy, his cravat awry. On entering a smart soirée, the crowd would part afore him as he cut a swathe through the swooning, simpering high-born fillies who'd been told by panicky chaperones not to catch his satanically magnetic gaze. Then he'd glower with devilish charisma in the very centre of the ballroom, refusing all food and drink that was offered to him. Although, rather unfortunately for the Byron myth, after leaving the party the same guests could often catch a glimpse of his vampiric lordship in the window of the local chop house, stuffing his face with the lowest of company. Don't you just love Byron?

Quite possibly one of the most self-aware self-publicists ever, Byron was brilliant at art-directing an atmosphere. At ruinous Newstead he created a series of sumptuously draped Regency Maximalist rooms, like priceless pillow forts in the near-roofless Medieval chambers. All the late Georgian decorating tropes of gilded glory, tasselling and fringe were displayed beside oddly personal items of his Lordship's devising. Weirdest of all, tartan, which at that time was a banned substance thanks to the Jacobite movement's opposition to the ruling royal house of Germanic

Georges. Let's face it, that mix is the mark of a mega-Maximalist.

After Napoleon's defeat (Byron *adored* Napoleon), his Lordship fled boring, judgemental Britain and the circulating gossip that he had been intimate with his own half-sister. Well, she was very lovely. Inspired by Napoleon, he commissioned a Maximalist travelling carriage with kitchenette, dining nook, four-poster bed and plenty of room for writing poetry and being moody. It was the first designer camper van in history.

In it, he prowls Europe. Byron is there at the inception of Frankenstein's monster, when author Mary Shelley starts to transcribe the horror story she'd been sharing with her Gothic book club while holed up in a Swiss lakeside villa. Byron is there when poet Percy Shelley washes up on a Sardinian beach after 10 days gothically decomposing at sea following a yachting accident. In Venice, he keeps a large menagerie of exotica just to tease the locals (and scandalized British tourists).

But we've come to love Lord Byron

for the most Maximalist death ever. All his passion wasn't merely a pose... Lord Byron heroically expires in his campaign tent, the night before he'd planned to lead his own contingent of the Greek Army against the forces of the Ottoman Empire, who had been occupying the cradle of Classical civilization since the mid-1400s. In Greece, Lord Byron is a national nationalist hero.

When news broke back in Britain of the death of their exiled rock-god poet, Britannia wept openly in the streets. After a hasty embalming, Byron's lordly remains were returned to Newstead and buried in the Byron crypt. A crypt that remained closed until 1938, when the odd-job man couldn't resist a peek inside the coroneted coffin... Byron's lower legs, arms and hands were skeletal, but everything else, including that famous face, remained astonishingly well-preserved.

We're advised to never meet our heroes. It can now be said that at the time of his death, Byron was not only quite un-heroically overweight, he was also getting perilously close to a state of middle-aged baldness. But because of his insistence on being buried nude, the odd-job man could also report (and did, for the rest of his life) that his lordship was not only mad, bad and dangerous to know, but also very much a biological Maximalist.

BECOMING MAXIMAL

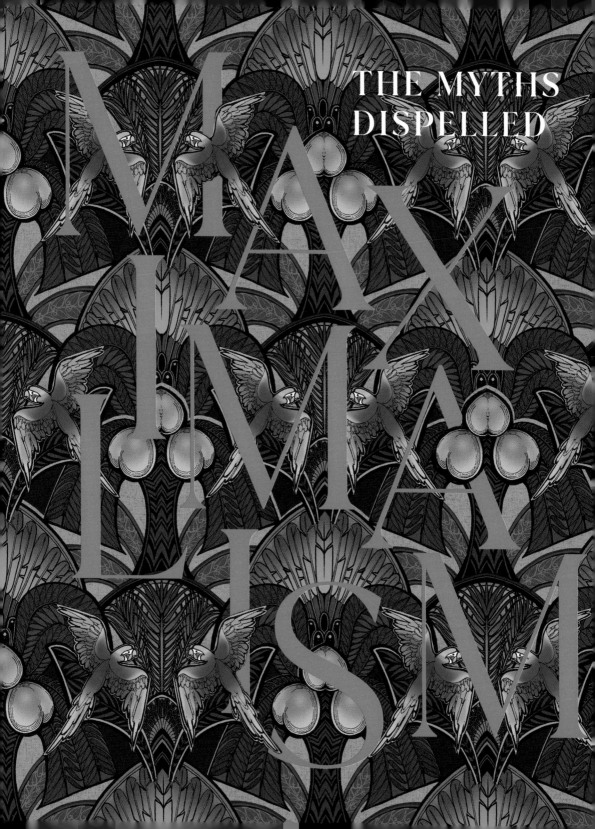

MAXIMALISM

THE MYTHS
DISPELLED

Maximalism vs Minimalism, surely it's just a War of the Poses?

Like beauty, lifestyle is so much deeper than skin-deep. To be a Minimalist requires a personality of weapons-grade hubristic optimism. An unswerving belief in the rightness of iron-rod control in life and a slavish interest in the rules that make that rod so irony. Whilst Maximalism is an expression of inner balance, grace and a glorious acceptance of the natural order. (Plus Maximalists are much more fun).

Isn't Maximalism a frightful dust trap?

Well, guess what? Dust happens. Dust falls on Minimalist kitchens just as much as castle walls. Removing everything fun from a room just to make it easier to clean will never bring pleasure. It would be much easier to wipe our bottoms if we didn't have to unzip or unbutton, but humankind hasn't abandoned clothing simply to allow a trip to the WC to become hassle-free. Besides, with no dust, how on earth would one leave cheeky notes for one's loved ones on the furniture?

Maximalism smells.

Yes it does. And it smells *lovely*.

Maximalism is the same as hoarding.

Oh no, it isn't. Maximalists are curators and choreographers of what muggles might call 'clutter'. Yes, Maximalist rooms are full, but they are full of love, life and happiness, because every object and each element in the space has a charmingly particular and personal story to tell. Although, if you look around your room now and see stacks of yellowed newspapers, empty bottles of bunion lotion, a single Wellington boot, cracked computer monitors and cats – *lots* of cats – then you've not got Maximalism right at all.

Isn't Maximalism just not putting stuff away?

A key philosophical point, this one. If an object takes root because you believe it more practical to have something you use regularly on proud display, then it's time to lift the lid on your motive. We may use a deodorant rollette every morning and, yes, taking it from the cupboard each time and returning it straight after is indeed more effort, but is that rollette

Maximalism is an expression of inner balance, grace and a glorious acceptance of the natural order.

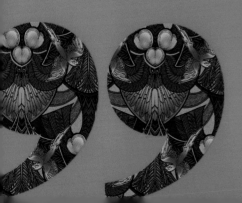

really worthy of an iconic position in your bedroom's interior design scheme? If not, then *do* put it away. But if you simply can't bear to be parted from your rollette, then find a fabulous way of celebrating said rollette within the gorgeous intricacies of your displayscape. And enjoy the fact that Maximalism drives a tractor through twentieth-century design's obsession with practicality. Venice isn't practical, wearing velvet to mow the lawn isn't practical, gold-leafing your toenails isn't practical, but they're all bloody wonderful. And Maximalism is bloody wonderful.

Maximalism is Hoity Toity.

No, no, no and *no*. Maximalism is *mojo*. It's an expression of incandescently shining self-esteem and thus is classless. Yes, the privately educated, nanny-reared trustafarians often confuse the congenital silver spoon in their mouths with coolness. But their museum-quality tchotchkes don't make for a better-flavour Maximalism. Maximalism is, in fact, open to all.

Isn't Maximalism just OTT for the sake of OTT?

Look, there are plenty of Maximalists out there that do it for the attention. But that's not such a bad thing, if – and this is key – they are actually *worth* the attention. The overwhelming *meh* of modern society discourages the tall poppy whose glorious flower is so much higher than all those around it. And let's not forget the term OTT originates in the infernal battlefields of World War I, specifically referring to the first soldiers who climbed out and *over the top* of the trenches to face relentless enemy fire. Over the top means brave. It means having the courage to do the thing you do no matter what.

Surely Maximalism is bad for the planet?

Spheres. Actually, Maximalism, with its credo of acceptance and its lack of judgement, means an end to the Modernist arms race of newness and the hysterical pursuit of the contemporary to replace all you had before. Imagine an anti-Maxer inheriting a Maximalist house: they see all that wonderful stuff as simply landfill - and that's where it would go. Planet Earth weeps every time a Maximalist dies.

WHOSE ACTUAL FAULT IS MINIMALISM?

Minimalism is the last late flowering of Modernism. And Modernism is a particularly unhelpful way of seeing the world that is now something of a period piece in its own right.

Modernism came from Europe, where its revolutionary philosophy started to ferment in the swampy cafes at the heart of any number of Western, Eastern and *mittel* European capitals. Cooked up by middle-class intellectuals who really should have known better, the whole ghastly thing wouldn't have happened if they'd spent more time outdoors, gargled less absinthe and had more constructive fridge magnets.

Imagine – Modernism could have been entirely avoided.

Even the name doesn't work. Modernism is meaningless. John Evelyn, diarist, celebrity garden designer and busybody at the court of Charles II, worried himself into a corner about the dome of Sir Christopher Wren's Saint Paul's Cathedral looking too modern. And that was in the 1680s. Calling anything Modern is a mayfly lie that exists for a micro-moment before immediately becoming something of the past. Think about it.

And Modern isn't even what Modernists were doing.

Humankind's desire to celebrate its progress is predominantly expressed through stuff. Once we've bossed the basic needs of food and shelter, we have time left over for lifestyle and leisure activities like story-telling, art, conceptual dance and ornamentation. The history of design follows the same trajectory as the history of social evolution (what the old boys called civilization).

What the Modernists wanted to do was to strip away everything that the world had carved, woven, inlaid, embroidered or sculpted, and reduce life to an existence within a simple box, with a few machines for company. In many ways Modernism was about going backwards: becoming less civilized. Primitivism in a dark grey turtleneck with unflatteringly small pince-nez.

Modernism began its coup d'état on the twentieth century just when, everywhere you looked, someone was staging a coup. Generally, it was the same grimy mockneys causing all the trouble. This philosophy of anti-loveliness was bound to appeal to these overeducated, over-opinionated, social re-booters. Loveliness had, after all, been spitefully lavished on them throughout their cosseted childhoods by their hard-working über-bourgeois parents, in the hope that little Karl or Vladimir or Charles-Eduard might grow up nice. The worst thing you could ever say back then was *bourgeois*. I'm still unclear what the bourgeoisie did to be so hated other than be the parents of Modernists.

Modern Modernism's official progenitor is often said to be the Bauhaus (or *boo hiss*), that particularly humourless gated community based around art and design. They wanted (very forcibly) to make their 1920s German world better. But only by following *their* definition of better, to the letter. Bauhaus Modernism was so pared-back in its avoidance of any unpleasant whiff of bourgeois comfort that it became proto-Minimalist. The steely-eyed zealots behind the Bauhaus prescribed a vegetable-only diet to go perfectly with their indescribably fibrous architecture. This led to Bauhaus Breath, a well-documented and extremely unpleasant side effect of the ridiculous quantities of garlic they surreptitiously chewed in an effort to cheer up teatime. No surprise that our old enemy Mies van der Blah-Blah was a Bauhaus graduate. For anyone unwise enough to commission the Bauhaus to build anything, or indeed unlucky enough to live in it, inconvenience was the order of the day.

As European politics got increasingly anti-bourgeois, politicians decided to use Bauhaus Modernism as one of the architectural stepping stones that would guide the proletariat to an enlightened dawn. Poor proletariat. The joke ends up squarely on the patronizing Bauhaus Bullies because there was nothing the Proles liked more than a comfy sofa spread with a cheeky antimacassar or a bobble-fringed mantel on which to show off the gee-gaws. White boxes with draughty Crittall windows and slimy linoleum floors could never feel like home. So the first thing the Proletariat did when they moved into their 'machines for living in' was bourgeois-up their Bauhauses. Ha. Modernism was, and remained, a decidedly middle-class taste. In America, Mies glass boxes and Le Corbusier white cubes are still the go-to glamouflage for those with *Succession*-scale wealth. From their redacted eyries, the intelligentsia could look down with contempt at Prole World, where animalistic plebs, like magpies or dresser crabs, encrusted their nests with the shiny shards of loveliness that had been so violently scattered when Old World Elegance was executed at dawn.

And so Modernism, like all pathogens, quickly understood that to survive it needed to keep rebranding. Particularly important for a concept pegged so incontrovertibly to the Right Here Right Now. Futurism, Dadaism, Surrealism, Vorticism, Expressionism, Abstract Expressionism (finally the Americans join in, in the late 1940s), until there was nowhere left for the –isms to go apart from the ultimate redaction: Minimalism.

Hilariously, Minimalism's big break comes on the coat tails of fashion. For such a worthy New World Order to be popularized by the super superficialities of the glamour industry is too funny for words. Back in the 1980s, couture houses were running out of the thin and rich, so they started opening shops in which to sell cheaper versions of their schmatta to the less rich (but still thin). Some of the more old-fashioned frock jockeys just took their haute couture Grand Salons onto the high street but the more avant-garde among them wanted a new-start new look. Minimalism was perfect. The lack of any distracting comfort or luxury made their clothes look even more enticing. At this stage in fashion's spin cycle, the look was very mechanical, very simple, very black, very body-con – so what could be better than a clinically Minimalist space in which clothes that were barely more than a shoulder strap and a gusset could be excitingly well hung? In fact, it made the whole experience look so much more authoritative and, weirdly, helped to justify the Maximalist price tag.

Quickly Minimalism became associated with expensive. Which it was. There's nowhere to hide in a Minimalist room. Every light switch, every socket and every hinge is on show, so even these rather ordinary components in a design scheme needed to be engineered.

The 1990s saw in an explosion of Minimalist concept decorating. It was particularly popular in kitchens. Which is so weird. Historically the kitchen always was the heart of the bourgeois home. It was the engine room that kept the family ship sailing: nourishing it, loving it and being the warm and welcoming background to family get-togethers and feasts. Not in the 1990s. If the magazines were to be believed, the ultimate kitchen had nothing in it but kitchen (certainly no people). And that kitchen was a machine for cooking in. Although cooking in it never looked that convenient. It was 'all about' lines and surfaces but in reality (and I've been in more than I care to remember) it was about appalling acoustics and an overwhelming sense of being surrounded by fascistically expensive engineering. During the food cult of the Noughties, restaurants used Minimalism as one of their principal weapons against their arch-nemeses: their customers. A Minimalist restaurant eroded a diner's confidence, subduing them and leading them with their head suitably bowed to the culinary high altar. Conversation was impossible thanks to the clatter of cutlery on china, endlessly ricocheting around polished plaster walls, and any sense of relaxation or enjoyment was perpetually discouraged by the barely-there chairs imported from the House of Torquemada at great expense.

Minimalism, like its big sister Modernism, is predominantly an architect's style. By its very nature it's architectonic rather than decorative. Sure, there are interior designers out there who will minimize your house for you, but it remains, at its core, something you need to sort out on a building level. And to be done properly it has to be done by creators who don't care about people. Minimalism will always look untidy with humans involved, but spectacular in its magnificently contrived emptiness. And, weirdly, these hubristically mechanical man-made spaces looked so darn futuristic. They were exactly what we'd been told the twenty-first century was gonna look like by *Star Trek*. Maybe that was a comfort.

Actually, as we'll find out, much of what Minimalism and Modernism were about isn't that easy to reconcile with the real twenty-first century at all. In terms of economic impact, in terms of bums on seats, in terms of how many people actually bought into Minimalism and lived Minimal lives, Minimalism was a flop. Sure, it became a style goal. Dinner parties tintinnabulated with conversations about clearing surfaces and decluttering, but in reality it just led to a near-ubiquitous rash of interior guilt trips.

It's so much easier to be a Minimalist failure than a Minimalist success.

THE BLONDE
LEADING THE BLAND

Modernism would never have become the twentieth-century style behemoth it was without the Scandinavians. It's weird to think that the piney fresh region that gave humanity Vikings, smörgåsbords and ABBA (three of the most Maximalist things ever) also made modern Minimalism so dominant.

And so-called 'Scandi Chic' is hugely important to our story because it has become the super-intransigent commercial iteration of Modernism. It has dominated the high street as the essential constituent in the wet-cardboard style of soft Modernism that tastemakerdom recognizes as contemporary good taste. Actually, calling it good taste makes it too exciting: appropriate taste is a better way of putting it.

And this is where my Scandi-phobia comes from. If, as an aesthetic approach, it did the job it had to do, but played nicely with all the other styles, merrily making a mess in the sandpit of taste, I'd be less vengeful. But oh no, Scandi has become the orthodoxy. I weep for the poor huddled masses in flat-pack furniture stores, wandering like lost souls around out-of-town retail parks, who have allowed the sedative of Scandi Modernism to dim the light of their style. They really believe that pale ash furniture and paper lampshades are all they deserve inside their four grey walls.

Even higher up in the market, where you'd think opinions might be more evolved, the catch-all phrase 'mid-century Modern' has department store furniture departments firmly in its thrall. True, mid-century Modern does include a few other sub-species, like Italian Modernism and Hollywood Regency (both of which we'll wallow in later), but it's fundamentally high-street Scandi gone high-brow.

So how did this particular style become a super-brand?

Before the twentieth century, the Scandinavians lived in the most charming homes. In such a sparsely populated region, it's no surprise that local materials played a huge part, so wood featured big-time, as did a bit of moss. But, interestingly, their wood was colourfully painted. Being so surrounded by the stuff, once wood stopped being tree and started being chair, they figured it was worth a few celebratory coats of paint.

Brits hate painted wood. Wood takes them straight back to their pre-Roman Celtic ancestors who worshipped the trees and almost certainly got a bit inappropriate with them after too much honeyed ale. Throughout British history, wood has remained defiantly naked. Just sloshed in several coats of candy-apple varnish. British men are such timberphiles they'd live in garden sheds if they could.

Scandinavian countries are forced to battle manfully and womanfully against a famine-and-feast relationship with the sun. In winter it doesn't rise. In summer it doesn't set. Traditional homes would factor this in and have two different decorating settings. In the winter: heavy velvet curtains, deeply upholstered furniture and lush, dark cocooning colour palettes. While in the summer, the sunshine was celebrated with a change to light, chalky colours, putting cotton slip covers on the upholstery, hanging muslin at the window and placing house plants on the sill. All very endearing and a jolly good idea.

We've established, therefore, a love of sunshine and a love of wood. Fast-forward to a world pulverized by war. The defeat of Hitler's Germany had come at a huge price for the once-grand towns and cities of Europe. And like the buildings, economies had been ruinously crushed in the gargantuan effort to rid the world of evil. Wounded and bereaved, but not demoralized, Europe was looking for a way to rebuild itself quickly, efficiently and cheaply.

In the years before the war, the old-school Modernism of the Bauhaus *et al* was really rather running out of steam. As storm clouds started to clash in the greying skies of the late 1930s, Modernist optimism simply couldn't stand up to the mechanized and muscular bullying of fascism, and the Modernists themselves were charmless and intractable. Post-war, however, Modernism's flat-pack simplicity starts to look a lot more appealing.

In 1947, an absolutely mouth-watering exhibition of life and style started a hugely successful stadium tour of the world. Displayed in spot-lit pools, Scandinavian design looked almost indecently decadent to people forced to sit on badly repaired three-legged chairs in homes where the dust of blitzkrieg still lay heavy on mantle shelves. Forget the perma-grey vistas of bombed-out neighbourhoods at home. Huge posters of mighty Scandinavian forests in rolling Scandinavian springscapes put this show-stopping style in its proper context. Clever.

Unlike the heavy, brown soup-coloured furniture at home, this new Scandi stuff was as pale and happy as the eyes of its pipe-smoking Scandi designers. Everything just looked so new and felt so hopeful. A fresh flavour of Modernism, peddled by chunky-jumper-wearing Danes, blond, bearded Swedes and outdoor-fun-loving Finns started looking a whole lot more wholesome.

But the 1947 Scandinavian Design exhibition comes with a much darker back story. Like everywhere after the war, the Scandinavian countries, by which I mean Sweden, Denmark and Finland (even though the Finns aren't technically Scandinavian) but not Norway (important – I'll get to that shortly) needed to rebuild their smashed economies. Promoting a combined design style that relied so heavily on the wood they all had in abundance was so straightforward. Particularly if it also presented a global PR opportunity that could rebrand the area as a stylish, forward-looking modern society. An opportunity Scandinavia desperately needed if it was ever going to be part of the new, post-Nazi planet. Because Finland had fought alongside Nazi Germany against the Russians. Denmark was occupied by the Germans and, while Sweden remained neutral, both countries continued to supply the ravenous Nazi war machine with Scandinavia's minerals and raw materials. Only brave Norway stood up against Hitler.

It's probably one of the greatest PR successes of the twentieth century: a snow job (literally) of epic proportions. The world hungrily devoured this newly reincarnated Scandinavia with its outdoorsy liberal attitudes, pitch-pine panelling, beaten-copper light fittings and bent plywood dining chairs. The war was brushed under the Flokati area rug, never to be referred to again. Well, at least not until the press inconveniently unearthed the links of Ingvar Kamprad, the founder of IKEA, to a Swedish youth Nazi organization.

Having a murky political past is one thing, but having a murky political past and somehow becoming the poster style for a light, bright, distinctly un-murky present is a serious achievement.

MINIMALISM: THE (*INEVITABLE*) CONCLUSION

Why do all those footballers, rap stars and TV talent-show judges love Minimalism so very much? Why has it become the go-to for oligarchs and wannabe-garchs to strip their homes of all but a few wenge wood sideboards and a stainless steel fire pit?

Think about the current evolution of the taste vs power continuum. Previously, power made money and money bought *stuff*, exquisitely wrought by the artists, craftsmen, sculptors, artisans and composers who created the Renaissance, the Age of Reason, Romanticism, neo-Classicism and every other flavour of gorgeous shade of rainbow-hued culture in history.

Today's rich don't want any of that and they certainly don't want stuff because there's now one thing that's so much more expensive than stuff, and that's s p a c e. What they conspicuously consume is now pure void. Their rubric is cubic.

In the past, the ceaseless transactions of buying things built civilization. Now, power still leads to money, but it's used to buy nothingness, a blank, an expanse of emptiness. And I'll tell you what shows off empty space a treat… a vast quantity of nothing at all.

It's all so desperately sad and horribly lonely. The super-rich (whom I feel we should all now pity) have fallen out of love with life and happiness. Instead they now actively seek out pointless vacuums in which to exist. It's almost as if Oscar Wilde wrote it with a tear in his eye.

Heavens, thank goodness we're done with all the ghastliness. Now it's time to unleash the lovely…

You *own* ordinary. Give everything you own dignity. Display it like it's Ming.

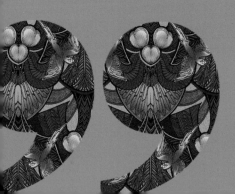

MAXIMALISM – OWNING ORDINARY

I hope you're now beginning to run out of the excuses that have previously held you back from embracing Maximalism.

Maximalism is the path of least resistance which leads to a happy home and a happy you. No, Maximalism doesn't need designer labels or museum quality artefacts to work. Maximalism is at its best a celebration of the simple abundance of that which surrounds us.

For those poor etiolated and constantly nervy Minimalists, there's an instant stigma that brands everyday objects as unworthy. For them, perpetual social insecurity means that anything's status must be sanctioned by others: style writers, designosaurs, influencers. If none of these false prophets have sanctioned an own-brand tin of beans as worthy of ownership then it becomes an object of shame to be hidden in the dark, purgatorial limbo of storage.

Now, I'm all for tidy-up time. We're all aware of the perils of utterly clutterly cat-lady interiors, but what if all you have in life are own-brand beans? What if you have no doors on your kitchen units? What if you have nowhere for the ordinary things to run to, nowhere for them to hide? Simple: You *own* ordinary. Give everything you own dignity. Display it like it's Ming.

These quotidian, common-or-garden-variety things are essential to your existence. Your teeth need cleaning, your toenails need clipping, your super-seed ready-sliced bread needs toasting and your stairs need hoovering. The ordinary objects that keep your world turning need respect.

My solution is to stack them with an eye for the overall design. Arrange them with labels proud to the front, cluster them by colour, graduate them by tone, choreograph them by height and welcome them as worthy of being part of your Maximalist world.

Poking around an anti-Maxer's bathroom cabinets is always a laugh. The room may be a sleek haven of uncluttered Minimalism, but break the seal on their storage and the true horror of their anal retention is revealed. You'll find a tangle of clutter, a seventh circle of hell represented by half-squeezed-out toothpaste tubes, hairy hair brushes, crusty cleanser and lidless jars of desiccated Anusol garnished with a sprinkling of pubes.

FURNITURE THERAPY

This is where the rest of your Maximalist life starts. Right here, right now, with Furniture Therapy.

It's a simple enough exercise, designed to inspire a new lease of love for the stuff in your life. Maximalism will never be an off-the-shelf experience. Buying Maximalism by the yard isn't just cheating, it's actually disrespecting the strange and particular beauty that comes to those who love what they own. But keeping on top of the stuff you've got is an essential part of getting Maximalism right. Remember, things that are where they are because they've just been left there aren't Maximalism – they're clutter.

Making a pyre-like pile of your rooms' contents is the most efficient way that I know of seeing the everyday in a new thoughtful way. To get Maximalism to work properly, it has to be thought through. Yes, I know Maximalism's about emotion, sentiment and falling in love with your living room, but trust me. To stop the heart running away with the head, thoughtful curation of a Maximalist space is essential.

Those anti-Maxers are always so annoyingly and judgily condescending about what they see as Maximalism's lack of intellect. And yes, compared to the painful levels of overthinking that come as part of the Minimalism package, Maximalism does indeed score less on the overwrought brainiac stakes. And hurrah to that.

But not engaging the brain at all simply won't help a Maximalist room. In fact, when everything is just left to settle, to take root where it's left, Maximalism tips the scales into Messymalism.

Furniture Therapy takes everything away from its comfort zone and forces you to reintroduce yourself to it. This is the moment when you ask that vase the big questions…

QUESTIONS YOU NEED AN ANSWER TO:

♦ Do I actually like you?

♦ Are you worthy?

♦ What memories do we share?

♦ Are you up to the rest of our lives together?

QUESTIONS YOU DON'T NEED AN ANSWER TO:

♦ How much are you worth?

♦ Are you useful?

♦ Are you impressive?

♦ Does owning you make me look cool?

Now, assuming that vase is indeed worthy, it's time to reintroduce it into your Maximalist world. Hey, let your freak flag fly, put it back in absolutely the wrong place. Go on, try it. Keep your particular flavour of Maximalism fresh and juicy by turning the objects in your world on their head. If it works, it works. If it doesn't, you can always put it back where it was before.

Furniture Therapy is the Maximalist art of throwing everything you've got in the air and seeing whether it lands somewhere better than it was before. Think of your room as a snow globe of gorgeous.

THE PRINCIPLES
OF LAYERING

Layering is Jedi curating across at least four dimensions of space and time. Which is scary, but it shouldn't be.

Start by thinking of your room as one of those *olde worlde* pasteboard children's toy theatres. Imagine, in your mind's eye, that your space has a cloth backdrop on the far wall and then a series of cut-out and painted flats coming towards the audience: you. Instantly, you'll see your chosen view of your room in terms of background, midground and foreground.

As a super-simple rule of thumb, think of each of these planes as being the perfect decorative environment for things that grow in heaviness of colour, pattern or detail as they recede backwards away from the eye. Visualize a gravitational pull away from you, with the dense and the massy stuff being drawn away first.

As in a painted backdrop, broad brushstrokes and big planes of colour merge at a distance to evoke an Impressionist vista. Then it's time to start furnishing the foreground with the smallest and most visually delicate objects. Frame them or support them with simpler, bolder objects just behind them in the middle ground.

The whole should be fabulously set off by the big guns: the heavy cavalry of eye-catching colours, patterns or just plain density bringing up the rear.

Whether this theatre of you is an entire room or just a mantle shelf, having an impresario's eye for staging the theatrical extravaganza that is you is, without doubt, the loveliest way of spending a wet afternoon.

TOUCHING THE VOID

I know plenty of Maximalist rooms that hit you with a chatty cloud of interest and detail the minute you set foot in them. Like aviaries, there's so much going on, in a never-ceasing, feathery, chirrupy whirl - the effect is quite giddying. Which is great, if giddying is the effect you seek.

These are rooms where the layering has been deliberately contrived to hit a consistent pitch of ornamentation, pattern, colour and detail. It's an opulent look, a strong look, and a look that suits those with old-school Maximalist ideals. But I'd like to introduce you to my own preferred school of Maximalism, a modern Maximalism, which embraces the use of visual punctuation as a framework, a bone structure, on which the glamour of Maximalism can shine.

I like contrapuntal moments of calm on which I encourage the eye to rest betwixt the Maximalist glories. These are visual palate cleansers, allowing digestion time for the previous aesthetic experience before munching into the next mouth-watering Maximalist morsel. It's a great way of focussing the story-telling in a room and creating defined chapters, where a visual theme or colour story can be eloquently conveyed. Calm is as calm does and your calm can be anything you want it to be, but I've grown used to relying on a set vocabulary of architectural elements of doors, windows and chimney breasts.

Now, unless you live in the Grande Galerie des Glaces at Versailles (where a particular *horror vacui* has led to absolutely everything getting super gussied-up under layers of Baroque ornament), doors, windows and chimney breasts usually come comparatively understated. And vertical. Like big, tall slices of calm in a cozy, chatty Maximalist world, these dependably strong and silent architectural types create wall-heightening pieces of peace. Between them, you can then assemble Maximalist vignettes in paragraphs, with a decorative beginning, middle and end.

But I hear you cry, 'I live in an Arts and Crafts house and my windows don't rise from floor to ceiling like an elegant Georgian column of supermodel refinement!'

Well actually, neither do mine. My home is seventeenth century, and back then, glass was expensive and super-draughty, so windows were small and high. Therefore, to counteract the squitty proportions of my fenestration, I've panelled below the window and painted it in the same shade as the window frame itself. This instantly creates a visual plinth on which the window sits, improving its vertical proportions. The whole is then given an effect of further heightening with full-length, down-to-the-floor curtains.

I do advise you all to never play host to short curtains, no matter how high the windows. There's something stunted about seeing curtains that don't reach the floor and therefore do not 'stand proud' on solid ground.

VISUAL WEIGHT

Some things are heavy: they are dense, they are colourful, they are eye-catching. Some things are light: they are ethereal, they are floaty, they are subtle. Some colours weigh a tonne: red, aubergine, brown and black, for example. Whereas other colours are as light as a feather: cerulean, grey, lilac, turquoise.

Guessing the weight gets easier and more instinctive with practice, but if you want a quick solution to fast-track you to the front of the Maximalist queue, then pretend you've just had an entire bottle of Sauv Blanc to yourself. Yes, blur your eyes and sway slightly. Seriously. You'll find that seeing less detail and less context will prove enormously helpful and you will notice that some items are immediately discernible. Those'll be the heavyweights. Other things remain teasingly intangible and mysterious: our featherweight friends.

Now, I know what you're like. If I don't get to the point soon you'll be asking me why this is important. So here comes the point…

BALANCE

If there's one thing an utterly clutterly cat-lady room isn't, it's balanced. No thought has gone into it, no decision-making in its Messymalism. Instead, like a coral reef of clutter, everything arrives to where it resides through casual accretion. Yuck.

Balance is (and brace yourselves) something good Minimalism does extremely well. Obviously, there's nowhere to hide in a Minimalist room (believe me, I have tried). The very guts of the space are laid bare for all to see so you are inspired to appreciate how everything fits together: the relationships between things. Inevitably, this becomes an exercise in understanding how the room balances. Where is the weight? How is it answered?

You begin to realize that the television in the left-hand corner is balanced on the right by a large frameless painting in dark shades, which has the same squareness… and, yes! The same visual weight. The big glass vase at one end of the annoyingly un-embellished concrete mantle shelf is anchored at its opposite end by three shiny green apples. God, how irritating. But yes, there you have it:

BIG GLASS VASE (large but light)
divided by
THREE SHINY APPLES (small, but heavy in numbers)
Equals **B A L A N C E**

Basically, think of that mantle shelf as a seesaw. Now, let's play seesaw in our very own Maximatorium. Start skipping amongst your shizzle and randomly picking one of the many lovely objects that make up the museum of you. Look at it. Consider how heavy it is. What would match that particular weight? You can use the sum of multiple objects to equalize another. Answering an artefact with a multiple of other artefacts is, in fact, the very point where Maximalism takes flight.

ASYMMETRY – A TRICKY BALANCING ACT

The fact that the majority of us are largely symmetrical casts a long and deeply dangly shadow over the whole history of styling.

Humankind, while arranging its bits and pieces, will instinctively try to balance everything on an imaginary centre line. This is sheer hubris. Humankind is literally trying to reorder its surroundings at the expense of the natural state those surroundings have so joyously enjoyed. It's because nature is so outrageously, gorgeously and unrepentantly anti-symmetrical that poor, fragile humans choose to force their own freakish symmetry on it. *Bless*.

Nearly everything we promote to the canon of beauty is there because it's symmetrical. Matching pairs – or better still a matching pair with a solo show-stopper object in the middle – quickly became a logo for civilization. A celebration of the unnatural, the man-made, the contrived-by-human-hand. This trio, be it a pair of candles and an urn, mirror image vessels and a bust, or perhaps matchy Capodimonte ceramic tramps and a carriage clock made to look like a vintage caravan, has become the knee-jerk way to display for generations. It's a very Western thing. It goes with chunky columns and buildings on super self-important pedestals.

In the Eastern tradition, symmetry is part of a particularly thought-through aesthetic balancing act. Since symmetry is so very made by man, balancing it with asymmetry (which is so very made by nature) creates a state of stylistic equilibrium that's hard to not gush over.

The joy to be had is a joy of balance. Yes, it's yin and yang, in perpetual creative motion, spinning in the way that only opposites do. But the point is that neither wins. And that's probably one of the biggie Maxims of Maximalism: there should be no winners. Balance can be brilliant, but there's another fella in all of this I'd like you to meet and he's Mr. Rhythm.

Rhythm is pattern. It's the disco bass beat that allows the Maximalist synth to soar in ever-ascending circles. Try it – you'll have a lark ascending.

Using the rhythm in your displayscape is instinctive and relies on your own perception of how you want to break the pieces down: into chords, bars, dots or dashes. Use all you've learned about the importance of void and the usefulness of peace because one of the best ways of defining your rhythm is by the punctuation points you place between the elements. Negative space is every bit as important as positive.

Counting plays its part too. Even numbers, like straight lines and symmetry, ooze control and the hand of man. Odd numbers are jazz and nature and organic excitement.

As with symmetry, the mind is wired to see even-numbered things as potentially human or at least human-made. Which is why, on the first page of the floristry rule book, you'll find the commandment to use flowers in odd numbers. Otherwise the eye starts trying to count them or decipher a potentially significant pattern behind them. Nature grows in threes, not fours.

There's a similar lesson to be used with pattern. If the repeat of a pattern is an even number, the mind becomes unsettled. It instinctively feels it needs to be concentrating, perhaps recognizing something like a face with even-numbered features or a body with even-numbered limbs. Keeping pattern repeats in odd numbers takes all that irritating responsibility away from the brain, allowing it to simply wallow in the lush undulations of pattern, as if it was authored by Dame Nature herself.

This is a lesson I'd like you to consider. Strive for balance, be a slave to the rhythm, by all means worship equilibrium at all times – but find your own way of weighing up what you're displaying. Understand the drama of asymmetry and appreciate the obvious serenity of symmetry, then use them *both* to create light and shade in your Maximalism.

THE GOLDEN SECTION

Having bigged-up the East for its enlightened embrace of asymmetry, there's actually a moment of great and powerful asymmetry at the heart of Western aesthetics, which I find super-useful when it comes to the setting out of a Maximatorium. Now, please bear with me because I'm about to use a term that has for several centuries sent design students instantly into a hypnotically slumberous state:

THE GOLDEN SECTION.

Arrrrrggghhgghhhhh! Yes, I know.

But let me sort this out for you. Forget all the mystical, mythical *Da Vinci Code* claptrap and complicated maths, the Golden Section is actually just a simple method of division. Old Master paintings tend to be oblong. Divide them with three vertical lines and the line that separates the first third from the second third is…

ONLY THE BLOODY GOLDEN SECTION!

You can go one further, dividing the oblong again horizontally, and the point where the first vertical line makes a cross with the first horizontal line, is the sweet spot. In an old painting that will be where the artist will put the most important bit, the thing he really wants you to see so you can understand what he's saying.

The golden section surrounds us everywhere – shop windows, photography, films, advertising, patterns. To get asymmetry to balance properly, you place your heavy thing – your important thing – on the golden section, then balance the hell outta the other end with apples. Or whatever. There you go. You are now, dear friend, Illuminati.

MASSY PLAYTIME

Of course, bringing stuff together is what this Maximalism thing is all about. But what happens if you simply don't have the right stuff? If, in trying to balance something you love, you can't for the life of you find an object that's heavy enough?

This is when you ask for help and call on several objects that can work perfectly as a group – but let's hit another level of gaming with this one. Let's up the stakes and say that you've got something that's the perfect colour, that tells a fabulously complementary story *and* it's something you simply can't live without… but it just ain't massy enough.

Poo. We've all been there.

It's a question of emphasis. Why not make it massive by putting it on top of something else? A book or stack of books, a box, a brick, a log. A candlestick, if it's a small thing. Try an upturned glass, a jam jar, a child's wooden building block. *Anything* to plinth yourself out of a crisis.

Chinese supermarkets often sell carved wooden plinths designed for pots or ceramic objects and these are the perfect solution to increase the height – and therefore importance – of one or two things in a collection.

If plinthing doesn't appeal, try framing. Literally, use an empty frame (sans glass and packing) and lean it against the wall behind your underscale object. Or use a piece of mirror, or make a colour block mount for it by propping a piece of coloured or wallpapered card behind it.

I love these tweaks. It's like giving the little fella a bunk up, so he can see the Maximalist parade march into town.

TASTE THE RAINBOW

The assumption is that a Maximalist room is a super-colourful room. A chromatic assault. And, by thunder, it can be if you want it to be – but for a lot of us of Maximalist bent, colour is something we use for its near divine ability to emphasize *and* enhance. It's not necessarily the star of the show, but an important cornerstone that ensures the mighty Maximalist edifice rises true and straight.

Despite what people say, no one actually has a favourite colour. When someone says they love orange or pink, what it means is that their personal sense of style is weighted towards warmth. And contrary-wise, blue people or green people like it cooler. Understanding this immediately allows a much wider net to be cast into the choppy waters of the paint chart. An all-pink room is, let's face it, pink pink *pink*… But a pink room that also glissades into corals, satsumas, blokey bricky reds and soft sandy tones creates a colour experience that feels effortlessly natural. This is because colours in nature never come as an 'end of' statement. Nothing is ever solely pink or blue or green. Light bouncing on and around any shade will impart a thousand different chromatic subdivisions as textures change and shadows fall. For a Maximalist, this is useful stuff to know.

Maximalism loves the spaces between things as much as the things themselves. And the space between colours is such a lovely place to spend time. As the colour wheel slowly turns from true blue to fire engine red, a million and one mystical shades of shifting hue sparkle into life. It's these neither-one-thing-nor-another colours that create the perfect backgrounds for Maximalist collections. You'll see them change and transmute before your very eyes as the colours or patterns of your Maximalist hoard are displayed afore them. It's seriously better than watching telly.

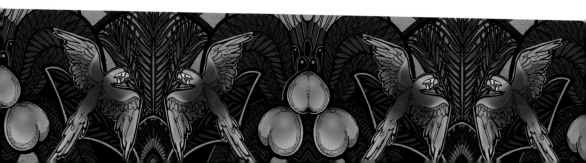

I'm going to give you some hard and fast scientific rules on colour shortly, provided you play your cards right, but now, let's talk *tone*. In many ways, tone is a much more important element for Maximalists to understand than colour. Tone, or the contrasting lightness or darkness of a colour, is critical in showing your tchotchkes off to their best and most fuckulent advantage. And, let me share with you now what all museum curators know, which is that large collections of objects sit far more cohesively in front of darker colours. Dark bookshelves make book spines look more ordered; darker walls show off the paintings so much better; an occasional table with a dark surface will turn frankly ordinary tablescapes into a Dutch master's masterpieces.

The colour (or hue) is up to you, but do please turn up the tone. And concentrate, because there's a science bit coming up:

Different colours are processed in different parts of our eyes. Our retinas are made up of cones and rods. In essence, the red gang goes to the middle while the cool blue kids get processed on the edge. Now, remember our retinas are the back wall of our eyes, which are spherical. This means at its centre, the retina is closest to the brain, which is why red will always be the super-shouty colour bully that grabs our attention and catches our eye. Literally. Meanwhile, cool, moody blue hangin' out on the edge is that much further away, which is why blues, greens and lilacs are so much softer spoken.

This explains a lot. Stop signs, traffic lights, McDonald's and lipstick are all specifically conceived in red to grab you by the visual love handles and not let go. Whilst distant mountains and far horizons are always such discreet shades of those calm and super-polite blue hues. Interesting stuff, yes, but also super useful…

A red wall will always feel much closer than a blue wall. To make a room big, use the cool blue family of colours. To make it smaller, cozier, more enclosed, throw open the doors to *Roister Doister* reds.

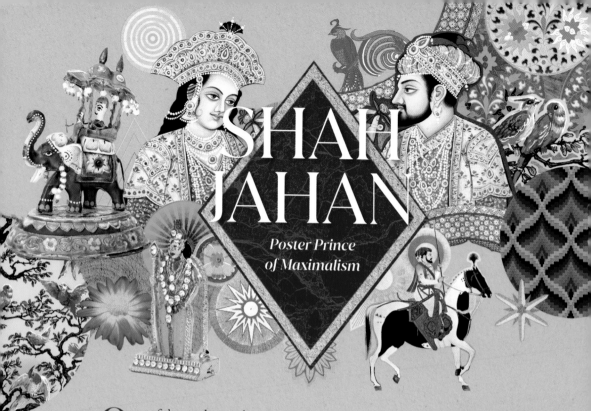

SHAH JAHAN

Poster Prince of Maximalism

One of the coolest and surprising things about the Mughal dynasty is their name. These days Mughal – or mogul – is constantly spliced with 'movie' to denote the biggest of the big cheeses in the film industry. The term oozes achievement, power and excessive success. It's a straightforward throwback to the Mughals, whose glittering empire dominated India's multi-cultural culture for more than 300 years.

Should you be looking for a historical period when the very best art, architecture, jewellery, music, poetry, painting and glamour all occurs at the same time (and offers considerable enrichment to humanity),

look no further than the age of the Mughals. They did science and tech too, but that's a bit of a whatevah from me. Think Renaissance – but so much better.

It's the brand name Mughal that's so fabulously amusing because for all their evolved aesthetic civility, Mughal derives from Mongol. Yes, these sultans of swing traced direct descent from Genghis, Kublai, Timur the Lame and all the other ruthless baddies who made the Mongol Horde one of the most feared fighting forces ever. At one point, it's estimated that the Mongols put 11 per cent of the globe's population to death. Impressive.

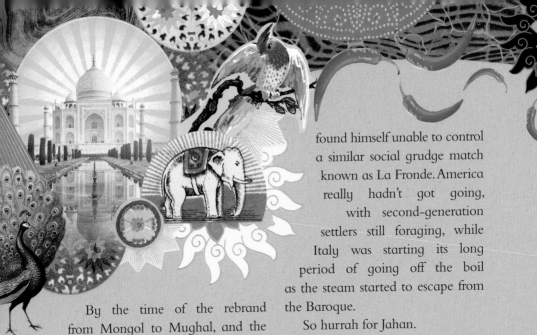

By the time of the rebrand from Mongol to Mughal, and the relocation from Persia to India, brand Mongol had relegated its tented tendency for barbarism firmly to the past. Instead, the Mughals started creating some of the world's most dizzyingly beautiful buildings.

It did help that the Persian architectural traditions they took with them had a planet-stopping elegance and a decorative language of sublime sophistication.

Shah Jahan was perfectly placed in the Mughal timeline. Too early and the culture wasn't yet properly baked. Too late and it all started to get a bit dog-eared and rather over-fingered. But Jahan hit the top job just as Mughal style hit its ascendancy. In the rest of the world, the English were tearing each other to pieces in the Civil War while Boy King Louis XIV found himself unable to control a similar social grudge match known as La Fronde. America really hadn't got going, with second-generation settlers still foraging, while Italy was starting its long period of going off the boil as the steam started to escape from the Baroque.

So hurrah for Jahan.

In a world being sliced and diced by hate, the Mughal Empire was a beacon of rather evolved tolerance. The particularly fragrant iteration of Islam practised in Persia sat side by side with the far older theological complexities of Hinduism (as well as Buddhism and Christianity). Jahan's grandfather, Emperor Akbar, made such enlightened declarations of tolerance and compassion that they cast shade on the social achievements of today.

Love was very much in the air. It's love that motivated Jahan's greatest achievement. Shah Jahan loved one woman above all others – something his Mughal contemporaries found extraordinary. The court structure encouraged emperors to appoint numerous wives and countless concubines to ensure as many healthy, vigorous, empire-inheriting heirs as possible. Jahan was no different… until he met the fabulous Mumtaz.

Big courts need big buildings. Big empires need big cities. And a big personality like Jahan did big brilliantly. He was fabulous at Maximalism.

His Maximalism was a Maximalism of precision and exquisite curation. He understood how to vary the intensity of effects to ensure the overall aesthetic story

destroyed, Peacock Throne of fable. This nonpareil of imperial state furniture relied on countless jewels for its glory, including the Koh-i-Noor diamond, which now sits, plump and dazzling, in the centre of the Crown of England.

Under Jahan, haute cuisine flourished. He personally endorsed the use of chilli, recently imported by Portuguese traders. The impact of this introduction on Indian cuisine could not have been greater. He also sanctioned a new approach for the

> *Big empires need big cities. And a big personality like Jahan did big brilliantly. He was fabulous at Maximalism.*

was as easy to read as possible. He also knew how and when to bend the rules. Although Islam proscribed visual depictions, the court of Jahan subtly, and with suitable humility, fostered a school of painted illustration that remains one of the most exquisite ever. Intimate and thoughtful evocations of court life in beautifully painted frames.

Applied arts reached a height of creative sophistication that resulted in the world famous, but soon

court physician to plan all meals, so that the magnificence of the food should be matched by its health-giving properties. Under Jahan a very twenty-first century philosophy of wellness flourished.

But it's the buildings surviving today where we really see the Maximalist icon that is Shah Jahan. The Red Fort in Delhi, the Wazir Khan Mosque in Lahore and a mausoleum for his father Jahangir in Agra all feature his signature love for elegant architecture, rising in shimmering domes and minarets from lush undulating parkland. Long established in Persia, the so-called 'Mughal arch' gets a do-over by Jahan to make its geometry extra perfect, making the sharp point of its sinuous ogee apex taller and more refined.

Materials being enjoyed for their own particular personality is a very modern architectural philosophy. So rather than heavily gouged, carved decoration, architectural enrichment is kept shallow, which leaves the veining of the marble or grain of the stone visually consistent and a part of the decorative language.

The Maximalist impact comes from the sheer scale. The buildings are huge. The genius way that arched openings and overhanging canopies are used to cast shadows, which in themselves become essential decorative elements, is perfection. From afar, the structures have great bones. Up close you're quickly lost in the intricate inlays of contrasting semi-precious stones, performing an exquisitely controlled choreography of repeating arabesques.

Shah Jahan's greatest legacy is shaped not only by his incredibly evolved Maximalist sense of style, but also by his love as a husband. His most famous building, probably the most famous building in the world, was created as a memorial to the love of his life, who died following complications in childbirth at just 28. During their marriage, he had involved Mumtaz in everything. Hers was the opinion he sought first in matters of state, war, politics, religion, architecture and art. And after she died, he was inconsolable, pouring all his grief into the erection of a tomb for her that he hoped would celebrate for posterity the beauty, the perfection, the grace and the power of his beautiful dead wife, Mumtaz Mahal.

The Taj Mahal always makes me cry.

Colouring in is in

Allow me to help you tiptoe through the tulips and join me as I unpack hue for you.

RED King of the rainbow. This fella knows he's at the top of his game when it comes to readability and recognizability. Red teams win far more often than teams wearing blue and red has always been the favourite shade of conquering armies. Painting a room red makes it look smaller but it's also supposed to stimulate saliva (good for dining rooms), be an aphrodisiac and encourage you to lose track of time (great for brothels). Actually, *everyone* looks so much livelier in a red room thanks to the rosy light bouncing off rubicon walls on to nearby skin. Is it an aphrodisiac or simply more flattering?

SHADES OF RED As an all-powerful *pater familias* with little to prove, red gets on beautifully with its chromatic descendants in all their different hues. The red family are at their happiest when they're all hanging out together, which is how we see them in nature. Reds, pinks and oranges are a regal and warming dynasty.

PINK Pink is the only lighter shade of a primary colour to get its own name, but pink actually means crinkle-cut, just like the delicate petals of the perma-pink flower of the same name that inspired it. Hence pinking shears. With the warmth of red compromised by plenty of white, be aware that pinks can get scratchy with each other. On the wall, pinks that nudge toward blue (say Barbie, or shocking) can appear cold, whereas pinks on the way to yellow (such as salmon or apricot) can look dingy and brown.

ORANGE Sunny, juicy and fun, orange is a surprisingly underused hue in the home. When it basks towards the browny tones of terracotta it's a perfect colour for northern walls. It's natural and subtly warming. When it's shiny, orange sure gets you up in the morning with a hit of vitamin C as vigorous as a bag of satsumas around the chops. Which is perhaps why the unsubtle 1970s used it rather too often for family kitchens.

BROWN Feared by many, brown can actually be a super-sophisticated choice for larger, higher rooms. The secret is to treat it like coffee and add cream to taste. Adventurous Maximalists know brown can take off-piste accenting: jade, damson, fuchsia and peacock all bounce off a brown base with decorous joy.

BEIGE Literally translated as underbelly, the Norman cognoscenti prized the softer wool from the underside of the sheep and left it undyed. Beige on a sheep becomes beige through prolonged contact with sheep poo and wee. Still fancy a beige sofa?

TAUPE This is what happens when beige gets stale and starts curling up at the edges. Taupe is beige with added green-grey mould.

GREIGE Created as a tease. Ignore it and it'll go away.

YELLOW Officially the most difficult colour to get right in interiors. Yellow is like leaving uncovered rice in the refrigerator; it will soak up everything you put next to it. So a bright yellow room with a window over a lovely garden breathes in all that green and ends up seriously snotty on the wall. There are two ways of getting yellow right. The first is to keep it rich and yolky so it's borderline orange. The other method is using it with black. I know that combination is nature's way of telling us something is dangerous but the black (particularly if it's lacquered) is the only colour macho enough to make yellow compliant.

CREAM If you're turning the colour dial down to neutral there's a lot to be said for dear old clotted cream. It's uncomplicated, untainted by Modernism or Minimalism and creates walls that offer you a soft and gentle knitwear nuzzle.

GREEN We're surrounded by greens. Infinities of shades of green that are all busily and contentedly photosynthesizing like there's no tomorrow. And all of them are a different hue. This is why the green family truly profits from the inclusion of as many different shades of itself as possible. But anyone who's decided to go floor to ceiling in leprechaun or Robin Hood will tell you how quickly overpowering it feels. We never see one green on its own in nature. Green needs to be treated like a salad to succeed. If the walls are spinach-shaded, add lime curtains and keep layering accents and opposites until you're ready to toss it.

BLUE Unlike green, we rarely see different shades of blue in the natural world. There's sky, sky reflected in water, and that's it. Very few animals or plants come in true blue and the majority will, in fact, be slowly sliding round the colour wheel to purple. Blue is unusual and is mostly found in crystals or minerals, which is where science finds its blue. But beware… blue is the colour of convention and control. It's also the most difficult shade to use within its own family. Blues that slide towards red will always hate blues that slither towards yellow. Blue clashes with blue big time, which is one of the many reasons why double denim is so hateful.

TURQUOISE, AQUA, PEACOCK, KINGFISHER Chromatic heaven. Maximalists adore the shape-shifting properties all these bluey-greens and greeny-blues give to their lovely Maximatoriums. Used with gold for imperial splendour, satsuma for oriental drama, cocoa for urbane sophistication or copper for peacocky perfection, this bend of the rainbow rocks. The Venetians invented their own shade, Turcino, which included plenty of grey and an undertow of emerald, which they said was based on the exact shade of their lagoon.

PURPLE Most natural blues err towards the red, so purple is a big player in the blue story. In fact, violet, which is pretty much 50/50 red and blue, exists in a perfect place of interior balance. Mauves are more pink than blue and can develop a rather unpleasant visual aftertaste that is both cloying and surprisingly metallic. Most people believe my favourite colour is purple but in fact it's…

PAVONAZZO Yes, you read right. While pavonazzo is mentioned regularly in Renaissance writings, we have no proper recipe for it. It is described as being both green and blue but is predominantly purple, so you can see how I instantly fell in love. It should be declared the official colour of Maximalism.

GREY The new beige. This is the shade that everyone hopes will protect them from everybody else's questioning taste antennae. On its own, grey is a disaster. On its own and accented with more grey, it's a disaster of national proportions. If grey is accented with a sparkle of gold, with shiny white to anchor it, plus plenty of sunshine, it can be understated elegance *sine qua non*. To really get grey going, see it as the camera-shy background to jewel tone accenting, in which case it becomes the true Greynaissance.

WHITE I'm oddly fond of white. Bright white. Hospital sheet white. Brilliant white is the most modern colour since it didn't exist until chemistry created it in the 1920s. Hence the Modernist's obsession with it, but that doesn't put me off it. An all-white room is a very active and energetic experience. There's something committed and gutsy about decorating with white.

BLACK Black isn't ever really black. To create black you need every other colour, which means it can tip to green, red, blue or brown – for which I love it. One black wall in an otherwise pale room is Jedi colour theory, particularly if the black wall becomes the curatorial background for a Maximalist collection.

A QUICK NOTE ON

CLASHING

Clashing colours is such
a wonderful way to describe
the collision between shades.
A collision can also be an
energetic collusion. A clash
can be violent and painful but
it can also be astounding and
exciting. Think cymbals.

A FEW PENSÉES ON COLOUR COMBINATIONS

Putting certain colours next to each other opens portals of Maximalist joy, for which your eyes will be ever thankful. As with all things Maximalist, it's in the combination that poetry is found.

Colour science tells us that complementary colours (a funny term for opposites, but it's lovely that it's so positive) have a near-magical ability to egg each other on to heights of intensity impossible on their own. This is the whole basis of Impressionist painting.

Questing for after-effects that would more accurately describe the lush French light, Monet *et al* started using unmixed colour on their white canvasses, presupposing that the viewer's eye would combine the yellow blob with the blue blob to make green. Which it does. The end result is evocative and conjures up paintings that not only capture their subject but also, somehow, the air around the subject too. The struggle with Impressionists is to forgive their draftsmanship, which is often borderline schlocky.

When the opposites are united you get a charged, chromatic gear change. Red next to green makes the red much more racy and the green… a whole lot greener.

Back when colour was a much rarer commodity than now, colour combining was a deliberate exercise in intensity. Colour was precious, so to make your hues go further, alternating them with their opposites seemed a clever thing to do. The term 'gaudy' actually means 'to trick' and describes the *trompe l'oeil* deceit of making colours stronger by putting them next to others.

Colour combinations can calm, too. An overwhelmingly cool scheme will take warm accents with relief, just to knock the chill off. These combinations can actually just be a matter of hue. Using a palette of greens that swing from the blue end of the spectrum to yellow is the best way to turn the dial down on green's photosynthetic intensity.

My top tip for getting the alchemy right when combining colour is to look for precedents. Let's do peacock. Fabulous! Blue with a top note of green, it's one of the most elegant, yet powerful, colours you could use. It's also, in untrained hands, super-unflattering. Light reflecting off blue-green tones gives faces a sepulchral pallor, for which you'll not be forgiven in a hurry. The solution is to be found on the peacock himself. Next to the blue-green you'll find blue *and* green in a clever bit of chromatic planning that should inspire some genius accessorizing. There's also plenty of greyscale wing, which is a lovely inspiration point for a black-and-white floor. The peacock's glory rests in the extraordinary cleverness of the iridescent copper that makes up the majority of the tail feathers. Warming and soothing, it's the ideal accompaniment to the deep sea shades. In interior decorating terms, copper is the perfect antidote to the cool blue light which gives everyone in the room a fabulous Saint Tropez tan.

PATTERN GATEWAY –
CATNIP FOR MAXIMALISTS

Adding colour to a room changes the way it feels, but adding pattern changes the way it speaks.

The gorgeously convoluted brain is hardwired to find order in chaos, to help it disentangle the millions of visual messages that hit the retina every second. Like Wordle-addicts or Sudoku-junkies, the cerebella love it.

When faced with a flat surface covered in marks, the human mind puts the kettle on, finds a comfy corner and starts to contentedly decipher the visual code. It's as gently stimulating as Miss Marple with a schooner of sherry.

The brain's first call is its own archive. It flicks through the Rolodex of experiences to see whether those jeepers creepers peepers have seen anything like it before. This is where pattern's role as fabulous fabulist steps to the fore. Memory starts overlaying similar recollections, like a slapjack waiting for a snap.

Let's role-play. Your eyes discern a leaf shape. Your memory starts to scrabble around for other leaf shapes and maybe a feather, which it pops on top. That feather sparks a memory of a stylized palmette-frieze, based on a stiffened honeysuckle vine… moving from ancient Greece, your visual shuffle leads to a single paisley motif or dhoti… and from that, you head to the undulating paisley extravaganza you once saw on a Rajasthani wedding sari… and that dense, organically inspired pattern experience inevitably leads to Austin Powers's pyjamas.

All too often, one ends up at Austin Powers's pyjamas. That's the key. Alongside every visual reminiscence there's a buy-one-get-one-free memory. A story unique to you that gets triggered every time you see a particular motif or pattern. Ahhh.

Now Maximalist patternistas do this, and they do it Out and Proud. They'll externalize their inner aesthetic dialogue and welcome the leaf, the feather, the palmette, the dhoti, the paisley and of course the pyjamas into the same room. All of them get on famously, like an exquisitely orchestrated drinks party with a seemingly unrelated guest list of design invitees that actually have one thing in common: you and your library of visual experiences. Refining the choreography of this *corps de ballet* of patterns requires you to get in touch with your inner Billy Elliot.

Don't be put off. I understand that a pile of pattern can look dauntingly similar to a cataclysmic explosion in the combined hand luggage of the cast of *The Golden Girls* on a dinner and dance tour of Acapulco. But this is where a keen eye for visual weighting and measuring comes in.

Densely undulating, autumn-hued paisley equals heavy. Sparsely sprinkled sprigs of summer blossom equals light. Obvs. But don't forget the help we can get here from sister scale and her ability to make the weak strong (and the strong, meek). Super-sizing your summery blossom to be big enough to be used as a parasol by a passing Sumo wrestler means it can legitimately step forward and be the prima ballerina in your ballet of pattern. Whereas shrinking the paisley not only reduces the detail, but also causes the colours to merge. The same repeat at half-scale becomes almost neutral and a perfect background pattern.

Ultimately, grasshopper, getting pattern to work for you will always be about trial and error. There aren't rules because of course Maximalism is a lawless place for aesthetics. Let me pour honey in your ear, and repeat: You Got This. Enjoy, play, combine. Treat patterns like a toddler treats crayons.

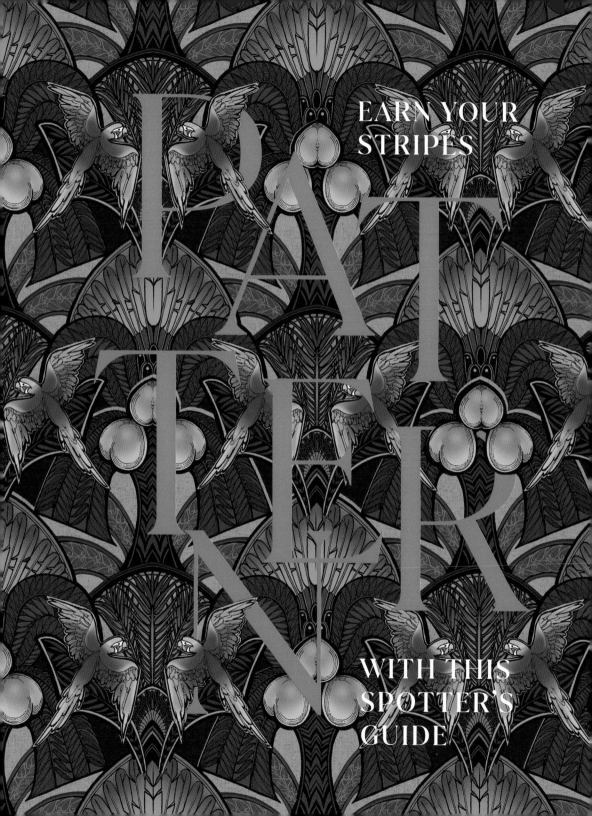

EARN YOUR
STRIPES

PATTERN

WITH THIS
SPOTTER'S
GUIDE

Pattern is exactly that: pattern. Making repetitive marks that together combine in a regularly repeating rhythm. The brain loves to lose itself in pattern. Brains love rhythm too. It helps them measure spaces and define where one object ends and another begins.

As an illustration of the power of pattern, camouflage proves that pattern can actively do the opposite, subverting the mind's ability to understand the shape or extent of an object. This is why the right sort of pattern can be useful in hiding a clunky chimney breast or a ground-to-air missile.

Pattern is often assumed to be geographically and sociologically specific. Historically, a particularly exotic pattern might have been chosen specifically because of its far-flung glamour. Most of the time this was just marketing; pattern is a much more international language than most people realize.

ANCIENT GEOMETRICS   Humankind's first mass-produced pattern was tweed. The weaving process means that the rhythm of the warp and weft creates a geometric repeat that leads the patternista into the vast majority of trigonometrical patterns. There's check, chequerboard, Y repeat, cube repeat, flame stitch… As techniques evolved, the world found itself enriched with designs that can be planned on a grid but that show off far more complicated or capricious geometric repeats. The perfect example of this is the Greek key pattern.

ANCIENT FLORALS   Early florals are heavy on the deliberate symbolism of particular flowers, which later became abstracted and refined. Honeysuckle is as synonymous with happiness, midsummer and love today as it was in ancient Greece. The honeysuckle shape, stylized into a curlicue-filled oval, crops up everywhere in architecture, pottery, wall paintings and on clothes. It could become a stencil very easily and thus was used as a border and all over repeat.

CHINTZ   Originating in India, chintz is a corruption of a Hindi word meaning spotted or printed. The European pattern tradition was held back by a rather pig-headed insistence on weaving pattern, whereas in India printing pattern allowed far more freedom (and many more colours).

Indian chintz started as depictions of the Tree of Life, which could be printed from intricately carved wooden blocks in a characteristic undulating repeat. To service the thirsty taste of overheated Western consumerism, Indian artists started to focus more on flowers (and less on trees), revelling in the plump reflected light trapped in the heart of cabbage roses.

DAMASK Although the term refers to Damascus, where damask was famously sold, the technique is Chinese and relies on the relationship between a matte background and a shiny foreground motif to create a self-coloured pattern. Usually silky, damask became a byword for high-ticket luxury in the Middle Ages and was often specifically reserved for the elite and the papacy. Chinese damasks are typically naturalistic trails of flora, sometimes alternated with Chinese characters. European damasks have a particular characteristic pattern. Derived from late Roman motifs that were adapted and remixed to suit the burgeoning Roman Christian Empire, they typically feature symmetrical repeats using stylized curls of acanthus often growing into abstract spirals.

THE GLORY OF ISLAMIC GEOMETRY Having inherited a mistrust of the depiction of living creatures from Judaism, Islam filled the decorative void with maths, science and calligraphy. While Christianity punished knowledge, Islam used the God-given complexities of trigonometry to create geometric spectacles that seem endless and powerfully infinite. Vegetative ornament, suitably stylized into what the world has come to refer to as Arabesque, is used as counterpoint to the lacy layering of interconnecting straight lines. Included in the scheme, calligraphic teachings or declarations encourage viewers to contemplate the divinity that inspires such thought-provoking intricacy.

SPOTS AND DITSIES Small scale, closely repeating patterns have a homespun simplicity that harks back to their below-stairs origins. In the past, the posher you were, the bigger and brighter your patterns. Minute ditsy florals and simplistic spots were printed, or perhaps woven, on cotton, which gave hard-working, low-income patternistas a smattering of jolly but low-budget ornamentation.

STRIPES In the Renaissance, walls were often furnished with strips of woven pattern in alternating colours to create a bold circus-tent effect. Bizarrely, stripes were, at various stages, specifically singled out to be a badge of prostitution. The bellicose burghers of bourgeois provinces were so concerned that decent ordinary ladykind be protected from being thought of as immoral that they came up with a whole list of specific fashion statements that should be forcibly worn by sex workers. It makes the concept of the pinstripe suit far more interesting, no?

ORIENTAL ASYMMETRY Hand-painted Chinese silks and brightly coloured strips of paper were used to furnish oriental folding screens, and they inspired European tastemakers to become far more organic with their pattern making. The screen panels themselves became early wallpaper, as seventeenth-century importers sold this packing material on to homeowners looking to do something dashing in the boudoir. Rebranded by European patternistas as Chinoiserie, these trailing asymmetrical patterns felt fresh and novel compared to the traditionally ponderous repeats of the by now old-fashioned damask.

TARTAN AND PLAID The idea of specific colours and combinations of colours denoting which clan or family group a specific kilt-wearer belonged to is actually Victorian. Queen Victoria loved anything Scottish and, looking at her interior decoration at Balmoral Castle, one must say she loved tartan a little too much. The tartan look, being a basic tweed weave, is simple to create and crops up in nearly all textile cultures. Today, tartan's place in contemporary style is not just iconically Scottish but also ironically punk. Thanks, Vivienne Westwood.

PAISLEY Most know this pattern is named for Paisley, the port town in Scotland that imported the intricately embroidered or printed shawls that bear its name. The Victorians loved its voluptuous detail to distraction, which egged Indian makers into ever more fantastical repeats. The main constituent of the paisley itself is the vaguely tear-drop shaped dhoti which is often said to be an abstracted depiction of the cypress trees fabled to grow in paradise. Others (me included) say that the dhoti traces a decorative lineage back to the Greek honeysuckle, to which it bears a doppelgänger-esque kinship. This is easily explained by Alexander the Great's military excursions into Northern India, the cultural legacy of which not only left us the dhoti but is also accepted as being the sculptural inspiration for the early classical depictions of Lord Buddha. Small world, isn't it?

THE OLDEST, AND THE NEWEST, PATTERN IN THE (JUNGLE) BOOK Our forebears and forebearesses wouldn't have worn animal print, they would have worn actual animal. Obvs. While patterned animal pelts crop up throughout the history of style, it's not until the exotica-obsessed Art Deco 1920s that they begin being printed. In ancient times, wearing the skin of a powerful animal was supposed to impart that animal's particular characteristics to the wearer. The same train of thought goes through the head of any animal print wearer today, who sees the adoption of leopard spots or zebra stripes as a way of advertising their untamed wild heart and forceful sexuality. Or so says Auntie Rita.

Pattern is a much more international language than most people realize.

USING PATTERN LIKE A PRO

Understanding Maximalism as I do, I know that the perfect visual symphony comes down to one thing, one truth, one perfect, perfect piece of arcane knowledge...

We old designosaurs are fond of saying 'It's all in the mix' and conventional interior design wisdom will have you dividing patterns between wheat and chaff, innies and outies or, more usually, rice and sauce. You'll find sauce patterns centre stage, blazing in spot-lit glory, while rice patterns are the carbohydrate-based, doo-wop backup singers.

Rice patterns are neutral and self-coloured: woven designs, grown up-ish geometrics, ditsy spots, stripes and tonal plaids. The idea is that they say what they've got to say in a strong, semi-silent fashion. Meanwhile, a typical sauce pattern is chilli-hot, brightly coloured, exotic and eye-catching and, when used in quantity, likely to incur a serious sugar rush. Hence, classically speaking, one is supposed to use them sparingly. As a method of interior design synesthesia that transposes taste for... well, taste... it works.

That's all well and good for conventional spaces but what of us Maximalists? Does the rice and sauce theory work for us too?

Yes, except the volume knob in our world is turned right up to eleven. Therefore the patterns the muggles may say are their sauce are, for Maximalists, merely rice. Now, Maximalkind quickly discovered that animal print, along with its luxurious, badass sexiness, is ideal rice for rich Maximal schemes. So, imagine, if you can, the pattern-coma our sauce patterns would induce in the minds of mere mortals.

HARD CORE
SOFT UPHOLSTERY

Comfort is *so* important for Maximalists. Purring is impossible on a bony-arse sofa with the bitter wind whistling through gappy, draughty blinds. The Maximalist state of grace is a state of *grand luxe*, where the room feels as much of a delight to the butt as it is to the sparkling eye.

The temptation is to furnish your Maximatorium *à la Seraglio*, with almost insurmountable escarpments of soft 'n' squishy cushions. Prosaically, that kind of thing is bad for the back and, in my experience, it's all too easy to mislay the TV remote. Indeed, our term 'sofa' derived from the *souffa*, that amorphous pile of upholstery to be found in the sultry corner of an Ottoman harem.

Something way too many people get wrong is seating and what my quiffy designer friends call 'softscaping'. Comfort is not synonymous with quantity in any way. All too often, buffet blindness leads to some hopelessly eyes-bigger-than-the-stomach choices. Sofas are often to blame, because they take up so much space. Their voluptuously rolled arms and generously adipose backs just gobble up way too much of your living room.

What you need, dear friend, is a settee. Oh dear, oh dear. I can hear granny turning in her urn with arch disapproval at the term. But please, let's not be snobby. Particularly since settee is a contraction of that good olde English piece of jolly furnishing, the settle, and it denotes a seating solution on legs. Far more nimble in frame than a sofa, a settee floats discreetly, where a sofa sits resolutely. A dignified back and straight arms may look less opulent but the point of all of this ain't the piece of furniture, it's the Maximalist array of cushions it hosts.

And good heavens, cushions really are top of the Maxima-list when it comes to upholstery. Accommodating the Maximalist in a soft feathery embrace, cushions are the ultimate expression of voluptuous comfort. Visually, they provide an ever-changing, ever-changeable art gallery of colour and pattern. The Maximalist world is divided betwixt the Maximalist cavaliers who like to leave their sofas in a sweet disorder of rumpled cushionage that looks racily post-coital and those who like a straight array (me included, curse my Roundhead tendencies). P.S. Never ever chop.

PUSHIN' FOR THE CUSHION

Since we're in the wonderful world of cushions, it's time for some pillow talk and the most bizarre bit of vestigial sexism.

The battle of the sexes was won most victoriously and most glamorously by ladykind. Hurrah say I – I love a woman on top. But a weirdly unresolved domestic conflict still rages with aggressive passivity in the bedroom.

Cushions on the bed (and I mean *cushions*, I'm presupposing the presence of pillows) – it seems all too many men see them as irrational and deeply suspicious. Perhaps they believe beneath the silk and tassels lurk steel-teethed mantraps? Anyway, get a grip, guys. These are items of soft upholstery but they're also highly symbolic. Bed cushions need to be seen as offerings. Dedicated to the household gods and the love gods, they turn an ordinary, everyday duvet-draped bed into an altar of Romanticism and a transport of delight.

The last thing Venus wants from her Mars is for him to be kicking the soft upholstery onto the floor with his back legs, like a terrier down a rabbit hole.

I can't help sniffing the unmistakable *odeur* of Bauhaus Breath here. It's as if blokekind has been ever-so-subtly brainwashed by some weird Modernist mind ray into the total disapproval of soft femininity in the home.

If only blokekind understood the significance of these super-feminine fripperies. If only they decided to not only *respect* the bed cushions but perhaps even come home from work with a bed cushion of their own choosing to lay on the altar of love… Then perhaps they'd find *all* sorts of lovely things to do and see in the bedchamber.

Surely Maximalism is *just* Boho *for* Grown-ups?

Yes it is, and if you want it as an equation:

BOURGEOIS + BOHO = MAXIMALISM

There is a cyclical symmetry to the equation. Don't forget that if those unamused revolutionary Modernists hadn't decided to fall out with the bourgeoisie and bohemians in the first place, the last hundred years might not have been quite so drab. Let me share the birth of Bohemianism – a term everyone takes for granted but never really has the time to Google.

It begins with the bourgeoisie of the 1850s, who wanted a way to let their hair down, take their bras off and live a little dangerously. Rather than owning the moment and spending the week in a negligee, the middle classes needed a brand to give their urges stylistic integrity. The French obliged with a series of steamy literary heroines whose lust-in-the-dust antics were patronizingly described as typical for ladies of gypsykind. In the way that the English word for Romani 'gypsy' alludes to a supposed Egyptian origin, the French term *bohème* suggests Romani culture, which was born in Czechoslovakian Bohemia.

Bohemian became shorthand for Parisian punk.

It was a style to be adopted as a way of showing how hip you were, how on trend. Very quickly, any suggestion that living a Bohemian life required an uncomfortable drop in bourgeois living standards was abandoned by the so-called Haute Bohémienne (who wouldn't be seen dead in a caravan).

What they wanted to focus on instead was free love (or the implied suggestion of free love) and shopping. Strongly coloured peasant embroidery was an obsession, as were layers of pattern, faux patches and a supercilious 'let them eat cake' evocation of the gritty life real Roma lived.

Boho has never fallen from fashionista grace. The yummy mummies of the Noughties threw themselves at boho the minute the first cuckoo of spring was heard off Portobello Road or in Greenwich Village. More than anything, boho was used as a way of proving (to themselves) how different they were from their own mothers. Mothers who, thirty years earlier, had thrown themselves at boho the minute the first cuckoo of spring arrived in Sloane Square or the Upper East Side. But boho remained seasonal. It floated in during spring and left after Labor Day. Frivolous and prone to being too pastel-toned, boho's butterfly fragility evaporated at the first sign of an autumn mist. But then along came Maximalism, boho's all weather big sister. The rest is Style History.

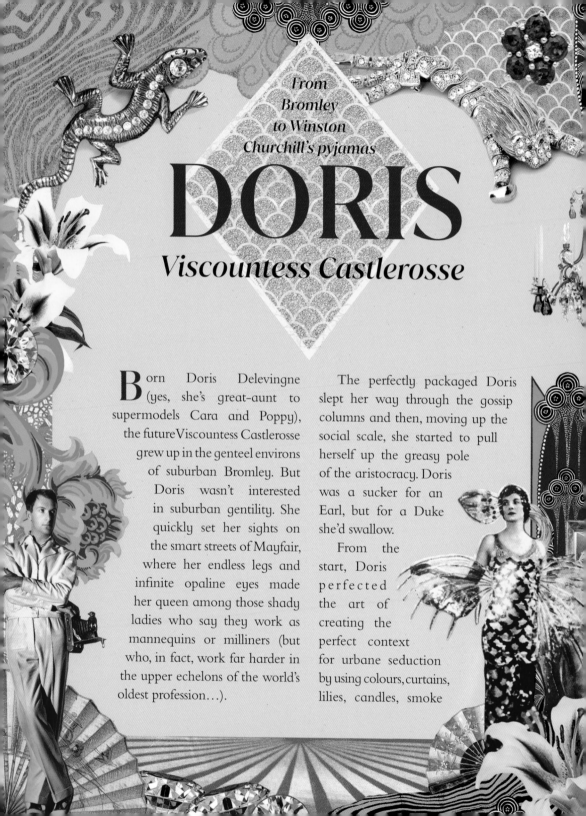

From
Bromley
to Winston
Churchill's pyjamas

DORIS

Viscountess Castlerosse

Born Doris Delevingne (yes, she's great-aunt to supermodels Cara and Poppy), the future Viscountess Castlerosse grew up in the genteel environs of suburban Bromley. But Doris wasn't interested in suburban gentility. She quickly set her sights on the smart streets of Mayfair, where her endless legs and infinite opaline eyes made her queen among those shady ladies who say they work as mannequins or milliners (but who, in fact, work far harder in the upper echelons of the world's oldest profession…).

The perfectly packaged Doris slept her way through the gossip columns and then, moving up the social scale, she started to pull herself up the greasy pole of the aristocracy. Doris was a sucker for an Earl, but for a Duke she'd swallow.

From the start, Doris perfected the art of creating the perfect context for urbane seduction by using colours, curtains, lilies, candles, smoke and mirrors to show herself off like the branded product she was honest enough to know she was.

She used close relationships with style arbiters like Cecil Beaton and showtune superstar Gertrude Lawrence to burnish her shining celebrity. Doris even seduced the confirmed homosexual Beaton, who enjoyed every minute (very loudly and several times a night, apparently). Legendary owner of a Singapore grip (look it up; it's worth it), Doris has long been credited with the aphorism 'There's no such thing as an impotent man, just an incompetent woman'. In fact, she made the salacious act of turning gay men into something of a sport, while also occasionally turning herself.

Doris's marriage to Valentine Browne, Viscount Castlerosse was glamorously chaotic and mutually abusive. Their fights were legendary. After ten years of matching black eyes, the Castlerosses divorced. But dishy Doris wasn't on the open market for long. She was snatched up by American heiress Margot Hoffman, who started house-hunting in Venice for the sort of spectacular *nid d'amour* in which Doris would look at her most fuckulent.

The *Palazzo Venier dei Leoni* was a *palazzo nonfinito*, basically a single-storey bungalow of epic, unfinished magnificence. These days it's best known as art collector Peggy Guggenheim's gallery of mid-century Modern masters.

But it had also been famously chosen as the background for Lady Gaga look-alike Marchesa Luisa Casati, during her Venetian incarnation before the First World War. Crowds would gather to watch the heroically over-made up Marchesa cross the Grand Canal in a gondola dripping with tassels and piled high with candelabra and two cheetahs in jewelled collars, while the gondolier (a near-naked American jazz singer) flexed enormous gold-leafed muscles as he got on with the gondoling. There must have been something Maximal in the water of the canal because when Doris moved into this stumpy palazzo she stripped out the Marchesa's old-fashioned, camp, silent-movie-style Maximalism and sprinkled her Venetian fixer-upper with 1930s luxury.

Society magazines gushed over the highlights. Black marble bathrooms with sunken baths and Liberty-style stucco panels... Back-lit etched glass murals... Super-costly Fortuny fabrics... Bank-busting Bevilacqua cushions dotted on uber-modern furniture to rather surreal effect. It was the epitome of international, jet-set, jazz-age Art Dago (as Dame Edna Everage used to refer to the excesses of continental Art Deco).

Yet Margot and Doris, despite having such a great couple name, weren't a match made in heaven. Doris quickly bored and started going AWOL. Finding solace in the plush villas owned by her glitterati pals that studded the French Riviera, she started drinking and screwing to forget.

There's a real consensus of opinion to support the idea she slept with Winston Churchill, and plenty of compelling evidence that a few sin-drenched, sun-drenched afternoon delights occurred with the old bulldog. The steamy paintings he did of her speak volumes, for a start.

It doesn't end well for Doris. She escaped the devastation of war-torn London by fleeing to the States, where she was broke and horribly unhappy. Her society circle were appalled that she'd refused to take World War II on the chin like everyone else and cut her dead when she finally returned to Britain and established herself in a suite at The Dorchester hotel.

Financially in peril (she was down to her last pair of nylons), losing her looks (or so she thought) and socially toxic (only Castlerosse visited her and he left furious), Doris took an overdose and expired in as controlled and as orderly a way as possible. Her exit was suitably Maximalist, surrounded by arum lilies and scented with Joy by Jean Patou in the Deanery Suite of The Dorchester.

Doris perfected the art of creating the perfect context for urbane seduction.

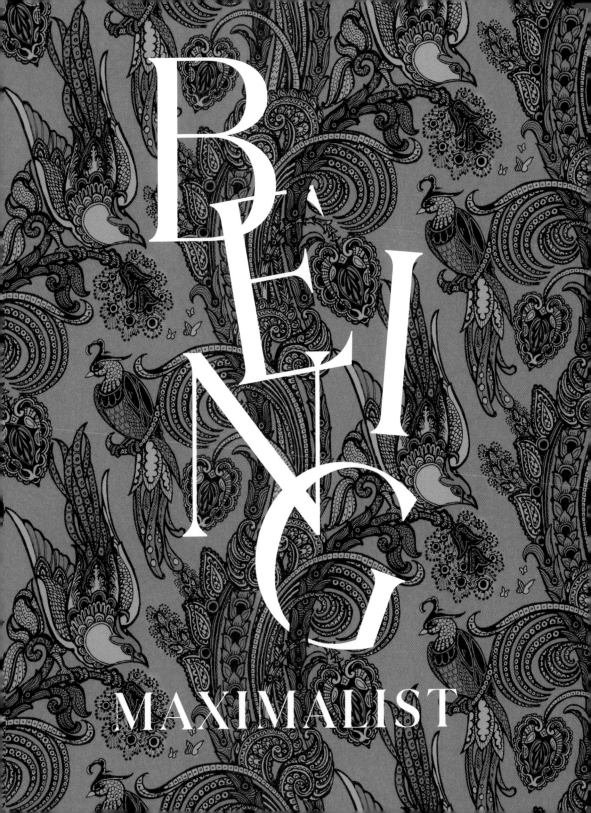

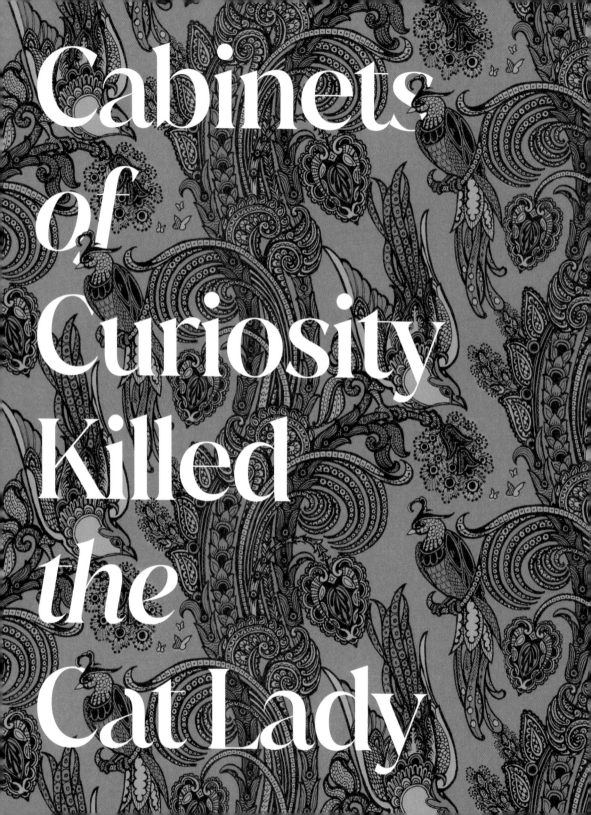

Cabinets of Curiosity Killed the Cat Lady

NOW IS THE TIME TO PLAY MAXIMALISM'S HISTORICAL TRUMP CARD...

And introduce you, dear seekers after the Maximal, to the *cabinet of curiosity*. Warrior princes of the Renaissance were masters at showing off. It went with the territory. They soon found the limit to just how big sleeves could practically be. And Renaissance-ifying your bastion with some Classically inspired architectural flourishes was all well and good. Obviously, it was nice to have a court painter to memorialize you in your super-shiny *haute couture* armour... Plus a court poet to stanza your achievements... And, of course, wall to wall antiquities — some of which could even be actual antiques. But the Renaissance wasn't just about great shopping. It was also about a new way of thinking. And, indeed, a new way of thinking about shopping.

The key to Renaissance ostentation was visibility. There was no space for subtlety. Every penny spent on Renaissance culture had to be worth its literal weight in gold. The Übermensch at the centre of his own Renaissance web had to be publicly seen to be powerful, virile, fertile, literate, courtly, knowledgeable, wise and thoughtful.

Now, *thoughtful* was not easy to advertise using architectural bombast. Out of all the princely values, thoughtful was the most personal, private state. So thoughtful couldn't be carved on castle walls. Instead it ended up enshrined in its own highly private little room.

Since the death of the Roman Empire, Western civilization had rapidly demonized learning. Weird, I know. But science, technology, medicine, history and drawing perspective were all aggressively repressed for a thousand dark and ludicrously Luddite years. Until the bright dawn of the Renaissance, that is.

There is way, way, way too much to say about the hows, whys and whats of the rebirth of culture in the early fifteenth century. It certainly wasn't the overnight *volte-face* school history books would have you believe, but the incontrovertible truth is that within one generation, the swanky cognoscenti of Northern Italy stopped feeling perpetually damned and started feeling a lot more optimistic about the human condition. This new sunny disposition went hand in glove with the vigorous revival of Classical culture, art, architecture, poetry, technology, science and a renewed enthusiasm for thoughtful philosophical curiosity.

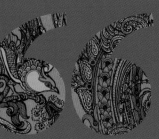

The key to Renaissance ostentation was visibility. There was no space for subtlety.

So back to our Renaissance Prince. He's got it all going on. All the boxes on the Renaissance list are ticked. But wait… now there's a new box in town. All the other big-sleeved princes are making themselves 'thought rooms'. *Stanzini*. In the many princedoms, fiefdoms and teeny tiny countries that made up Germany, Austria and all the *mittel* European lands beloved of comic opera, they were known as *Wunderkammer*.

The *stanzino*, *Wunderkammer* or – let's call it what it is – "the dudeoir" was, by its very nature, sequestered. Of all the big bouncy show-offy rooms in the palace, this one was defo off the guided tour and only shown to mates and intimates.

For a start, it was likely to contain bits and bobs considered mildly racy at best and, at worst, full-throttle blasphemous by the ever-circling, never-forgiving inquisition. But more than that, it was supposed to be a very personal mind palace, a museum of you, with a myriad of extraordinary and peculiar objects collected for their ability to pique the curiosity of their collector.

So *stanzini* quickly became the most illuminating room that the illuminati could create for themselves, devoid of any preordained social or cultural tropes. Every *stanzino*, every *Wunderkammer*, every cabinet of curiosity was as different, personal and complicated as its individual owner.

The collections themselves were deliberately unprescribed. The point was to follow your own idiosyncratic inquisitiveness down rabbit holes of inquiry. They were Renaissance Google.

The combinations of items were beyond surreal and covered anatomy, biology, geology, gemmology, mythology, geography, anthropology and – because you rarely invited the missus in for tea – quite a lot of pornography too. These items could have cost a king's ransom. Literally.

Kidnapped aristos were sometimes swapped for a narwhal horn or two… which were placed next to a pebble with a hole in it, found on a beach walk that morning. The thing was that whatever was included was super fascinating.

Which is why they're so damn Maximalist.

TABLESCAPES –
A MAXIMALIST ART FORM

Tablescape always sounds like a wince word. You know, those often-used terms that make you pull a slightly strained face like you've licked a lemon. It's a bit too snappy, like smasual (smart casual) or brunch ('I'm too disorganized to eat breakfast but too impatient to wait for lunch').

But tablescape comes with an impeccable, even royal(ish) pedigree, since it was first coined in the 1960s by super-boujee geshmakateer David Hicks, to describe the art of tabletop display. He was an incandescently talented designer who married into a rather low-growing twig of the royal family tree. Hicks maintained a masterful command of the energy and originality that propelled 1960s interiors to do some super-improbable stuff and his particular genius was to do 1960s swing-your-pants style in the historic homes of his upper-class clients.

With one eye on the Georgian rule book he'd pull off some really quite rock 'n' roll decorating combinations. He would throw oriental lacquer, smoked glass, cola-coloured gloss paint walls and cherry-red patent leather bean bags into the taste blender with a set of Hepplewhite dining chairs and a twice life-size Cambodian Buddha head.

Hicks's style became the benchmark for jet-set decorating in the 1970s, until punk pulled those palaces down towards the end of the decade, and the very keystone of his style was the tablescape. Which sometimes featured an actual keystone.

Having stuff 'out' used to be considered supremely eccentric. You'd be allowed a gentle arrangement or garnish on your mantelshelf, perhaps a classical pairing of vases, a centrepiece clock, a bud vase or two and a family photograph or three… but little else. Good-taste interiors imprisoned shizzle in large, glazed cabinets or under glass domes on high shelves for fear the objects might escape and have far too much fun.

Hicks sprung those tchotchkes from their upper-class jails and allowed them to frolic unfettered around the drawing room.

Built into this release was the presupposition that the newly liberated bric-a-brac was eclectic. Hicks's vision had much in common with that

Renaissance favourite, the cabinet of curiosities, where the only criterion for a collection was that it made you curious. Hicks wanted to be the (evil) genius who pulled together a bizarre pantomime of disparate characters into a highly original and highly personal tableau. *Très* Maximalist.

And to help his methodology, he embraced the un-embraceable. He allowed coffee tables into his schemes, despite their Modernist overtones, and he left the door open for more or less anything – any style, any period – to join the party. However, the really clever bit was keeping the stylistic bone structure rigorously classical.

Alongside the coffee table, a Hicks scheme would offer potential tablescape space on occasional tables, lamp tables, console tables and sometimes, since this was the 1960s, a corner of the floor.

What the Dickens is a tablescape – and how does one create one?

A tablescape is a highly stylized and theatrically inspired grouping of objects. Think still-life meets Harrods' sale. It's an opportunity to express the design direction of the entire room scheme in miniature. A bit like an *amuse-bouche* or an overture. It's also the point where you can create a specific choreography for the things you feel benefit from close up attention. It's the essential edit.

Tablescapes allow Maximalists to order objects so they may be appreciated through 360 degrees of loveliness as the viewer progresses around the room. Tablescape is so much more exciting than the traditional single-point, fixed frontal view of a mantelshelf arrangement.

With this in mind, relative height is far more important, as is axis. I like to imagine the tablescape as an imaginary townscape. Sounds weird but bear with… Imagine traveling around the monumental knick-knacks that a giant version of you has placed with thought and care. Imagine going for a gentle and relaxing walking tour and enjoy the changing vistas, as your eye moves from one thing to another. Turn a corner and a new view is revealed while unexpected combinations and unanticipated relationships make your mouth water.

The joy of tablescaping is that it's like bonsai furniture therapy. Toy town decorating, without the commitment of turning your whole room upside down.

The usual rules of display apply. Seek out new life and harmonious relationships between objects that can be as disparate as you like because, hey, they're yours and you love them. Keep an eye, as ever, on their visual weight. If something you love needs a bit more emphasis, then place it on the shoulder of a giant. Use a box or stack of books as a Maximalist plinth to help it stand loud 'n' proud. Don't be frightened to add the ordinary either. David Hicks himself was not above sneaking Christmas decorations from Woolworths into tablescape compositions that were predominantly museum quality.

He was also super-cunning with glass vases. He used straight-sided chunky bottomed glass tanks, so beloved in the 1970s, in a variety of sizes which could be turned upside down to become modish pedestals or used right way up as receptacles for small and precious collections.

If you're feeling like a space wizard, there's a whole new dimension to play with in your tablescape, which is reflection. Putting a particularly diverting object on a piece of mirror will create an *Alice Through The Looking Glass* upturned twin, which can make a surreally exciting centrepiece. I've trawled flea markets and thrift stores for old mirror pieces cut to fit into unusual shaped frames, which work particularly well. The older and more blotchily foxed, the better. Hang it all, you could even put a mirror across the whole tabletop, doubling your tablescape for free.

Don't forget lighting in your miniature *mise-en-scène*. Tealights integrated within the tablescape will sparkle and glimmer, adding new shadows and highlights. I'm not a fanboy of fairy lights, and their ubiquitousness doesn't make their effect classier. Fine for Christmas (to which classy should always be a stranger) but I have seen tablescapes where battery-operated fairy lights, concealed in opaque opaline glass vases, created rather magical effects. Although, having said that, I had been drinking rather a lot.

The final word goes to floristry. Finding space for a few containers in which you can put flowers (or branches if you want to upscale the effect with added drama) will give your tablescape a topical florescence that stops you becoming bored. The secret is to design the composition so that it works without the floriculture, so when you do treat yourself to the flowers, it's a special addition, not a stylistic necessity.

CURATION EXPLAINED

So, world, you're a funny old place and constantly surprising. The way that words slide from thoughtful obscurity into pop culture ubiquity never ceases to amaze, and it is irksome to suddenly find that curation is now a T-shirt slogan for the generation hooked on the neurotrash of social media. Everyone is curating everything, from their mental health to their Instagram feeds. These days, if you're not curated then you're not truly alive. Get curated or be cremated. Yet curation is actually an incredibly delicate and quite complicated art. It's essential that we proud Maximalists, in our lovely Maximatoriums, become near divine in our curatorial capabilities. And to do that, curation needs to be understood.

Curation is the ability to take an object and understand it. Understand it so very well that you can express everything about that object, the essence of the object, by the way that you present it. It's not just about something simply looking good in the corner of a room. Actually, true curation has a depth that's possibly deeper than that irritating iceberg that almost did for some of my in-laws on the Titanic. And that's deep. And also a story for another day.

At the heart of curation, I've always found a degree of good ole-fashioned Celtic magic. My shaggy forebears and plaited forebearesses believed that anything could be controlled, if you knew its true name. This is why we Celts are so deliberate about using people's names casually in conversation. There's a lot of magic that could go more than a little dark if one inadvertently says Blodwin three times. Gad, look at *Beetlejuice*. This is why we Welsh are particularly prone to peppering our intimate conversations with *darling* and *duckie*. It's not that we don't know your name – we do – but we're also super-respectful of the power that comes with it.

Back to the curatorial and this magical, mercurial commitment to knowing the name. Learning the story, getting under the skin of the detail, is essential in getting it right. But I think it's extremely important to understand that the knowledge I'm telling you to seek isn't necessarily to be found from a solid Googling.

It's self-knowledge. There are plenty (me, for one) that will take pleasure from knowing an exact incept date, from translating a maker's mark, from learning all the ingredients. But I want to point you towards a level of knowing that's yours and yours alone. Tap into your own memory bank and retrieve the specific reasons why, whatever the object is, it gives you pleasure. What are the associations? Exactly what has illuminated the synaptic sparks that leap from one side of your brain to another, opening up vistas of memory, enjoyment and pleasure?

Is it because your Mum had one and, although she's dead now, owning this thing will conjure her back into your life with an intensity that looking at a photograph will never achieve? Is it because your Mum didn't have one, but always wanted one?

Is it because every time you look at this item it takes you to somewhere far, far away that you've never actually been to? Or is it from somewhere you have been, and you bought it at the airport, after a few at the bar?

- ♦ Did you buy it with a friend?

- ♦ Were you given it by an enemy?

- ♦ Do you love it because it makes you feel doomed and beautiful like Marie Antoinette? Or indeed Gary Antoinette?

It all boils down to coming clean about your motives for ownership. This is one of the most important cornerstones of Maximalism. Own too much stuff, by all means, but own it thoughtfully. Own it respectfully. And above all, know *why* you own it.

LAYERING IN YOUR MIND PALACE

So you've written a full length biography of your vase. You've psycho-studied it from every angle, talked to the other vases it grew up with and even tracked down its potter. You now know your vase.

The good news is not just that it's passed the vase test, making it worthy of ornamenting your life, but also that you've also given yourself a good steer on its compatibility.

Now it's time to slide into the hot, soupy waters of aesthetics. You'll need to summon your inner stylist and make a full visual inventory of that thing. Start by weight. Ask how heavy, how light? What sort of massy impact does it make on your retina? Consider the shape and architecture. Horizontal, vertical, angles, curves and general shapeliness? Then make for the surface… Look at texture and pattern. Do they augment or undermine the outline? Does the ornamentation make a greater impact than the shape?

The vase is now thoroughly surveyed, inside and out. Its links to your own very particular and peculiar psychology are catalogued, alongside a full-size scan of its aesthetic impact.

 *The ode to joy that a Maximalist room sings to its owner is one of total inclusion and magnificent peculiarity.*

Now we can indulge in the moment we've all been waiting for… Now is the point in our Maximalist journey when, with a proud tear in your eye, the vase is released into the wilds of your home to gambol with its friends. But importantly, let's now consider who those friends should be.

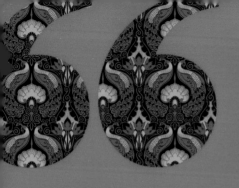

When you look at two *objets de vertu* together and they embrace, they unite (yet remain obviously distinct), they rhyme.

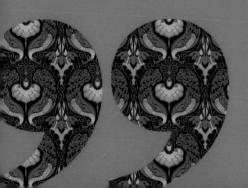

to tickle and dandle all that surrounds you, all those things you get such very great pleasure from owning. It's a great opportunity to start a dialogue with your Maximalism and then keep the love alive through engaged conversation.

The menial act of cleaning can also be used as stealth furniture therapy. Assess how you've arranged stuff as you move it to dust beneath. In a techno world where cleaning solutions abound and new machines are created to achieve unprecedented levels of futuristic cleanliness, Maximalists know the best solution to spring cleaning a Maximatorium is unrepentantly lo-fi. The good old feather duster. Anyone with a feather duster in their hand feels fabulous, making one the very epitome of pantomime glamdom. And they allow you to dust your collection *in situ* without the imperative to move it all around.

Hurrah to the inventor of the feather duster (who was actually an inventrix). The patent awarded to Susan Hibbard in 1876 is a feminist landmark. After a lengthy legal battle, she proved that husband George had no right to the invention because he played no part in its creation. Up to that point, the husbands of women who filed patents were automatically entitled to half the revenue. The assumption being that the little lady really couldn't have come up with the idea on her own. But thanks to Susan, the world of innovation became a fairer place.

But I think the final word should really go to the Icon that is Quentin Crisp, Gaytriarch and anti-lifestyle guru. Crisp welcomed dust into his Maximalist New York lair, seeing it as a great visual leveller. Like Vaseline around the lens or an Instagram filter, a fine layer of dust gives everything a flattering soft focus glamour. It works on people too, if they stay still long enough.

HOW HIGH MAINTENANCE *ACTUALLY IS* MAXIMALISM?

As Aladdin's Uncle Abanazar was keen to point out, always keep your old lamps polished like new. Maximalism is, and will always be, high maintenance. That's the point. Maintenance is esteem. If you love it, then keep it polished. Ask any boarding-school-age teenager: that which they love the most gets a stonkingly thorough polishing on a near-daily basis.

For all those who look at a Maximalist space and instantly cry, 'Oh my God, what a dust trap.' remember it's Minimalism that is the high-maintenance decorative option that one constantly needs to live up to.

Minimalism will never forgive you if you leave the Sunday papers by the sofa until the following weekend. Whereas Maximalism is always much more easygoing – especially when it comes to dust. Maximalism offers you the choice to clean or not to clean. If you want your Maximalism to be glossy-magazine-cover-shoot ready at all times then you will indeed spend much of life's precious time a-dusting and a-fluffing. But guess what? It's not necessary. Dusting was never mentioned in Maximalism's operating instructions manual, and tumbleweeds of dust are so much more spitefully visible on a bland, blonde Minimalist ash floor than on a cozy, densely patterned Maximalist magic carpet. In fact, I think there is something rather lovely and very Maximalist about a very fine coating of dust to knock everything back.

But the occasional flick around with a soft duster is charming cardio with a lovely end result. And as for the heavenly scent of good, old-fashioned beeswax polish… well, *oh my*. Polishing is, let's face it, stroking. How lovely

Thanks to your deep vein knowledge of all the ins and outs of the stuff you live with, you're in the most BABOOSHKATASTIC position to start making tchotchke matches in heaven. Pairings that aren't just about skin-deep beauty, but also psychologically profiled relationships, like you're the best mofo matchmaker in the village. Ever.

The ode to joy that a Maximalist room sings to its owner is one of total inclusion and magnificent peculiarity. Hell, what you've got to realize is that Maximalism is thoroughly possible with the mass-produced. Remember to *own* ordinary if you own anything ordinary.

You could have a room whose contents constitute a set number of items, an inventory that is identical to your neighbour… But your Maximalism will be totally different from their Maximalism because the way you put your Maximalism together will be about you, while theirs will be about them. Curation, like fingerprints, will always be different from individual to individual.

When Maximalism is at the top of its game it creates casual, but unbelievably powerful, relationships that are allowed to develop between objects that would never normally exist in the same sphere. On the other side of the coin, chez anti-Maxer, the level of control means there will never be the happy accidents on which Maximalism thrives. And no joy either.

Maximalism is the quest for you to open a museum dedicated to you. The perfect display of everything that's important and different about you, allowed its own space, to speak on its own, and as part of a powerfully particular personal chorus. Hallelujah hallelujah hallelujah. Your mantelpiece will never be the same again. All you own will become combined within thoroughly thoughtful and exquisitely composed still-lives that tell the story of you.

Looking at one of my own mantelpieces, I'm glowing in the highly charged, personality-rich joy of a pair of museum-quality and intricately pornographic Georgian candlesticks, a raffia donkey from Acapulco airport, a Roberts radio and a pebble or two from a recent walk. Heaven.

If you're looking for a Maximalist masterclass, rearrange those in your head, until you're happy with the effect.

GO
MAXIMALIZE
YOURSELF

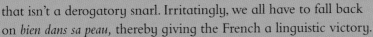
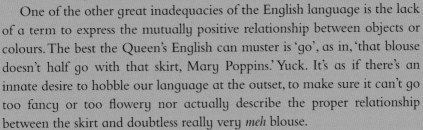

Sometimes English fails us. There are 145 words for 'posh' but nothing to describe a state of positive self-esteem that isn't a derogatory snarl. Irritatingly, we all have to fall back on *bien dans sa peau*, thereby giving the French a linguistic victory.

One of the other great inadequacies of the English language is the lack of a term to express the mutually positive relationship between objects or colours. The best the Queen's English can muster is 'go', as in, 'that blouse doesn't half go with that skirt, Mary Poppins.' Yuck. It's as if there's an innate desire to hobble our language at the outset, to make sure it can't go too fancy or too flowery nor actually describe the proper relationship between the skirt and doubtless really very *meh* blouse.

Anyway, I'm here to help, as always. Let me share my time-honoured, tried and trusted solution. Instead of 'go', use 'rhyme'. Because that is actually what's happening. When you look at two *objets de vertu* together and they embrace, they unite (yet remain obviously distinct), they rhyme. There is a reason the rhyme rhymes… keep reading, and I'll tell you later.

COLLECTING
VS ACQUIRING

Look, I'll not lie, *of course* Maximalism can be bought off the shelf. Actually, by the yard. It's how they furnish sports bars or the more remote corridors of country house hotels. But Maximalism bought from the Maximalism shop (however fresh) is Maximalism without a heart. And Maximalism without a heart is Maximalism without a point.

As a thoroughly efficient barometer of just how popular Maximalism is, check out the glossy advertorials you find in the weekly chat mags. Collections reign supreme. For a series of manageable monthly payments, you too can own an exquisite set of 12 (yes, 12) hand-embellished figurines depicting the 12 ages of Elvis. Each beautifully modelled, cruelty-free porcelain statuette will be dispatched direct to your home on the third day of every fourth month until (decades later) you have the full resplendent set. Voilà, you've acquired a collection. But you won't have acquired much of an experience to augment the pleasure of owning your collection.

OK, there are times when an off-the-shelf collection can play a part in a Maximatorium. There have been times when finding six matching Victorian fruit plates or two pairs of monkey candelabra have got me more than a tad excited. And it's because I can see these sets or suites providing a moment of choral structure, or Maximalist rhythm, around which more informal groupings of stuff may revolve. I like a bit of bone structure in my *sweete* disorder.

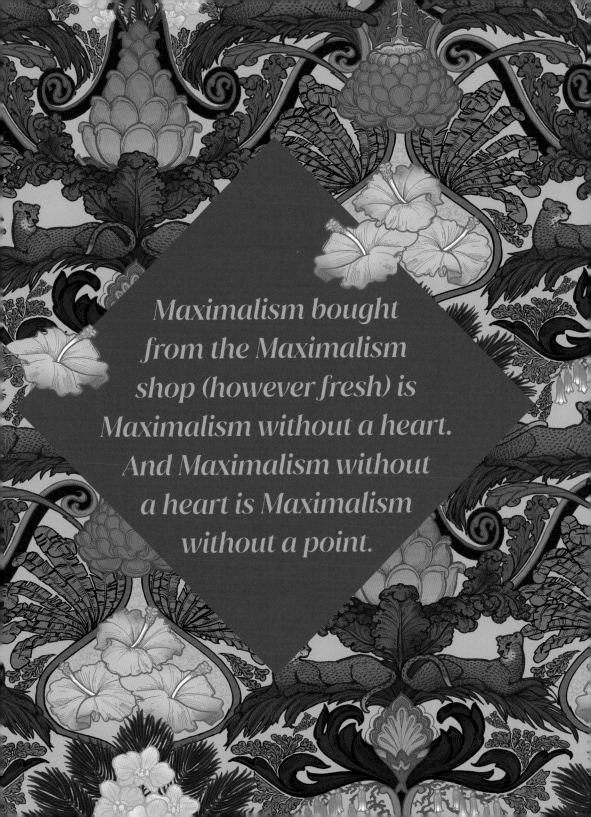

Maximalism bought from the Maximalism shop (however fresh) is Maximalism without a heart. And Maximalism without a heart is Maximalism without a point.

STORAGE

TO STORE OR NOT TO STORE?

Well, there is no question. Don't. Storage is a ghastly confection of twentieth-century origin which simply didn't exist before the 1950s. Unless, that is, you were an apple farmer and needed to store an excess crop of applage, or you were a Venetian merchant with more bales of gorgeously figured silk than could be plausibly sold on the Rialto in one lovely Venetian afternoon.

Storage, as a destination or as a desirable utility, rather than an understated convenience, would be considered thoroughly eccentric to our forebears and forebearesses.

Before we stored, we displayed. Before we jimmied all our less photogenic shizzle into the understairs cupboards, we proudly composed our chattels in beguiling still-lifes on the sideboard. We showed off all that we owned because we loved it – and it loved us back.

Sure, some stuff didn't get a thorough outing on a regular basis. But even that tropical butterfly net, pith helmet or patent anti-yeti visor might find a less visited corner in which to lurk, out of mind but still in sight.

But two things changed – two things that hate each other with deathless loathing. First, faced with the mouth-watering smörgåsbord of consumerism that late twentieth-century society presented, humanity started suffering from a really bad case of buffet blindness. Conversely, humanity quickly realized that the average real-estate footprint of the average life simply didn't have enough room to contain the sheer quantity of all-you-can-consume excess it desired.

There was an entitled aggression to the way the world shopped like kids with their pocket-money clenched in sweaty palms.

Meanwhile, as if there wasn't enough friction in the air, design orthodoxy deliberately and spitefully dreamt up Minimalism.

Minimalism was for the enlightened, the evolved few, who weren't seduced by tawdry gee-gaws or distracted by the siren call of *buy one get one free*. Minimalists saw themselves as a cerebral elite who owned a perfectly edited inventory, thoughtfully chosen from the best designers that lifestyle had to offer.

OK, maybe somewhere there are a handful of these shining higher beings, but most people realized that to keep up with the careening Minimalist bandwagon as it gathered repulsive momentum, they'd have to start compartmentalizing their interiors. They realized that perpetuating the glossy-magazine fiction of Minimalism meant they'd need to find hidey holes for all the furtive clutter they didn't have the moral fibre to skip.

If only they had made a bonfire of their own inanities on their own front lawns, at least we'd all feel they were actually committed.

The funny thing is that, although none of them said it, all those whey-faced Modernists with paper-cut smiles saw housing as storage anyway. The way Le Corbusier prattled on about the modern home, you'd think he wasn't just describing storing humans but actually filing them. As we've all come to agree, Modernists didn't like human beings making their lovely clean-lined schemes messy. Couldn't people be put in drawers?

You should be careful what you wish for. The contemporary obsession with storage does actually include storing ourselves, or at least our lives. The smartphone that has become a digital life-support system now also stores our souls. Everything that makes us who we are is locked behind a PIN. Not least our memories. Time was, photographs were proudly catalogued in photo albums, with the best or most important in frames on the piano. Now they exist only in the ether of storage, unless we specifically conjure them from our phones. Surely it's impossible not to be deeply unsettled, scrolling through a smartphone photo library at high speed? Science tells us that that's exactly what the brain sees in its last 15 seconds of existence before the oxygen runs out. Literally, life flashing by before our mind's eye.

Back to storage and its egregious effect on what poor storaphiles feel is – and isn't – worth showing off in a room. If storage is an aid to curation, then fine! However, it quickly becomes a home's backed-up colon. A dark, dank, malodorous jumble that explains the fact that most high-street modern rooms are martyrs to IBS.

Even at this point, another layer of complication gets applied to the modern room. Rather than a jolly good turn out, a new breed of genetically modified storage consultants has been created in the germy petri dish of the internet to show you (on Instagram of course) how to fold what you store into ergonomic pods. Panties crisply folded to look like fortune cookies.

Scarily, the suburbs are now hooked on storage. Who knew the understairs cupboard was a gateway drug to a life-destroying addiction? In these strange and terrible days, realtors will list off the storage solutions in a home with lip-smacking delectation before any of the more traditional selling points of real estate.

Store stuff, friends, by all means, store stuff. But, if you do, then why not take the door off the cupboards or the fronts from the drawers? Make sure you truly own the stuff you're storing.

Before Modernism, kitchens didn't have units, they had shelves. Shelves on which the ordinary and the useful was displayed with the same Maximalist pride as the valued and the venerated. It was storage with honesty. Honesty, integrity and pride. It was also the ultimate goal of marvellous Maximalism; owning up to ordinary.

VERONICA FRANCO

Putting the Cor into Courtesan

A gondolier slithers up to a cascade of worn stone steps spilling down into the Grand Canal. An older woman, dressed in a servile understatement that belies her hauteur, waves us in.

The hallway is dark and cool. A few wooden settles are painted to look like Istrian stone with counterfeit carved ornamentation. The upper portions of the walls and curved ceiling cove also set out to convince the eye that their flat surfaces are enriched with deeply moulded architecture. Which they are not.

We are shown a steep staircase that rises through a long tube of barrel vault, up to the first floor. The treads, thin fingers of blue-veined marble, force you to step on your toes as you ascend. Bravo for the velvet-covered rope that loops, helpfully, through cast bronze hands, offering welcome support to the scrambling climber.

And, as you reach the top, a little stooped, a little breathless and still on your toes, you're in a perfect pose of submission before the smile of the golden woman that greets you in deep blue damask radiating an abundant and generous welcome. Meet Veronica Franco.

The first floor is the most important floor of any Venetian building. Up here, above the canal, is where sunlight fractured by wavelets gilds the deeply coffered ceiling with blotches of Venetian gold. As is the custom, this ceiling has the most eye-catching ornamentation in the whole building. It's painted, plastered, gilded and carved to extremes. And cost as much as possible too. Ever practical in their ostentation, Venetians know that it's this ceiling that the world sees as it passes below on the canal. In Venice you are judged by your ceiling.

Stretched from one end of the narrow building to the other, this room is a particularly Venetian invention known as the portego. The end overlooking the canal becomes an open loggia, with a view framed by four sets of paired columns in the old-fashioned pointed style. The other end is a decent walk-away (portegos are welcomed by sequestered ladies as a place to exercise through walking), and slatted wooden shutters let slits of light in from the scruffy little square below. To be a Venetian wife in 1570 is to accept a life-long sentence of confinement. Kept under lock and key at home, heavily and un-recognizably veiled in the street, Venetian women are pale and private. It's punishment to be a wife, although it's a life of gilded luxury and self-determination to be a prostitute, and Veronica Franco is at the pinnacle of that career. This portego boasts of great taste, tact and learning. Objects are posed with a studied carelessness as if gently set down at our arrival. The whole effect is of rich opulence and casual confidence, allowing a mélange of patterns and heavy colours to converse with a mellow intimacy. Intricately chased brass lanterns, no two of them alike, betray Ottoman origins.

As do the folding tables,

The whole effect is of rich opulence and casual confidence, allowing a mélange of patterns and heavy colours to converse with a mellow intimacy.

whose geometry has a snowflake complexity. X-frame chairs become chimerical beasts, thanks to the carvers' art.

Look closer and tabletops, settle seats, mantle shelves and artfully chosen areas of the terrazzo floor each become a still-life for the visitor to unearth, as one discovers pictures in a gallery. A lute, a bowl of fruit, an unusual mineral, a skull, a brightly glazed pot full of rambling blossoms and books... Everywhere, books. And those covered with the finest leather and tooled with the brightest gold are the books of Veronica's own poetry.

Her other great achievement is her storied beauty, which remains the lustrous subject of several framed canvasses displayed on silk-draped easels. The glass-makers of Murano were delighted to provide la diva Veronica with panels of smoky mirror, as dark and cloudy as obsidian and etched in endless arabesques that reflect the bed from both wall and ceiling. And they

allowed their jealously protected artistry (it is a capital offence to share the secrets of glass-making) full licence in making chandeliers with myriad amber glass lustres. The colour chosen to resemble Veronica's own hair.

Despite the meniscus of grandeur, the majority of this building, this palazzetta, is occupied by others. Boatmen and their families, apothecaries, an artist or two...

But none of that matters because Veronica has created a Venusberg of such comfort and Maximalist luxury that you immediately feel that this reality must be the dream.

So, there we are. Veronica Franco in her Maximalist lair. She was an extraordinary character and her luminous personality shines through the glowering murk of five hundred years. Poet, feminist and, yes, courtesan, because selling your sex was the only key a Venetian woman had to unlock the patriarchal prison that kept all other females out of society and off the streets.

It's typical of the bureaucratic Venetians to create an administrative structure for the city's sex trade. There was even a guide book/price list/Trip Advisor-style review rating system called *Il catalogo di tutte le principali et più honorate cortigiane di Venezia*, in which Veronica gets a seven star write-up. In it, readers are regaled with the Maximalust details of Veronica's 11-day non-stop romp with Henry III of France, who was decidedly young, dumb and full of aplomb. He'd come to Venice to be impressed and Veronica didn't disappoint.

Venice invents the art of luxury shopping as early as the twelfth century. St. Mark's Square became one giant millionaire's trade fair, with stalls selling the world's most recherché desirables, to coincide with the tourist catnip of Carnivale.

By Veronica's day, luxury had come to define Venice. Venetian art, propelled by superstar painters like Titian, Tintoretto and Veronese, held the world in thrall and all of them, at some stage or other, painted la diva Veronica. Not, as was usual, beneath a euphemistic mythological filter as a Greek or Roman goddess such as Diana or Venus, but as Veronica Franco, businesswoman, tastemaker, Renaissance influencer and author. She was Bitchtorious. Until, that is, the inconvenient irritation of a city-wide outbreak of the Black Death. Veronica leaves Venice in a hurry and the next we hear of her is Veronica acting as her own advocate, fighting the courts for the return of all her marvellous Maximalist trappings, which were looted while she was in self-imposed exile. It doesn't end well, and poor Veronica dies in extremely reduced circumstances, supported by occasional hand-outs from her former clients.

Icon of self-determination, fierce Queen, feminist, Maximalist and poster girl for the late Renaissance generation, Veronica Franco used her shimmering life, her looks, her intelligence and her books (*Familiar Letters to Various People* was a Europe-wide best seller and a favourite of Elizabeth I) in a way we would now recognize as supremely Modern. Which is not a term I use lightly.

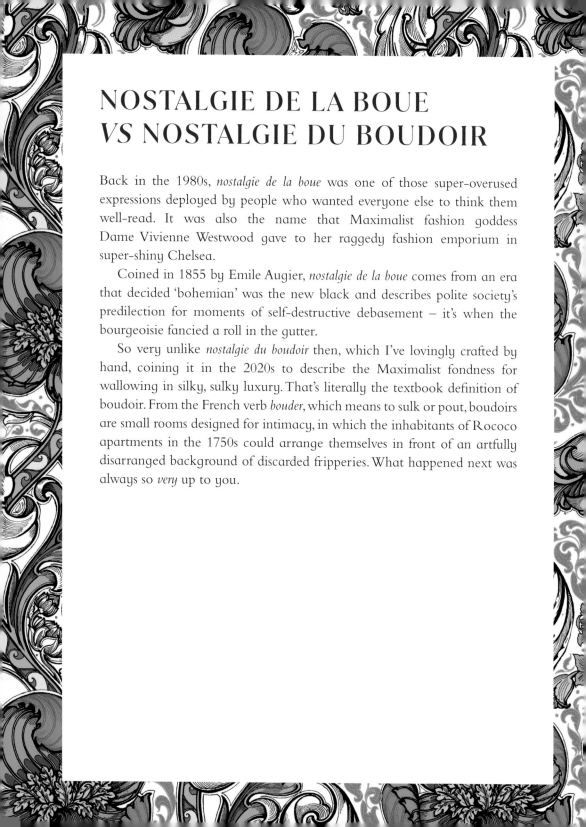

NOSTALGIE DE LA BOUE
VS NOSTALGIE DU BOUDOIR

Back in the 1980s, *nostalgie de la boue* was one of those super–overused expressions deployed by people who wanted everyone else to think them well-read. It was also the name that Maximalist fashion goddess Dame Vivienne Westwood gave to her raggedy fashion emporium in super-shiny Chelsea.

Coined in 1855 by Emile Augier, *nostalgie de la boue* comes from an era that decided 'bohemian' was the new black and describes polite society's predilection for moments of self-destructive debasement – it's when the bourgeoisie fancied a roll in the gutter.

So very unlike *nostalgie du boudoir* then, which I've lovingly crafted by hand, coining it in the 2020s to describe the Maximalist fondness for wallowing in silky, sulky luxury. That's literally the textbook definition of boudoir. From the French verb *bouder*, which means to sulk or pout, boudoirs are small rooms designed for intimacy, in which the inhabitants of Rococo apartments in the 1750s could arrange themselves in front of an artfully disarranged background of discarded fripperies. What happened next was always so *very* up to you.

WHAT'S THE ACTUAL PROBLEM WITH BEING BOURGEOIS?

The chokehold of twentieth-century orthodoxy despised one word beyond all others. Bourgeois. But why?

Well, everyone needs a villain and there's nothing more fun than blaming one's poor, blameless parents for being so damn *parenty*.

Back when Modernism was young, those passionately under-groomed firebrands that were trying to rebuild society, art, politics, music, architecture, poetry and living rooms more or less all started life in over-upholstered nurseries as the beloved apple in their over-upholstered mother's eye.

The prevailing pose was to despise all that had been before and *particularly* absolutely anything that your parents stood for. The language of the time was all about sweeping away the past, smashing tradition and crushing the bourgeoisie.

I accept that we all roll our eyes at dad jokes, and that mums can be over-annoying about whether we're eating enough (or maybe eating a little too much). Dad's sporting memorabilia and Mum's *you* memorabilia are the antithesis of any idea of what you may call good taste, but tread carefully.

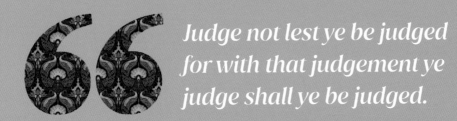

Judge not lest ye be judged for with that judgement ye judge shall ye be judged.

Historically, the bourgeoisie were always thought of as rather jolly. Roly-poly ruff-wearers responsible for a decent Christmas feast complete with lusty mumming. Occasionally they were heroic, like the grimy and emaciated Burghers who trudged out of Calais to surrender the city's key to Edward III after a particularly bitter siege.

The bourgeoisie were the urban wealthy, successful shopkeepers and merchants who built their power (unlike their aristocratic overlords) from trade, rather than the armed land grab favoured by the knightly classes.

They loved their merchandise. Billy and Betty Bourgeois sank their cash into fineries and fripperies. Unnecessarily ornamental carved crockets or showy gargoyles, over-large sleeves and a codpiece with a silver bell on the end (for Billy, not Betty).

Anti-bourgeois tee-shirt sales are at their highest in Northern Europe. Britain, rather wisely, saw middle-class energy as a great motivator. America was founded by the bourgeoisie and for the bourgeoisie, with bourgeois values engraved deep on its heart. The Chinese and Indian Empires held their merchants and middle classes in appropriately high regard and if you're looking for the bourgeois promised land, look no further than the Maximalist capital of the world: Venice. Here trade, ostentation and general showy off-yness were very much accepted as the way of the world.

But there's obviously something in the water of the northern corner of EUfordshire that breeds bourgeoisphobia.

Now, let's find out more about the case against the bourgeoisie, as submitted to the High Court of Civilization by the onion-breathed legal team representing the twentieth century. At the top of the list of crimes is Maximalism. The bourgeoisie, it was claimed, were to be condemned for…

A   Owning too much unnecessary stuff

B   Aping the style of their aristocratic betters

C   Unquestioningly following fashions and not knowing their own mind

We can trebuchet B right out of the equation. The aristos I know are certainly charming but neither they, nor I, would ever brand them as 'betters'.

A is more tricky because the idea of owning too much is up to personal decision-making, surely? C is where the battle is won. If your home is buried beneath a pile of stuff that you have no real engagement with, but feel you should own, then the Modern World's point strikes home. That's bourgeois bordering on cat lady.

BUT (it's a big but and I like big buts, I cannot lie) if all your bourgeois bits and bobs are there on their own particular merits, then you can simply shrug off a hundred years of anti-bourgeois Modernist orthodoxy and simply say: I display, therefore I am.

The Minimalists' own judgement has turned against them in one fridge magnet slogan. Modernism's only real charge against bourgeois Maximalism is a lack of intellect, which can be rebuffed by taking a moment to prove to yourself that everything you own means something to you.

Go on, have a catch up chat with your tchotchkes and tell the world that bourgeois rocks... Or as the urban young now call it, boujee – which is fabulously where it's at.

BRIGHTON PAVILION – A WARNING FROM HISTORY

We're all cozily used to its dotty outline and interior stuffed with fluffy random oddments, like an old lady's handbag. Familiarity has bred content for a building that we now caress in cosseting tones as eccentric and eclectic. But all this soft-focus pussy-footing only serves to mask the poisonous vanity and cancerous self-indulgence that caused Brighton Pavilion to be created with so little stylistic compassion.

It's no secret the Prince Regent and I would not have got on.

There are pro-Prince historians that would have him a great and important tastemaker, the style governor of the extraordinarily sparkling design era that bears his name. Nah. He was just lucky enough to live at the very moment when British aesthetics had started to flower after 20 years of going it alone, starved of all continental influence, thanks to Napoleon's wars.

There was no self-indulgence that Prince George felt himself un-entitled to enjoy.

He dove deep into excess. Not just food, not just booze, not just clothes with too much lace and wigs with too many curls, but also emotional states in which he wallowed with opera-scale intensity. He didn't care who saw it. He didn't care who was going to pay for it and he really didn't care who was going to clean it up afterwards.

Nobody liked him. The British are often quite good judges of character and saw him for the sham he was. Particularly when he tried to grab power after his sweet but ditch-water dull father, King George III, started to succumb to bouts of lunacy. The affectionate Brits had nicknamed their king Farmer George and liked his bourgeois ways. Unlike George, the son, who had become as vast and pink (and just as easily crushed) as a strawberry-syrup flavoured meringue. He was just as flaky, just as crumbly and just as campy too.

When architect John Nash started the do-over of George's bow-fronted beach house, which would become Brighton's Pavilion, it was the latest in a long list of failed, unfinished and abandoned palatial money pits.

Nothing hurts a royal reputation more than a string of half-finished palaces when most of the nation is struggling under the crushing tax burden of a post-war economy.

People hated George.

But they quite liked his puffed up mistresses… Over-powdered and smelling of rose like dainty, juicy morsels of Turkish Delight. And the people adored George's wife, probably because he hated her. She was wantonly unwashed and stridently opinionated and appalled by the fact that her husband, as she herself said, knew far too much about the fashionable cut of trousers. That's the thing about George, he didn't know much about anything useful and, worse, he didn't care.

Back to the Pavilion. Anyone else would have said to Nash, 'Let's go discreet on this one Johnny boy… You know, the economy isn't great, people are struggling… Let's do something nice, but not too ostentatious.' Hah. Not George, who had set his heart on a style that was the architectural equivalent of flipping a finger at his own subjects. Widow Twankey meets Danny La Rue, with slut-drop domes, panto-curtain verandahs and some very meaty tucking going on around the French windows.

The style was synonymous with exotica, yes; opulence, yes; extravagance, yes; but also synonymous with deeply despotic, unconstitutional rule. George had built a fantasy escape pod in which he could lose himself in a ludicrously lavish delusion of being an all-powerful Eastern potentate who didn't have to give a flying fanlight whether the people he governed liked him or not.

All of which I could take, if it had been better done. George (with his bra off, wig askew and breeches awry) was out of his box on hookah-smoke and hookers, cowering from reality in a structure designed with such negligent thoughtlessness it's given Maximalism a bad name for over two centuries.

And that was before it got hit by the Prince's shizzle stick.

George loved shiny. Like an opinionated bogan housewife on a rosé-fuelled mall trip, his taste for bling had an aggressive edge and a really quite morbid side. George's agents scoured the post-revolutionary fire sales of France for any over-ornate trappings once owned by his doomed and decapitated continental equivalent, Louis XVI.

Scalp-hunted gee-gaws flecked with royal blood shared display space with the sort of tinsel-tastic Chinese lanterns even your local takeaway would dismiss as too tacky. And just to make sure all oxygen is sucked from the room, enormous drapes of bumpy, grindy satin still to this day carry the *odeur* of Regency debauch.

Since you now know me so well, you can tell I'm enjoying myself far too much hating on George and his in-a-state pleasure dome. Although isn't hating simply exhausting? No matter how grumpy I may be about the Brighton Pavilion, when I'm actually there, I'll always find things to love.

But it doesn't help that the architecture is so crass. What should be light and elegant is lumpen. The whole gooey surface of the building makes it look like a macaron left out in the rain. Even after all these years it still has a camp passive aggression to it, a confrontational 'Yes I know I shouldn't be here looking like this but just deal with it' harrumphiness. Just like a blousy and underwashed old queen wearing a tiara to a decorously informal garden party with cross-patch belligerence.

In many ways, I pity poor George. He was the only national leader left out of the first-hand celebrations thrown with gusto to celebrate Napoleon's defeat at the Battle of Waterloo. In his cherry brandy-sozzled decline, he would declare he'd led the cavalry (even to veterans of the battle who'd actually been there). His suffering at the tragic death of his daughter Charlotte in childbirth was cataclysmic. For once, Britain and George put on a united front with national mourning on a scale that would have eclipsed the funeral of Diana, Princess of Wales. Princess Charlotte, had she lived, would have become Queen. In dying, she left the throne open for Victoria.

The very greatest tragedy about George remains that he was so reviled and so vilified by his subjects, when all he wanted was to be loved. Which is why the Brighton Pavilion is such an uncomfortable experience.

It's a big architectural lump of door-slam, fuck-you attitude that hides the hot tears of the lonely.

THE HEMLINE INDEX

Beloved by writers of fluffy lifestyle pieces in the glossier business press, the Hemline Index is a straightforward theory that skirts are short when economic confidence is high (1920s, 1960s, 1980s) and long when the prognosis is gloomy.

This isn't just about fashion, though. Because what does a short skirt mean? It means Thoroughly Modern Millie.

One of the biggest stylequakes in living memory happened in my childhood. I remember it. It was an almost overnight phenomenon and it was such a violent transition that living through it felt like living through one of the baffling and turbulent foreign revolutions that seemed to perpetually be the lead story of the evening news.

October 1973 is the point when all the lights went out. Suddenly, the world had no oil, and since it was the consumption of oil that made everything modern, time started to run rapidly backwards. By Saturday it was 1893.

Up to that pivotal point, suburban style had been revelling in the dense colour fields that man-made materials could achieve with retina-jarring splendour. Op Art was still inspiring textile designers to make flat surfaces look like chromatic vortexes. Everywhere you shopped, plastic was called upon to become coffee tables, upholstery, light fittings, room dividers, tablescapes and conversation pits. In fact sometimes there were only three non-plastic items in a living room: the shag pile carpet, the abundant house plants and you.

And what's the key ingredient in plastic? Naphtha. Naphtha comes from oil.

Overnight, not only had the economy and most of the world's transportation and infrastructure been irrevocably compromised, but so had the brightness and shininess of the modern middle-class lifestyle.

But there was an antidote that had been quietly bubbling away in cauldrons from San Francisco to the Welsh valleys. An alternative way of living that mistrusted the modern, hated the mass-produced, despised the mini but loved the maxi… At its purest, this alternative was super-alternative, advocating communalism, veganism, naturism and beard-ism. Super quickly the stylists in the newly invented Sunday colour supplements saw that, with a few tweaks, this new style, a new life (hey, let's call it *lifestyle*) could be promoted to be exactly what the world needed.

Like a painfully jilted lover, society slammed its bedroom door on Modern and – in revenge – put on a prairie dress accessorized with red-rimmed eyes and a teary, snotty hanky. Instead of Space Odyssey inspired white plastic kitchens, scrubbed pine dressers snuck back into the house from their exile in garages and garden sheds. Wallpaper in shades of denim or soft tones of autumn, boasting an infinity of botanically accurate floral sprigs, replaced shiny walls painted with colours taken from the periodic table. Where once was a tundra of shagpile, now a ship's-deck of gnarly exposed floorboards were sanded into submission and polished as shiny as a Hallowe'en apple. At the heart of the home, on a merrily sizzling hob was some enormous cooking pot as big and cartoony as anything you'll see in a fairytale, belching nourishing clouds of stewy steam.

All so that the dejected and stressed family could gain comfort from being safe at home.

Of course, gradually, after most of a decade in nostalgic hibernation, the economy that had bust now started to boom. Sentimental evocations of Victorian servants' quarters were very much out, replaced by a new, confident, optimistic, sexy tech look. Hemlines went so high they nearly hit jawlines on the way down.

And so on and so on. Within another decade the high-tech kitchen in an ersatz New York loft-style apartment became something shaker in a converted Wimbledon semi. This now well-established cycle of Modern-when-we're-happy, traditional-when-we're-sad seems to have created an automaton: a stylistic perpetual mobile on a roughly decadal rotation.

Unless, of course, you're a Maximalist, in which case you're happy all the time and you like your hemline in a daring asymmetric diagonal, with one side short and the other side long.

YOUR HOME
ON THE COUCH

There's no doubt that the home's symbolic power has been used to stir the imagination since time immemorial. It is after all a really quite significant member of the family, with its own quirks and eccentricities.

In the good old/bad old days (delete where applicable) there wasn't a lot of psychology attached to the home because there were very few homes. The vast majority had, at best, shelters. Twiggy confections of wattle, daubed with, well, daub. Even the top tiers of the feudal pyramid didn't have homes *per se,* but architectural avatars of might, iron-clad-fist buildings, designed to safeguard the haves from the super-muddy (and often grumpy) have-nots.

After a while, the middle classes, fresh from the social drawing board, saw before them a burgeoning urban lifestyle, with streets and comfy town houses looking to be lived in. In America, Canada, Australia and everywhere settlers found themselves plonked down in scary sci-fi netherworlds, home as haven was a reality from the get-go. In Australia, particularly, there's an epic dignity to the steadfast bourgeois ornamentation of a digger's home in the outback. Stencilling the wriggly tin in the hope it'll look a bit like William Morris wallpaper and fret-cutting the shingles in homage to Balmoral: this was steadfast middle-class aesthetic heroism in the face of the deadly environments that early settlers found themselves settling in.

Back in the Old World, even the newly minted bourgeoisie originally rented from an overlord or over-institution like the Church or the Crown. It's only when the home starts to become owned that the psyche starts to unpack its baggage. Suddenly where one lives gets a whole lot more complicated than a motto embroidered on a sampler. Home is more than where the arse sits.

Of course, mass home ownership coincides with that least loveable of centuries, the twentieth. And, as the era of much meddlement, there were queues of opinionators and designosaurs, all with didactic ideas about how home should be. Better home, better *you.* Better you, better *society.* Better being *their* better – don't for one moment think it might be *your* better. From the safe distance of a hundred years, it's both scary and moving to see the world's first global war as the first time war was overtly promulgated with the concept of *home* at its heart. Keep the *home* fires burning. *Homes* for heroes. *Home* is where the heart is. All become emotive slogans to simply get the poor trench-bound troops through the horrors. Before, wars were about nations or countries, but this one was made deliberately much more personal.

After the Great War, the British countryside yields to ribbons of suburban development, all to provide the jolly boxes promised to the tenacious combatants who'd survived the man-made inferno.

Despite the Modernists' best efforts, few were interested in their dystopian architectural utopia. Having survived the carnage of a futuristic, techno war, the last thing *anybody* wanted was to live in the contemporary. Instead, a soft mantle of nostalgia settled like rosy red brick dust on housing stock. Modernist haters called them *pastiche*, and with period-detail-inspired, mass-produced cosmetic ornamentation bought from the catalogue, these houses had an impressively mechanical sameness. The only tough decision was picking which Queen. Should it be Elizabeth I, with a riot of half timbering? Or the Blocky Bricky (Sir Christopher) Wrenaissance of Queen Anne, God bless her? No accident that both these historical periods were seen as times of political stability and economic security. We're all so much happier if there's a woman in charge, let's face it.

The psychology was simple. We made it. We survived. Less the odd appendage perhaps, and traumatized to hell, but now a new, better world could and should be built. And, psychologically speaking, that better world had one foot very firmly in the past. Yes, nostalgia is comforting, so the kind thing to do for those that so needed comfort was gently turn back the hands of time.

The giant gold plug that had kept all the wealth at the top of society had been wrenched from its giant golden plughole and money cascaded down through the social plumbing. The big change was that the ordinary sorts – the shop workers, bank clerks and librarians – now had the chance to call a home theirs.

It's a great idea. Give the majority of the population a handkerchief-sized share of the country. Make them stakeholders, shareholders in the National Corporation. Share and share alike; Nanny would approve.

And it's now that you get the idea that everyone's home is their castle. Instead of Mies van der Rohe's boxes or Le Corbusier's machines for living in, the suburbs became resplendent with tiny, weeny, mini country mansions. The perfect symbol for the smaller shareholders of Great Britain PLC, proving that they were every bit as crucial to the functioning of the state as the full-size mansion dwellers.

Two and a half bedrooms, Lilliputian inglenook, cookie-cutter stained glass panel over the front door and plenty of room by the porch for a pair of concrete beasts. Ersatz heraldry. Democracy in action, but instead of forcing the upper social echelons to survive in the plebscape, the proletariat were given a homeopathic-sized slice of the good life. OMG, the Modernists must have been fuming. It was all they hated on an unprecedented national scale.

But don't get too comfy.

Because Modernism does chalk up a victory after World War II. Having promised that global war would never ever happen again, it must have been the most appallingly dispiriting experience to come to terms with the fact that there would be no other way of containing Nazism than by physically defeating it.

The Nazi style stance was vigorously anti-Modernist. The majority of the Bauhaus-set scuttled to America as the Nazis rose to power. But that didn't mean that Hitler's aesthetes didn't do modern – in fact, the National Socialist style has quite a lot of streamlined Art Deco just below the surface of its preposterous redacted Classicism. But the vicious Nazi mindset of weaponized nostalgia for a mythical Germany was powerful architectural stuff, and when draped in those vertiginous swastika banners, power oozed from every poured concrete pore.

After the post-war clean up, Modernism is allowed to rear its ugly head. Psychologically damaged by all that had happened, it's as if this time around, society simply couldn't be bothered to resist. Besides, Modernist snake oil had polished up its act and claimed to have hardwired a new way of living into this new way of building.

Oh, also, it could be done on the cheap, using fabulous modern materials like asbestos and new techniques with concrete that would almost certainly not crack, leak or weep. Probably.

There was an optimism at the heart of the splay-legged amoeba-shaped refurbs that homeowners used to shore up and paper over the cracks of the war traumas their homes had suffered. It's when the term 'dust trap' suddenly becomes an epic enemy to be defeated at all costs. It's also when Doing It Yourself assumes the solemn duty of all civilians, to rebuild their nation in several shades of Formica. All terribly, terribly modern.

And so the idea that it was going to be much quicker, cheaper and easier to start again, architecturally speaking, takes root. This time around, out goes the pseudo Tudor and in comes the jovial (slightly Scandi) vanilla Modernism-inspired Tetris suburbs of flat-roofed, timber-clad, picture-windowed executive housing. Inevitably, in these Modernist suburbs, tower blocks and shopping centres proved themselves to be as practical in the damp as a cardboard breakfast cereal box and as habitable in the heat as a matchbox with a magnifying glass roof. So house buyers started asking house builders for something with more solid aesthetic values.

Despite the twentieth century being the century of Modernism, by the end of it everyone wanted to live in houses that didn't look twentieth century at all. And that is because the past, despite its dodgy politics and unforgivable wars, will always be so very much more comforting than the present (with its super-dodgy politics and super-unforgivable wars). And as for the future? Well, no one's got an optimistic word to say about that, these days. At least you know where you are with the past. There is something comforting in the knowledge that there have been countless souls before you who've lost their job, hated Monday mornings and buried the cat in the garden. Guess what? They survived! Bounced back, got on with life. They came home, put the kettle on and lowered themselves into their favourite chair with an unapologetic sigh.

Actually, maybe home is where the arse sits.

MAXIMALISM IN A TIME OF PESTILENCE

With the home so chock-full of psycho-drama, it's amazing there's actually room for us to live in it.

When we're busy, when we're distracted, we don't notice the household gods that inhabit our living rooms. When the economy's going great and the world's a fabulous place full of exciting opportunity and money to be made, the emotive associations of hearth and home are frankly irrelevant, if not embarrassing. Like kindergarteners, quick to lose the grip of their loving parents at the school gate to join their playing friends, all's well when all's well. But the minute a knee gets grazed, it's the soft bosomy maternal comfort of the home to which humanity turns. It's how you survive the zombie apocalypse, after all.

The first two decades of the twenty-first century saw homes becoming increasingly de-personalized. People stopped loving their homes and started capitalizing on them instead. Everything had a price tag. Everything was a commercial transaction. And the prevailing Minimal, wet-cardboard Modernist style trends were a gift, as Mammon started calling the decorative shots and squashing real estate into commercially appraised identical moulds. Homogenized, pasteurized product lines from which realtors and estate agents could extract optimum commission for minimum effort.

But then the world got sick. And the only way to mitigate the spreading pestilence was to close your front door and wait it out. Pray for Passover.

While we were isolating (the lucky ones surrounded by family), it was impossible not to take stock. Appraising the very, very big stuff – and

the irritatingly little. Meanwhile, with no work and no social life, came no distraction.

I think many realized, in the first few days of lockdown, that they'd locked themselves down into a strangely featureless, personality-less, greyscale cell of their own making. And then there were some that hoped that if they kept their idle hands at work, then the devil in the (lack of) detail wouldn't ambush them. So out came everything formerly confined to that 1990s obsession, storage. Garages, carports, garden sheds, under-stairs cupboards, boot rooms, mud rooms, lofts, attics and basements were spectacularly emptied in a magnificent global anal vacation of formerly constipated shizzle. What a void.

And, basically, much of it never went back. All those photo albums, keepsake boxes, bobble-trimmed lampshades, rattan peacock chairs, Meissen-inspired figurines, swimming certificates, school of Rubens altarpieces (or was that just me?) and, of course, raffia donkeys from the Acapulco airport, were allowed back into the light.

In triumphant celebration, and as a background to this magnificent renaissance, orders flew out on the fastest of fast internets for rolls of patterned wallpaper, gallons of rich-hued paints in shades of family nourishment and jewel-toned sofas the size of the Great Bed of Ware. And all to rekindle a love for where we live.

Mystical magical makeovers – the twenty-first century version of sacrifices made to the household gods for keeping us safe, keeping us dry, keeping us warm. And, as reaffirmation that we are special and we matter, because hey, we've got a raffia donkey from the Acapulco airport, and we don't care who knows it.

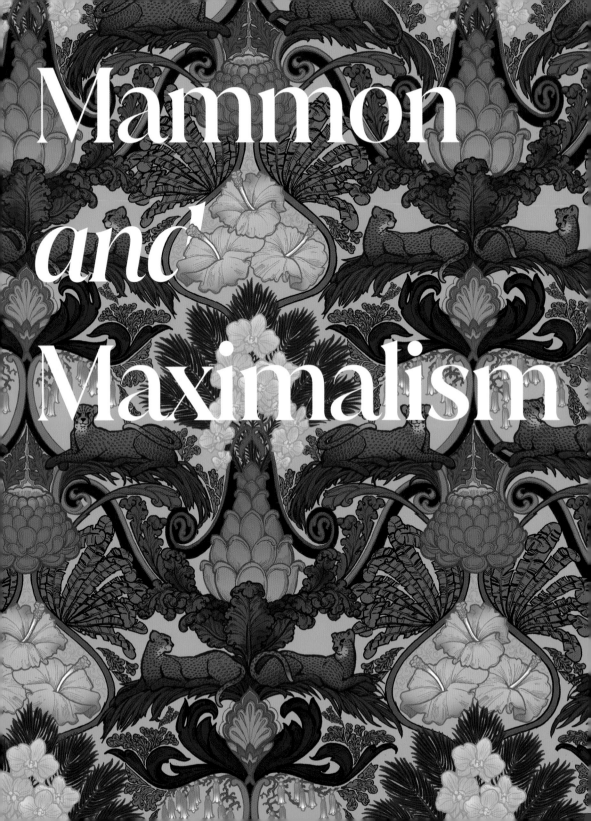

Mammon and Maximalism

It seems super counter-intuitive, but Maximalism isn't in any way comparable with conspicuous consumption. Yes, there's a lot of stuff in a Maximalist room, but the showing off that's going on isn't material, it's spiritual. So unless the consumption you're consuming conspicuously is soul, you're gonna be disappointed.

The vision of an opulent oligarchic surfeit is essentially anti-Maxer propaganda. If they can't get you with their cat lady clutter scare tactics, then frightening you into believing that Maximalism is synonymous with Putinism. Obviously, there are many very famous exemplars of high-ticket Maximalism: the Yves Saint-Laurents, the Cavallis, the Versaces. Haute couture autocrats always did mega-luxe Maximalism with a rare and near-hysterical compulsion. As their empires increased, so their real estate portfolios swelled like blood-engorged ticks. But, as creators, even these catwalk potentates knew how to play open house to the ordinary, the everyday, even the kitsch, if it could be relied upon to augment a scheme or chilli-up a tablescape.

And, as top-of-their-game aesthetes, they would never welcome even the faintest whiff of social insecurity in their opulence. So they are generally unlikely to play the Minimalist card as the ultimate luxury, in the way that less evolved species might (*vis* football players or TV talent-show judges). One thrilling exception to this rule is Kaiser Karl Lagerfeld – but more of him later. In fact, these high-ticket frock-jockeys are likely to deliberately pursue the Maximal via design styles or periods that feel anti-taste, demonstrating just how far removed they are from the bewildered and bourgeois hoi-polloi.

The fundamental problem with fiscal value in a Maximalist zone is that it upsets the balance. Unlike Minimalism, which is all about value. Designer labels, price tags and complicated provenances, all specifically chosen to dazzle the attention away from just how dull the Minimalists themselves are.

That, of course, doesn't mean there's no place for the expensive in Maximalism. Don't feel compelled to go Maximal Marxist and bonfire your vanities. The expensive, the valuable and the valued are all given space in God's Maximal world. But they're here on equal footings, all to be judged first and foremost as things, not price tags.

Thingship is king if Maximalism is to work, as we have by now thoroughly and most fruitfully explored.

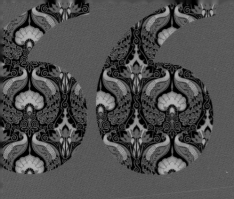

Love what you own and *own* what you love.

CULTURAL
APPRECIATION

The absolute joy of design is that it's a language without words. It crashes through borders, smashes barriers and speaks to all who can see.

By its nature, it inspires. It sparks into creative life more designs, new designs and designs that take existing design as a highly springy springboard that then propels a design idea onto a new, original trajectory.

I worry when design, and designed objects, get mired by nationalism.

Yes, a particular style of tchotchke may have been evolved by a particular collection of humans from a particular global zip code. But once that tchotchke is made, I believe it belongs to the world, for the peoples of our world (and beyond) to use, enjoy – and, indeed, emulate.

That said, objects of faith are another level. As a card-carrying Pantheist, I believe everything sacred is just that: sacred. So respect has to be super-baked into the way we treat artefacts that have any spiritual connection. In fact, take huge comfort and pleasure from the privilege of sharing your life with objects that can inspire you to explore other ways of being a human.

We are so often excited by what former generations called the 'exotic'. We love the idea of owning that which comes from outside our particular window on the world. But, as us Maximalists know, beware blind, thoughtless ownership. That unpleasant sense of keeping objects in captivity for show and to impress. Instead, love what you own and own what you love, remembering that love is impossible without deep vein knowledge of – and insurmountable respect for – the object of your desire.

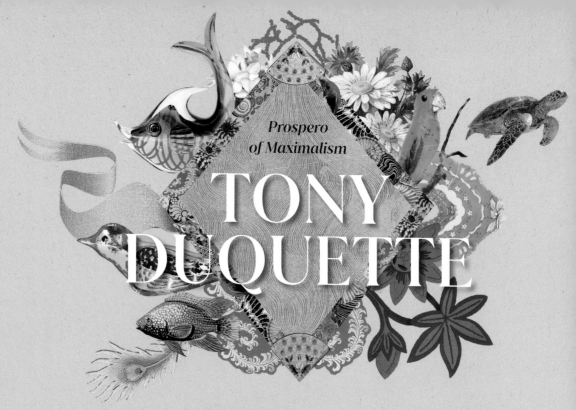

Prospero of Maximalism

TONY DUQUETTE

The only one of my Maximalist icons to actually know what the term Maximalism meant is Tony Duquette. And he was very much the Joker in the Hollywood Regency designer pack with a genius that lay in his own hands-on attitude.

The perma-ghastliness of the Modern era tried very hard to drive a wedge between designing and doing. Design was supposed to be a theoretical process that pipe-smoking salarymen in shirt sleeves did at big desks, under the sickly light of an Anglepoise lamp. The idea that a design could be dragged into being by the cleverness of fingers and the sweat of a brow, rather than just thinking about it, felt weirdly old-fashioned.

Making was Tony Duquette's genius. After art school, tall and genial Tony used his affable charm to chatter his way into jobbing design work on the sets of pre-war Hollywood films. Along the way, he was picked up by the redoubtable Elsie Mendl. Lady Elsie was a larger-than-larger-than life interior dictator, whose pronouncements on taste were treated as legal requirements by the white-on-white decorating set.

Charming Tony, with his WASPy style, was soon embellishing pieces of furniture for the enchanted Elsie, using an extended cast of fantastical, vaguely Rococo, motifs.

Counter-intuitively, it was actually World War II that gave Tony an aesthetic leg-up into Maximalism. Like many Americans, Duquette found himself deeply saddened by Europe, whose once-magnificent architectural icons now looked like they'd been made over by Surrealist supremo Salvador Dali, using a wrecking ball and a blow torch.

War was awful. But what humanity had done to its own exquisitely evolved civilization was heartbreaking for Tony. Paris, Venice, Rome, Prague and then Berlin maintained enough cultural landmarks silhouetted on their horizons to be recognizable, but close up all was contorted and infernally damned.

Sat in LA, the now demobbed Tony vigorously set about creating a parallel aesthetic fairyscape of the crushed Europe he'd left behind. Borders and boundaries were unimportant, as were the historical constraints of what designated one Louis style from another. Venice had cast a particularly profound spell, cleaving Tony's heart to the floating city of dreams forever. He never escaped its thrall. In gossamer and coral, he spun softly Baroque

vignettes that looked more Venetian than anything in Venice. Innately surreal, the iconic Venetian carnival mask became a cult object for Duquette, whose work was becoming increasingly sought after by a new technicolour Hollywood.

A Classic Duquette moment is seen in the 'This Heart of Mine' dance sequence from *Ziegfeld Follies*, where the timeless story of vampy girl meets Ruritanian count is choreographed in front of vertiginously tall, draped scarlet curtains. All protagonists wear black, white or buttercup yellow and a snooty ball is interrupted by the immaculately shiny Fred Astaire, who pitches up to do a dirty debonair on the heroine. But it's the candelabra that steal the show. Twice life-size statues of female deities are festooned with antlers bearing twinkling light bulbs. Duquette's signature trick of immersing cloth in plaster of Paris and then arranging it as classical drapery gives these horny goddesses a massy majesty that's wryly subverted by black carnival masks. And a beauty spot.

The craft is always very visible in Tony Duquette's take on Hollywood Regency. It inspired middle America to embrace a particularly collage-y style of light operatic Baroque design, which fitted perfectly with the fairytale fantasies with which Disney filled the movie theatres of the day. It was this insubstantial moonbeam Romanticism that Duquette brought to the designer jewellery collaborations that really propelled his work into high society. And there's nothing higher in high society than royalty (albeit abdicated and exiled royalty). Former British sovereign Edward VIII commissioned Duquette to drape his Duchess in Rococo revival bijouterie.

In a way, it's Duquette's jewellery that has a more ubiquitous legacy than the Tony-award winning styling or Oscar nominations. Chances are, your grandmother (or more likely your Auntie Rita) would have owned a brooch or earrings inspired by his eclectic take on Hollywood Regency glamour. Heavens, you'll still see Duquette-inspired costume pieces piled high in thrift stores and at vintage fairs today.

There's something so joyous about the Tony Duquette look, which made it highly attractive to anyone with fun to sell. Hawaii loved Tony and Tony loved Hawaii back. On top of all that deep, dark, sexy jungleliciousness, Duquette added a gussied-up tropical Baroque twist, which gave the tiki bar an upmarket internationalism. Stylistically, it was a two-way street, as Hawaii supplied an unceasing demand for nacreous abalone shells, which he used to construct eighteenth-century Rococo chandeliers and create gigantic architectural frames for ballroom-sized mirrors.

With its drapes, festoons, chandeliers and clusters of gilded cocktail chairs, Duquette style became the party style of the 1950s and 1960s. Tony and his astonishingly pretty wife, Elizabeth, known to all as Beegle, were dedicated party throwers. They bought a disused silent movie sound stage in Los Angeles, which became a perpetual wonderland of sparkling hospitality (with an elegant apartment for the couple attached).

It's Tony's final home, Dawnridge in Beverly Hills, that encapsulates the celebratory and joyous eclecticism of this most maximal Maximalist. Out of sprawling acres of tumbleweedy canyon, a cultivated and exotic evocation of a European pleasure park was shaped by the power of Duquette's aesthetic. Pavilions, follies and architectural assemblages stud the lush landscape around the main house. The walled estate has the air of parallel reality, as if a different path had actually been taken in early twentieth-century design, one where Tony Duquette, rather than Mies van der Rohe or Walter Gropius, became the apex predator designosaur.

For the interiors, Tony applied layers of oriental artefacts and architectural salvage to his enchanted ballroom style. Everything was topped off by the signature plaster of Paris drapery, painted to look like Venetian velvet. Coral and malachite effects turn out to be painted twigs and marbleized paper, whilst waterfalls of abalone shells reflect the Californian sun in flashing patterns, highlighting random details of Tony's Maximalism.

Like Prospero on his island, at Dawnridge Tony Duquette configured a Maximalist world in his own image, which turned its back on the seas of Californian monotony that surrounded it. There is an infectious joy that comes from the perpetual pleasure of new discovery. Every detail has a new and surprising element. It's what happens when an intelligent and affable designer of great talent transplants the concept of *Wunderkammer* to the Eden of the Hollywood Hills and opens the gates to a non-stop cocktail party. Magpie Maximalist heaven.

03

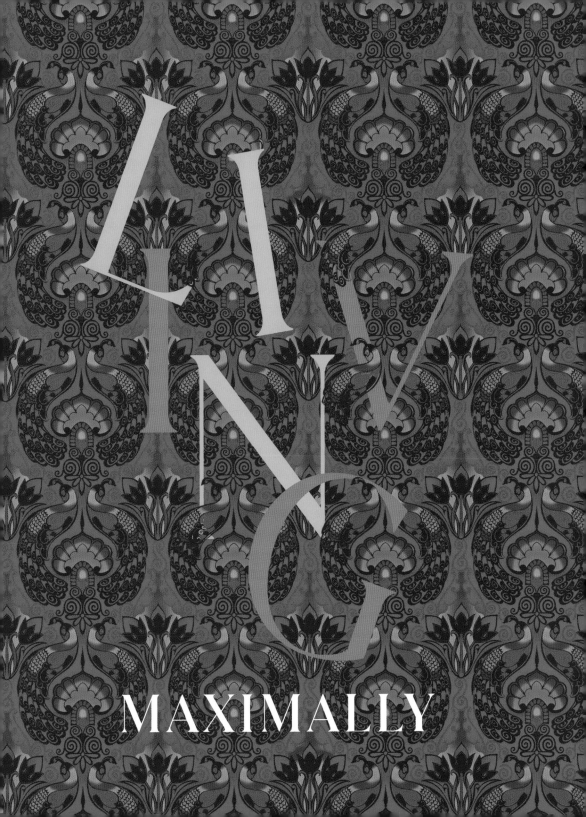

LIVING

MAXIMALLY

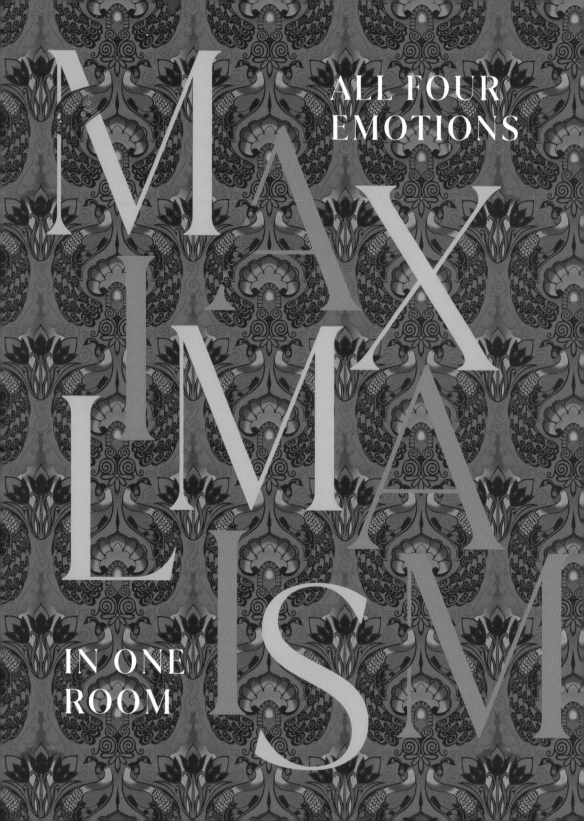

MAXIMALISM

ALL FOUR
EMOTIONS

IN ONE
ROOM

IF YOU'RE LOOKING FOR A DESIGN STYLE THAT WEARS ITS HEART ON ITS SLEEVE...

. . . look no further than Maximalism's big heart and super big sleeves.

I'll go further and say that emotion is essential in a Maximalist room. In many ways this is why it stirs such Marmite-ism in mugglekind. The gory intimacy of showing the real you through your choice of tchotchkes is beyond uncomfortable for them. But that, fellow travellers, is their problem – not yours. If their emotional immaturity and fragile sense of self are so easily irritated by the spectacular cultural evolution that makes you a Maximalist, then there's only one thing left to do. Pity them. Then pour them gin.

Modernism is a deliberately emotion-free zone. That's the point of it. Modernist law-makers hated what they saw as the crass sentimentality of bourgeois homes. The framed photographs of grandkids (living), enshrined locks of hair from grandparents (dead), ornaments bought to mark family milestones, ornaments inherited from family now beneath headstones… The fact that everything had a story was anathema to Modernists. Things that tell stories release unwelcome emotions and, even worse, sentiments. Modernists cannot bear sentimentality, that exaggerated emotional reaction to things that all humans have feelings towards, like babies' heads, kittens' ears, winter sunsets seen through snow-sprinkled branches and Christmas trees. I have it on good authority that The Grinch was based on Bauhaus founder Walter Gropius.

I adore being welcomed by the shades of a chair's former keepers.

There was a lot of subcutaneous sexism in Modernism's reaction to the pre-Modern 'Home is where the heart is' philosophy. A stifling emotional miasma that somehow seeped from the lady of the house, like the all-pervading smell of Parma violets. Their mechanically perfect man-made (literally) machines for living in used science, reason, ergonomics and glamorexia to create the ideal place in which humans should live. More accurately, they created the ideal place in which to store humans.

Charles Eastlake was one of those designosaurs from the Victorian period whose philosophy was polished to a high shine. These days, he's best known as the progenitor of Eastlake-style furniture, characterized by the sort of Scooby-Doo Gothic the American horror movie genre couldn't live without. His simplified fret-cut patterns and bobbin-turned spindles became wildly popular in the expanding American suburbs, giving them an aesthetic route map derived from the rich historicism that Old World England was busy shoehorning into its smoky cities.

This man was an unexploded IED of opinion. He hated fringe (bizarre thing to hate, in my opinion… perhaps he'd seen a loved one morbidly entangled in fringe at an early age… or maybe he just hated kittens having fun).

His biggest bugbear was rooms with a lack of ornament. Seventy years before Modernism outlawed ornamentation, Eastlake predicted that removing the curlicues from the ordinary rooms of the middling sort would cause housewives to succumb to a lingering neuralgia. Basically, Eastlake believed Modernism would make women mad.

Hate the overbearing patriarchal impertinence of the man, but his point, should one declaw the sexism, is that without the emotional stimulation of detail, a room is a pretty grim place. And for the ladies of his era who could barely hobble from chaise longue to whatnot, thanks to the whale-boned bondage of their bobble-fringed fashions, maybe neuralgia would result from indolent imprisonment in an un-ornamented boudoir.

Accepting that emotional design is a good thing (of course it is), then it's crucial to accept there are a thousand flavours of feeling embedded in each emotion. Everyone's going to have a different take on it. The associations that conjure the madeleine moment of emotion in the first place are triggers embedded since childhood, or booby traps left behind after war-zone relationships, or maybe they are simply reminiscences based on recurrent pleasure principles.

Luckily our mate Maximalism has this emotional subjectivity thing hardwired. Subjectivity is a great thing. Anti-Maxers will forever be in thrall to the latest Minimalist influencer, on a quest to find the most *au courant* flavour of Minimalism, the owning of which allegedly imparts aesthetic super status. Poor things. Maximalists who know that one person's meat is another person's poison, are forever open to find loveliness in anything and everything.

Objectively speaking, old furniture is haunted. Haunted by the emotions and sentiments former owners imbued their goods and chattels. The idea that the personality as well as the hair oil of previous inhabitants survives to stain the upholstery of a wing-backed armchair is an appalling thought for most Modernists.

But I love it. I adore being welcomed by the shades of a chair's former keepers. I particularly love the powerful engagement one gets with the actual makers of old pieces. The DNA of their skill and their craftsmanship impregnates the objects they made and is so very easily released as one uses and enjoys their work today.

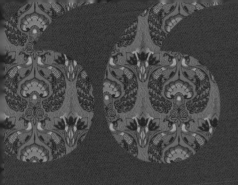

My dining chairs
are older than
America and
have more stories
to tell than
Agatha Christie.

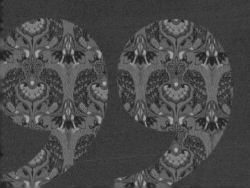

Whereas all you get from flat pack is a splinter or two and a heap of rage from deciphering assembly instructions printed in a rarely used dialect of Sami reindeer herder – my dining chairs are older than America and have more stories to tell than Agatha Christie.

With a magnanimity that surprises even me, I'm going to give the last word to the Minimalist camp. I came across a statement on a fellow interior designer's website of such bone-chilling, passionless frigidity, it near took my breath away. I'll not name her but I'm pretty sure you'll all do a Rumpelstiltskin and guess her name from the tone of what I'm about to share (it's best read out loud through thin lips, recently returned from the Botox clinic…):

"I want my interiors to be as peaceful and refreshing as a nice green salad or a gentle work out in my home gym."

There we have it. Rooms of such underwhelming understatement the best way to describe their flavour is lettuce-y. My mind is really, quite vigorously, boggled by the fact that there's a design orthodoxy at work on this planet that somehow accepts this super-floppy über-vanilla-ism as a dynamic sales statement. It remains the best advert for Maximalism you'll ever find. I'm currently planning to have it tattooed on my butt.

SHARING THE MAXIMALIST HOME

When two Maximalists come together and share the same space you'll find a mighty conjunction. The fusing of two personalities and merging of two great Maximalist collections into one.

Of course, the same cannot be said for when – heaven forfend – a Maximalist and a Minimalist throw their lots in together. I mean, I love that love has no boundaries… It's wonderful that for every teapot, there's a lid. But what on earth is to be done when the anti-Maxer crosses the threshold and drops their bony tush square in the midst of the Maximalist sofa?

Gin.

Moving on, let's now turn to how to deal with the *un*-invited, which is now more of a quiz. In particular, what on earth does one do with the children?

I'm a child owner myself. Several children, several grandchildren… As well as being the loveliest things in my universe, they're also – all of them – card-carrying agents of chaos. And not ordinary chaos. I'm talking Tasmanian devil, press the hyperspace button, truly chaotic chaos.

They also have no concept of independent, thoughtfully refined, individual taste. Personal style is something to be facsimlied from a few dominant members of their peer group. Unchanged. Unevolved. Literally copied straight from Aidan or Scarlett. And if it's not identical then prepare for detonation…

This, of course, makes all our beloved little blighters sitting ducks for the pan-global character licensors that have become such insidious aesthetic behemoths. Like fish being shot in a barrel, action figures, pyjamas, tableware, bed-sets and confectionery all rain down on our wee ones, who flap and flail in the confines of the water butt, unable to escape. And once one of them has the lunch box or the rucksack, they *all* have to have it.

So what to do? Nothing. Every bit as inevitable as taxes and death, children will grow up. And quicker than you think.

Meanwhile, be the open-hearted Maximalist you know yourself to be and welcome the kid-etritus with a benevolent but wry tolerance. Actually, sometimes it's not *that* awful. I have a grandson for whom avenging superheroes are catnip. Given the right lighting, sometimes these little musclebound plastic fellas have a hint of Myron's Discobolus. *Ish.*

If there ever was a super-strong case for winding in your aesthetic neck for the sake of family, love and concord, then this is it.

Instead, see these highly visible bits of much-loved moulded plastic like *kintsugi*. Forever looking for a philosophical solution, the Japanese invented the art of mending ordinary china with molten gold. It's super-Maximalist in its intent, celebrating – literally crowning – something everyday with regal gold. But, at the same time, drawing attention to the fact that what was once broken is now fixed, and to the object's imperfection. So do reverse *kintsugi* on the darn plastic action figure: think of it as the gold and think of you and the child as the pieces of pot it holds together.

There we go, Jedi Maximalism. A Maximalism that sees stories in the everyday and loves them just as much as the swanky stuff.

Try to love the objects that are loved by those we love.

DOES MAXIMALISM WITHER WITH AGE?

No. Actually, it's one of the only bits that doesn't.

Age brings an incremental notching-up of the opinion dial. So a born Maximalist, by the time they die, will be Maximal to a state of near weaponization.

It's bizarre that modern thinking has human capacity declining with the years as a foregone conclusion. The Japanese artist Hokusai – the guy who created the original wave, which beach-side tattooists all over the world offer to copy (badly) on your butt – felt he was only getting going when he hit 80. Which is certainly borne out in his work. Then there's Ninon de Lenclos, a celebrated courtesan at the court of Louis XIV's Versailles, who negotiated a glittering deal with a young nobleman in return for a night of unparalleled passion to be enjoyed in exactly 3 months and 13 days' time. 'Why 3 months and 13 days?' the impatient young man asked, to which Ninon languidly replied that she wanted an especially succulent treat to look forward to on her upcoming 84th birthday…

Old Maximalists never die, they just start curating the way clear for new Maximalists to ornament.

So it's important to get that Maximalism is not an old-people thing at all. It's often called 'grannycore' or 'cottagecore' in the style press, but most cottage-dwelling grannies these days can't bear the idea of Maximalism. The elderly you see cruising the Bahamas and riding mobility scooters at ramming speed were actually nurtured throughout the twentieth century by the nanny society of Modernism. They're by far the most likely stratum of the population to snarl a wrinkly lip at clutter and dismiss ornaments as dust traps. Although one supposes dust is a sensitive subject, for those so close to becoming it.

In fact, the growth in Maximalism comes from the young and funky. Like you.

With Maximalism's exciting stance on anti-taste as a draw, the *jeunesse dorée* are wild about the aesthetic adrenaline hit they get from grannycore and cottagecore. It's like taking the bed cap off Little Red Riding Hood's grandma and finding, not a toothy wolf, but Anna Wintour. For the young it all feels fresh and new. And *so* unlike the tired wet cardboard interiors their middle-aged parents created to make their energy-less lives look more modern.

All the claptrap about property value is wasted on a youthful generation of renters who need to furnish where they live with stuff and things because the landlord won't let them do anything to the walls.

Maximalism is as revolutionary for the young as Modernism was for their great grandparents, only without the boring bits.

Or the Bauhaus Breath.

It must be amusing for this essentially bourgeois design language to find itself, with more than a whiff of rebellious glamour, pitted against the concrete orthodoxy of Modernism.

With none of the irony that crochet, collections of kitten plates or rattan peacock chairs deserve, the urban young are buying into the romance of Maximalism wholesale. For them, it's a portal back to a design time that reflected a much more stable, much less environmentally overdrawn, geopolitical world. A powerful but misguided nostalgia, since this planet has been perpetually on the cusp of destruction by its human inhabitants ever since some fool invented the wheel.

But it's not just Maximalism's Insta-appeal or its rule-less *laissez-faire* collectibility that's the draw… it's the fact that it really does have a heart, and where there's a heart there's hope. Or so it says on the T-shirts that the young so love to wear.

INSTAGLAM –
MADE FOR MAXIMALISM

No one here is a technology-bashing Luddite. There's no point in turning back the clock to a time when candles were king just to make a point. Although, saying that, candles do make rooms much prettier than LEDs ever will.

The past couple of years have seen something of a small domestic triumph for camp Maximal, when it comes to tech.

The twenty-first century dawns and the home of the future becomes the home of the present, with all the techno tropes you'd expect. Doors that automatically open and close with a *scchhpfff*, just like on *Star Trek*. Lights that come on when you walk into the room. Living pods devoid of all comfort or furniture but with plenty of backlit milky glass. It's all exactly as it was on prime-time TV from the early 1970s.

It's clear that twenty-first century tech wouldn't exist if twenty-first century technicians had just been sent to bed early every night during their youth and missed the schlocky sci-fi shows from which they've lifted all their most profitable ideas.

Interior decoration's relationship with tech has come a long way. The early twenty-first century room would have been nothing without the glowering black monolith in the corner, connected to a series of featureless black boxes and mysterious subsidiary box forms by a Gordian knot of cables and tubes… Altar-like and all-pervading, this black totem bullied any attempt at softscape into tearful submission.

Noughties TVs were behemoths that gobbled up 25 percent of the living room in one greedy gulp. Credit where credit is due, that Hadron Collider-sized cathode ray out the back of the box made all of us who appeared on the screen look like gods. Slightly fuzzy gods in shades of rose and jade.

Huzzah then that, 20 years later, instead of taking styling tips from Hal the super-computer in *2001: A Space Odyssey*, tellies today are much more *Bridgerton*: as slim as an after-dinner mint and hung discreetly between the post-Impressionist watercolours. We watch TV like it's a painting hanging above the fireplace.

Making TVs into shrinking violets of discretion has meant that rooms are back to the way they should be. Focussed on the chimney breast, rather than shifted off-balance to align with the enormous screen on its NASA-inspired triangular stand in the corner.

This is a triumph for Maximalism, and it suggests the future can learn lessons from the past. Tech can play nicely with culture. Innovation is not the destination, it's the journey. Everything in a room, whatsoever its provenance, can work hard to make a cohesive and expressive whole.

In fact, there are plenty of bits and bobs of technology that are completely Maximalist. Shuffle being one. Randomly extrapolating an automatic playlist from an extensive and eclectic Maximalist library of aural loveliness is exactly the sort of service technology should provide humanity. So easy to do, and far less complicated than trying to convince a string quintet to skid from Scarlatti to Daft Punk just because they can. I've tried.

Lighting has become very helpful these days, too. You can go super-discreet, almost concealed, which is fabulously exciting if your Maximalism is crying out for highlighting with a series of dull nimbuses. Or you can choose high-intensity, sniper-accurate lights, so just one small bit of your collection becomes the star of the show. The colour can change at the clap of a hand. However, watch out for this impromptu ability to make rainbows; jumping from red to green will make the room feel like a busy traffic junction. Change colour, by all means, but only change within the same chromatic family.

There's one final bit of tech without which Maximalism would never have become the global glamdemic it is today: Instagram. I'll admit there is a point when digital life and social media become neurotrash, and it's that point when you stop focussing on what you're scrolling but can still carry on scrolling through muscle memory alone. However, used well and wisely, the digital connection of the world, for the good of the world, should be a lovely thing to look forward to.

Insta's instantness has been entirely to Maximalism's advantage. A dark blue drawing room in Mumbai is on screens in pockets and handbags across the digisphere the minute the paints dry and the picture is posted.

There's a hauntingly familiar historical resonance to this, and that's with the undulating loveliness of the divine design style known as Art Nouveau.

Who wouldn't want to Insta the hell out of their Maximalist home?

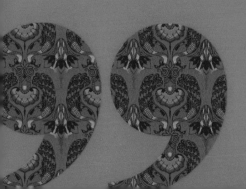

In 1893, technology wasn't digital but photogravure, which allowed photographs to be mass-printed in newspapers and what they called periodicals (basically Victorian Instagram).

To this day, no one can really say what started Art Nouveau. In fact, it's not even called Art Nouveau outside English-speaking cultures. In some corners of EUfordshire it's known as *Le Style Anglaise* and in Italy, it's 'Liberty Style', after the London design emporium that was early to stock it. But around 1893, drawing rooms, boudoirs, barbers, metro stations, hat shops, bread shops and knocking shops all broke out in a rampage of undulating ironwork, whiplash mosaic motifs and jewel-toned art glass. It sprung forth overnight like mushrooms or mould.

Never before had architecture been so thoroughly taken over by nature. Not even during the flighty and flimsy days of the Rococo had natural forms been allowed to reinvent man-made buildings to this extent. Dragonfly wings, beetle mandibles, contorted willow roots, coral, lava flows… Art Nouveau designers deliberately and cleverly refuted the rational, in favour of an all-encompassing, highly original, aesthetic effect. It's at this point in design history when original becomes a buzz word.

As if by magic, the new tech of photogravure was quickly press-ganged into the global promotion of this extraordinarily innovative new way of designing. It helped that Art Nouveau was so photogenic. Intriguing foreground shapes framed a composition where high-contrast combinations of materials made for high-visibility photo spreads in periodical interiors supplements from Kyoto to Kettering. Within months, international Art Nouveau burst into being, arguably the first instantaneous global style.

Talking of which, back to Maximalism, which was made for Instagram. Made for and made by Instagram. Compared to Minimalism's smudgy tonality, overall *meh* colour palette and sheer lack of visual excitement, Maximalism is super photogenic. Dense, colourful and unashamedly patterned. Maximalist posts are easy to like – which is why they are liked in their hundreds of thousands. But it's not just kerb appeal with Maximalism, Insta also celebrates an 'I did this and I did it my way' attitude at its core.

Authorship and individuality, coupled with drop-dead aesthetic intensity. Who wouldn't want to Insta the hell out of their Maximalist home?

DRESSING TO THE LEFT (OR THE RIGHT) – POLITICS AND MAXIMALISM

I know it sounds weird but despite Maximalism's inclusive and generous positivity, it has found itself, and indeed still finds itself, on the wrong side of politics. It's important to remember that Maximalism only become a democratic possibility in Britain following the social and manufacturing revolutions of the 1750s. Other countries took far longer to make High Street Maximalism viable. It has been all too easy for anti-Maxers to retrospectively weaponize the fact that Maximalism was historically an all-too-visible symbol of *yah boo, I have and you have not*-ness. And there's no one who was around at the time to put forth a decent case that was properly pro-Maximalism. Apart from me.

As we've been discovering, there's a world of Maximalist difference between the aggressive, conspicuous consumption of a Medieval warlord using bling like a bludgeon to subdue his peasantry and the cuddly, comfy Maximalism we love today. For those cursed from birth, with a chip on their social shoulder, anything vaguely schmancy betokens class. The problem with class is the inescapable assumption that one class is better than another. Which they're not. They're all equally horrible.

Maximalism hit the headlines when British Prime Minister Boris Johnson and his partner Carrie Symonds (quickly renamed Carrie Antoinette by the wagging tabloids) redecorated their flat in the Prime Ministerial residence on Downing Street. With the help of Maximalist torch bearer and uptown decorator Lulu Lytle, the Johnson *nid d'amour* was treated to a thorough and probably joyous dose of Maximalization.

I say probably because the Johnsons – rather foolishly – refused to invite the British public in for a nose around via the glossy celebrity organ that is *Hello!* magazine. That's where the problems began. Not seeing the wallpaper (reputedly charged at £700 a roll) or the opulent curtains, the suite's rattan furniture and the footstools in the shape of the ceremonial temple boots worn by Indian elephants, everyone has imagined it to be far worse than it almost certainly is. Meanwhile, 'let them eat cake' and 'fiddling whilst Rome burns' played constantly across the lips of nay-saying anti-Maxers smearing Maximalism with an ill-deserved and irritatingly predictable upper classdom.

Instead, the focus should have been on the exciting possibilities of presenting cutting-edge British design, in all its bat-shit eccentricity and buzzy creativity, right at the august heart of British government. Let's not forget, it replaced previous incumbent Theresa May's distinctly wet-cardboard, high-street, modern scheme, unimaginatively bought like a display home package deal from John Lewis. But Brits are monkeys for stirring it, when it comes to class consciousness. They even cut the head off a king just because of his overt Maximalist tendencies. And that was 150 years before the copycat French started me-too royal decapitations.

Charles I was short, flimsy and stuttering. He only became king because his far more rubicon and robustly healthy brother Henry turned out to be not robustly healthy enough to fight off a deadly dose of typhoid. Charles was a deep thinker. He was passionately spiritual and mystically attached to the arcane concept that God had specifically decided that he, little tiny Charles and his spindly royal beard, should be king. Charles was also deeply interested in art, architecture and design. Good for him.

Britain in the 1620s was just about as far as you could get from the dazzling glamour of Europe, where the sizzling comet of Baroque style was blazing a firework trail of sparkling gorgeousness at the very height of its ascendancy. Britain was muddy, beige and bolshy.

Charles concocted a quasi-religious belief that the God who ordained him as king would be best celebrated through the creation of a magnificent court made even more magnificent by the best art, the finest architecture and the most superior design.

This was Maximalism with a halo and very different from just shopping for the sake of showing off. Although, I suppose, his shopping was kind of showing off to God. I'm not sure God was particularly impressed. Certainly, there were those among his subjects who were deeply pissed off to see cartloads of continental paintings and gilded altars turning up *chez* Charles.

Charles I was absolutely dreadful at reading a room. He didn't clock that half his country was enjoying itself with a disapproving fundamentalism that made Puritanism look jolly. Charles, in his satins and his silks with big bits of imported Baroque covered with soft porn and cherubs, looked to them like he had enemy written all over him. And a dotted line with 'please chop here' across his neck. Which is just what they did, after eleven years of hideous self-destructive civil war.

Someone who got political Maximalism spot on was Napoleon. But then he did have a great team. The Empress Josephine was sophisticated, cultured and had style so surgically keen she got just about everything she did, said, wore, cooked, grew or built absolutely perfectly sharp.

But Napoleon's genius was trusting architectural duo Charles Percier and Pierre Fontaine to do the grand stuff – the nationally impressive, culturally important stuff. In their hands, desiccated Neo-Classicism became a style of enormous energy and (this'll surprise you) originality. Just when the world thought there was nothing left to squeeze out of Romanity, Percier and Fontaine revivified the high Imperial style of the Caesars and made it totally Napoleonic. It helped that his personal shoppers could follow the conquering French Army across Spain, Austria and, most importantly, Italy, filling their Emperor-sized shopping cart with the very, very, very best bits hand-picked from 2,000 years of European culture.

Napoleon's Maximalism had a dizzyingly controlled curation behind it. Splendour was made more splendiferous by areas of relative un-adornment around it. Whilst the look was unapologetically power-heavy, Napoleon's domestic politics were surprisingly enlightened, enshrining anti-slavery, anti-racism, women's rights and unprecedented levels of tolerance for the personal upstairs habits of others in his legal system. He just wasn't very good at sticking inside his own borders.

The Maximalism of today is of democracy, eco-responsibility and gender-neutrality and is fully Wokeahontas-compatible.

Born at around the same time in the twentieth century, Socialism and Modernism marched hand-in-unmoisturized-hand. As a style, Modernism was only too easy to politicize. With its aggressive unloveliness, it became the perfect kryptonite lid to imprison society in an inescapable Proletariat forcing-jar, squishing the juice of ambition and the pith of betterment out of every poor soul, to make a social pâté of grey, taste-free conformity.

The big joke about the way Modernism got used as a political battering ram by the tyrants and despots of the twentieth century was that when they got home, the same despots wanted their home to be Maximalist. Modernism, the great and ghastly leveller, obviously wasn't going to cut the mustard for the domestic decoration in the homes of the Ceausescu, Stalins, Khrushchevs, Castros and Maos. Modernism was never going to be a power look suitable for a power player.

A footnote in all this is Moscow's subway system. Despite Russia's chillingly humourless espousal of Modernism as the go-to Marxist style, Russia's mid-century municipal stylists decided to really get their Maximalist freak on when confecting the subterranean splendours of the underground. Like Old World ballrooms ablaze with chandeliers and glistening mosaics, each station seems to bow under the weight of its heavy hanging ornament. But these aren't palace interiors for cosseted Tzars. Among all the sculpture, paintings and opulent oom-pah-pah, shuffling office workers in macs the colour of Lowry landscapes were allowed a momentary bask in the sunshine of unapologetically over-adorned Maximalism. But only for a moment.

True, there is a rather off-colour Maximalism embedded deep within the politics of the 1980s. The sheer grandiloquence of designer curtains and the polyglot palette of disparate patterns sucked all oxygen out of 1980s interiors, and sure looks a lot like Maximalism. But there's no heart in its Thatcherite excess. In fact, worse than that, Power Rock Maximalism was an overt expression of success at the expense of someone else. A rather nasty Trumpian triumphalism. People got crushed under those shoulder pads, and the ozone layer is still paying the price for all the lacquering required to achieve a party-at-the-back, gravity-defying, achy-breaky mullet... I had left a few lines to sell you the political idea that the Maximalism of today is a Maximalism of democracy, eco-responsibility and gender-neutrality and is fully Wokeahontas-compatible but, bollocks, I've run out of room.

KITSCH MAXIMALIST SRIRACHA

Back in the olden days, when good taste reigned supreme, people would laugh at the strange, lumpen and gaudily coloured objects that common people kept in their homes. Childish gee-gaws with more than a whiff of Woolworths about them, they betokened an absence of education and a dearth of taste.

Plates printed with kittens or Elvis. Or Elvis and kittens. Anything onyx, anything ormolu. Crochet, rattan, lampshades with a frill. Palm tree prints, pineapple ice buckets and plastic flamingos… For previous generations, any one of these items would be strictly verboten by the Taste Police and would precipitate more eyeball rolling than a whole football team of freshly martyred martyrs on a Baroque altarpiece.

But these days, each and every one of those resplendently tasteless items makes a Maximalist's taste buds water. I am particularly excited about the Elvis and kittens plates.

Is it because we actually *like* plastic flamingos? Has our generational taste become mysteriously aligned with *The Golden Girls*? Or is it far more knowing, far more kinky? (Oooh, but don't we *love* kinky?)

In fact, it's confidence.

Maximalism has given an entire generation *cojones* of such bright shininess that they feel more than empowered enough to face down the bullying behemoth of ghastly good taste. In fact, we've all come to value the chilli heat that kitsch will bring into our Maximalist collections.

TEA WITH
A DUCHESS

A slut-drop name-drop: the late Duchess of Devonshire once had us LLBs over for a sleepover at Chatsworth House, which – as the world knows – is a repository of museum-grade treasures. And Duchess Debo, as well as being one of Britain's foremost duchesses was, far more importantly, a Mitford.

The Mitfords were an aristocratic clan that, beyond any other family, made the twentieth century bearable thanks to their wit, beauty, brains and filmic antics. Back to Debo. Rather than receive us surrounded by Canovas, Renaissance masterpieces or wall-to-wall Chippendale, we kicked off the weekend in her study which is where she kept her most prized and loved objects.

And these objects of duchessy desire? A large collection of Elvis kitsch and masses of mass-produced chickenalia (she was passionate about her hens).

CATHERINE

THE GREAT

Goddess in a man's world

Now, confusingly, Catherine the Great's real name wasn't Catherine. Or, indeed, Great. As the last reigning Empress regnant of Russia, her Russian subjects knew her as Ekaterina, but her parents called her Sophie. She wasn't Russian either. She was born and brought up in a small and rather tatty minor principality in German Pomerania run by her small and rather tatty father, the prince.

Before Catherine, Peter the Great took a look around at how the other kings ruled and decided Russia needed to move on up. Heavens, this was the 1690s after all. And so Peter decided to spend time hoovering up as much useful information as possible on the rules of modern rule during a hilariously incognito trip to the major royal courts of Europe. Disguising 6-foot-8-inch Peter as anything other than

6-foot-8-inch Peter was a significant challenge to the fancy dress-mongers of the day. Yet his royal recce stood him, and his subsequent reign, in good stead.

Unlike Europe, where the ballet of royal succession was choreographed to a pre-ordained tune, Russia was more likely to make it up as it went along. Also, unlike Europe, Russian rulers had to actually be popular. It wasn't really enough that your dad, the king, might have had the job before you; you had to prove yourself to be a crowd-pleaser or else the crowd would do exactly what it pleased with you and your broken, bloodied body. Peter was a tough act to follow.

The years after Peter's death were chaotic. The succession bounced all over the place for years until it settled on Peter's youngest daughter, the formidable Elizabeth. She had no children, so she settled the crown on a nephew called Paul who, you guessed it, had been married off to little Princess Sophie of Pomerania.

As a wedding present for the new in-laws, Sophie changed her name to Catherine or Ekaterina. At last, Catherine takes centre stage and my, she's a hard worker. She grafts at heir-to-the-throne-ing. She learns Russian, converts to the Orthodox Church and mounts gushing campaigns of girlish schmooze to woo anyone and everyone. Her charm offensive is victorious over all – apart from her charmless and oafish husband, Paul.

Following the death of Aunt Elizabeth (who knew she was on the way out and forbade the word death to ever be uttered), Paul became Emperor, and Catherine, Empress.

But underneath the doll-like drag writhed a powerful intellect and a fierceness that sparked a flame of loyalty in the hearts of the gold-braided, fur-hatted, commanding military men that surrounded her.

After a mere six months under the new Emperor (who still played with toy dolls and lost his rag with everyone), the more thoughtful factions at court clubbed together and decided to lose Paul and put Catherine in her rightful place.

Catherine had absolutely no legal, moral or constitutional claim to her husband's throne, but what she did have was a fabulous sense of timing and complete mastery of *mise-en-scène*. As her troops left the palace to oust Paul, she suddenly appeared at the head of the column wearing a super sexy uniform and riding a bucking stallion like it was a Harley. She had serious sass. Paul fell and was discreetly dead within the year.

Catherine got the gig on merit, no question. And she kept the gig for 34 years by sheer force of will and her personality.

For the Russian people, the muddily oppressed millions, she was a Mother, a Madonna, a Fairy Queen who led her troops into battle and cried when she saw the plight of their serfdom. For the court, she was undoubtably the best man for the job.

Catherine led an incredibly Maximalist life and that's before we even consider her mega-Maximalist architectural record. With all the money in the world our Catherine started building, converting, knocking through and fixer-upper-ing predecessor Peter's rather low-slung suburban Classicism. Taking a style lead from the prevailing taste for Louis (mainly the XVIth, but it didn't really matter), Catherine's real estate swelled until its wings had wings and its boudoirs occupied their own zip codes.

Everything shimmered in shades of pale gold and verdigris. But even the latest Louis could only fantasize about the oligarchic riches she had at her disposal to furnish these enfilades. Suites of rooms panelled in Baltic amber, gorgeous green malachite, blue John, porphyry or – the most lavish of all feature walls – super-expensive porcelain.

Catherine had a very robust taste for the erotic. It has been opined that she was in the habit of making sure her private chambers were fully stocked with porn, just to keep the eyes of her young cavalry officer lovers firmly on their driving. Particularly as she aged and thickened.

Which brings us to her most Maximalist achievement. It's a difficult choice to make because this minxy Maximalist owned so many contenders. There was the Wedgwood dinner service, named 'the frog service' due to the emerald-enamelled frog motif, numbering 944 pieces of world-class porcelain – the *sine non ultra* of table settings. There was the Amber Room, plundered by the Nazis and lost after the war (although now recreated by the Russian government, at the cost of millions and using enough amber to kickstart a million Jurassic Parks). Or there was the world's first outdoor roller-coaster, erected at the heart of a magnificent Chinoiserie amusement park, lit by 50,000 coloured lanterns and sound-tracked by the court orchestra. Oh, and then there's the small matter of Russia's national collection of loveliness, known as the huge and seemingly endless Hermitage museum, whose shimmering exhibits were all assembled by Catherine. But no, it's none of these exemplars of excess.

Catherine the Great's most Maximalist moment was the suite of hard-core porn boudoir furniture that she kept in her most private chamber. It leaves nothing to the imagination. The sheer craftsmanship and cunning that envisioned proudly triumphant genitalia as table legs, seat backs or foot stools is a hilariously knowing and fabulously fitting testimony to this marvellous monarch who achieved so much and, above all, knew how to have a laugh.

SHARING IS CARING – MAXIMALIST ENTERTAINING

Of course Maximalism is the party style. Even a Minimalist is going to push their measly, grey boat out when entertaining, thereby edging slightly closer to a state of Maximalist grace. Slightly.

The first element to get right is not how you entertain, but why. What are the motives that propel you to throw open the doors of your Maximatorium and invite others to share your Maximalist feast? The right answer is sharing. (The wrong answer is showing off.)

That said, there's actually nothing wrong with showing off for the sake of showing off. Done well, it's performance art. Done properly, it's performance art that really doesn't need an audience. It's all about showing off to the one person you want to appreciate the showing off, and that person is you.

Showing off under your own steam, on your own terms, is being an extrovert with the volume turned up. Doing it (whatever it may be) for attention works. Provided you're actually worth the attention. A good example would be wearing hi-vis, which carries a burden. If you're going to be extra-visible then you need to be worth looking at. Something I'm forever reminding builders and traffic cops.

But showing off to meet a criteria not of your own concoction is a soulless and tragic waste of space. Taking on somebody else's measurements of worth and inflicting them on yourself… Well, that just opens floodgates for every conceivable incarnation of low self-esteem, like Modernism, Minimalism and a heightened interest in collecting postage stamps.

Nearly all the anti-Maxers I've met are appallingly insecure about themselves. It's why they became Modernists in the first place. They are drawn to a way of living that has code at its core. It means they don't have to pester their own fragile morality to decide whether something is good, bad, worthy or unworthy as there's a concrete orthodoxy that does the job for them. So when their doors open and guests arrive, they've got an in-built tick-list of status indicators they will do their utmost to get recognition for. How sad.

What's even sadder is that that's why the guests are there in the first place. As witnesses, auditors, validators. Not revellers but valuers. We've all been to those parties and we've all left as early as we could politely leave.

So, back to the original question. Why entertain? If not to show the world how cool you hope you are, then what? Sharing, as I say. To share what you have, without promoting its value or status (but importantly, celebrating its worth to you).

When a Maximalist entertains, they do so specifically to share with others the surprise and delight they get from the world. The Maximalist maxim for any Maximalist fête should be 'We're here not to celebrate me but to celebrate us'.

The first thing Maximalists will want to do is make their guests feel welcome and very much at home. Putting people at ease is a wonderful Maximalist trait and comes from a place of tremendous self-security.

I leave to you the schmancy details of what cocktails to serve and how to arrange your rare or endangered nuts in decorative bowls, but as a Maximalist host (I've been around the hospitality block a few times…) let me share some of my entertaining hints and tips.

Put yourself in your guests' Manolos. Ponder, for a moment, how they will react to being face-to-face with your Maximalist largesse.

Think about where they will sit and what particular views or vistas they'll have of your Maximalism.

Consider a special edit of your knick-knacks. Think about whether there are specific things that might chime with the particular interests of your guests. Move them to the fore.

Conversely, weed out anything that might have uncomfortable associations for a guest.

Relax. Ensure that as the door opens, you are completely at peace with the evening's arrangements and entirely focussed on seeing your guests.

Set the tone from the get-go. I like my guests to find themselves walking into a wall – no – a cliff face of celebratory music and heavily heavenly-scented candle smoke.

Don't let the food take over. A Maximalist do can be quickly ruined by a high-maintenance menu. There's something rather too try-hard about being an Aga martyr simply to show off your culinary artistry.

Conceive the revels so that you're present for as much of them as possible. Nothing upsets guests more than absentee party hosts as they will start feeling guilty about not helping.

Remember, your guests are there to spend time with you.

When it comes to aesthetics, as always with the enlightened and evolved philosophy of Maximalism, the glory details are up to you. Hey, I know of a super-Maximalist couple who once threw the most extraordinary dinner party which had a Minimalist theme. Terribly amusing. The food was deliberately sparse and the booze trickled like it had prostate issues. The possibilities are endless.

When a Maximalist entertains, they do so specifically to share with others the surprise and delight they get from the world.

One of the joys inherent to Maximalism is the sheer quantity of stuff from which you could choose to create spectacular effects themed to express your hospitality. Now is your chance to raid the shelves and muster such surprising and diverting items as unusual vases, surreal candle stands, Baroque napkin rings, amusing place-card holders or something bat-shit crazy to serve the potato dauphinoise in.

Surprise and *delight* are your watchwords for the event. You may very well be inspired to set up your feast somewhere surprising and delightful – or deeply unconventional. There's something intrepid about being invited into not often visited parts of the home, like the upstairs landing, the attic, the front garden or the bathroom. Imagine the sheer novelty of laying on a spectacularly memorable off-piste entertainment in the priest hole. One of my favourites.

Don't forget to extend the unusual to the dress code. Unwieldy fancy dress can quickly become inconvenient after the initial entrance. Anything based on a large cardboard box with holes cut out for limbs will be difficult to steer at an intimate supper party. A Maximalist do is all about comfort and ease, so deliberately setting the tone by insisting your guests wear garments in which they can recline goes down brilliantly. But do stress that by *comfort* you're not anticipating leisurewear or towelling. Instead, gently steer your guests toward the opulent luxury of kaftans, djellabas or silky pyjamas – perhaps with a *femme fatale* turban to top off the effect. Pyjamas are every bit as glamorous as they are comfortable and come with the added excitement of high-risk fastenings that could leave the wearer decadently exposed without the slightest warning. Lush.

My heart slightly sinks when I'm told an evening's revels are to include games. I'm not a team player. Besides, elegant and surprising conversation is without doubt one of the most important constituents of a Maximalist do. However I concede that there are those for whom a party isn't a party without games. Do, however, keep them simple and sedentary. Anything that takes a lot of explaining or a lot of running around may run the risk of fracturing the golden glow that settles on the company after booze, food and witty conversation.

The exception is Sardines. Nothing eclipses the near orgiastic excitement of cowering in the inky dark of a remote laundry closet as fellow guests blunder backwards and forwards trying to find you. And when one does find you, the thrill of sharing so small a space is often so intense, it's borderline impossible to keep oneself to oneself.

By the same token steer clear of high maintenance 'entertainments'. Anything that requires the celebration to stop, sit up and pay attention runs the risk of derailing the organic enjoyment that's doing a jolly good job of making the evening swing under its own steam. There's nothing worse than needy tumblers or attention-seeking fire eaters tugging at your sleeve when you're in the midst of a fascinating conversation about yourself.

Let's talk table talk. Of course, the grand scheme of things is up to you but please allow an old roué a few constructive suggestions. Nothing says *ta-dah* more than a spectacular table. All that nonsense about not judging books by their covers is a very modern construct. Throw *everything* you've got at the table. Make it fit for the Queen of Sheba, Cleopatra, Abraham Lincoln, David Bowie *and* you. Hold nothing back in its creativity, opulence and louche luxury. Then serve everyone fish and chips from the takeaway, still in newspaper.

I like to use every last piece of dining accoutrement I own, even if there's no plan to serve snails, lobster or sheep's eyeball. It just looks so spectacular to have rows of cutlery, obelisks of table glass, pyramids of flatware all sparkling and scintillating in the dancing light of myriad candles. Meanwhile, I love the sense that the table has been laid in accordance with the type of *haute etiquette* only a very few Romanov duchesses know by heart (and *they're* dropping like flies). There's nothing more fun than driving a celebratory tractor through all that formality and deliberately drinking Coke from your Marsala glass, port from your Coke glass, using your fish knife to flick peas and your pea fork to flick fish.

My final word will be the most useful to you. There was a big innovation that swept dinner parties just before the Georgian age got going. It was the newfangled practice of serving courses one after another, in a set, orchestrated pattern. It was called *service à la russe*. I'd like to introduce you to the dinner party convention it replaced, s*ervice à la française. Service à la française* meant that *everything* you were about to eat was on the table as you sat down. The table was a fabulously indulgent still-life of food, wine, flowers, crockery, silver, candles, skulls (optional) and some extraordinarily figurative erotic napkin folding. It rocked. It is, without doubt, my top tip for making a Maximalist meal to remember forever. Cheese, bread, meat, fruit, salad… all gorgeously and artfully spread down the centre of the table for your guests to pick, chomp, flick, throw, roll into a little ball and thoroughly enjoy themselves with. It has its own built-in entropy so there's no tidy-up time required. Just let the whole Baroque ensemble gently and decadently get picked at by your finger-licking guests. And, too, enjoy the fact that you, their beneficent party giver, is not popping on a pinny every three minutes and anxiously dashing into the kitchen to check whether the butler has ruined the soufflé.

DÉJEUNER SUR L'HERBE

One word: *effort*. Making your life far more complicated than it need be, doing fancy for the sake of schmancy, refusing to be cowed by thoughts of practicality, suitability or doing the washing up: that's Maximalism, my friend.

Dragging dinner down to the end of the garden when you've got a perfectly serviceable kitchen table (usefully positioned between the refrigerator and the dishwasher) is the exemplar of Maximalist philosophy. But that extra, often superhuman, effort instantly enriches the experience.

Everything in your life should be an affirmation of how lovely things are. Even the ordinary moments. Even the sordid, naughty, dirty bits. Yes, even those, when pursued with commitment (and one eye on the styling) should be opportunities to celebrate life. There's nothing in existence that should be written off for its ordinariness or disposability and food, which can bring such pleasure, always cries out for celebration.

Maximalists throw everything, including the kitchen sink, at their lives for the simple reason that they know they're worth it.

And the most Maximalist you can be when it comes to *al fresco* dining? The onomatopoeia of picnic expresses its informality and, well, pickyness while a *déjeuner sur l'herbe* is dinner on the grass with all its fuss and glory. The point to be made and proven is that there are no lengths to which a Maximalist party giver won't go to, to make the moment magnificent. An ordinary dinner party at home is one thing, but the sheer joy of taking your landlocked dining room into the embrace of the wild is off-the-dial Maximalism, for sure.

Maximalism gets a lot of its impact from its sheer bloody-minded ability to exist in the most incongruous of contexts.

There's so very much ★*Ta-Dah*★ to be had from setting the table as far away from its habitual surroundings as possible. Back in the bad old days there'd be a cohort of oppressed servants to do the work for you but the fact that *you're* the one to have transported crockery, flatware, linens, table, chairs *and* wind-up gramophone yourself proves one thing. Love. Love of life, love of your guests, love of the moment and the sheer love of doing things love-ely.

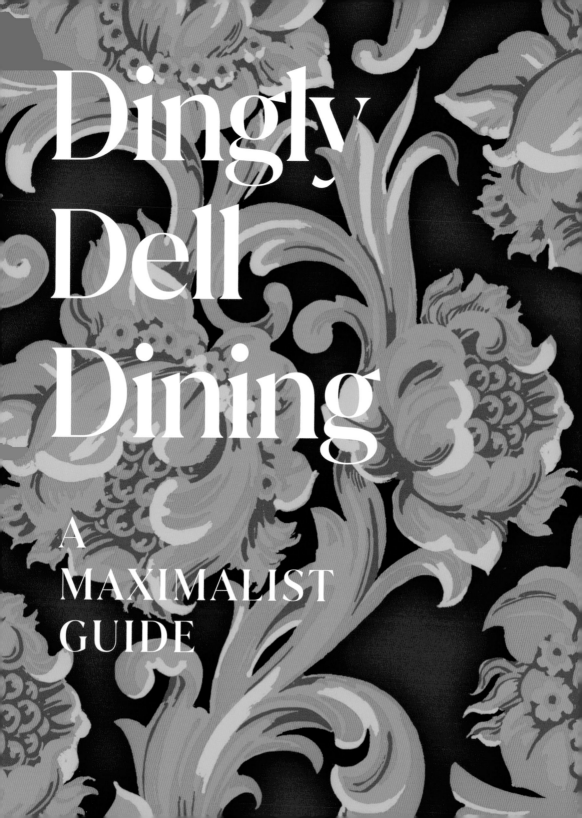

Dingly Dell Dining

A Maximalist Guide

- Do use gingham sparingly.
  In the *Wizard of Oz*, even
  Dorothy's Auntie Em only
  used it as an accent.

- Don't be too table-tidy.
  Allow all the constituent parts
  to tumble in bosomy bounty.
  Think Dutch still-life.

- Do drape your way out of a crisis.
  Too much sun, too much rain,
  or an over-lusty shower of frogs
  may be held at bay by lavish
  swagging from trees or lampposts.
  It's so much less urban than parasols.

- Don't dye lambs to
  match your napkins.
  The ewes may get confused.

- Do cool the white wine in a
  sparkling brook.

- Don't serve food that
  may be unlikely to survive
  the journey to the table
  in an Instagrammable state.

- Do be charmed by the surprised
  reaction of the local wildlife
  – and neighbours.

- Don't ever forget to believe
  in fairies.

- Do use shawls, drapes
  or patterned material as
  part of the decorations.
  Should the temperature drop,
  guests can decorously layer up
  and still be fabulously coordinated
  with your aesthetic.

- Do light the way to
  – and from – the table.
  The footpath through the ravine
  that takes you to the ancient city
  of Petra in Jordan is illuminated
  by brown paper bags filled with
  sand, which keep a stubby, lit candle
  upright and shielded from the wind.

- Don't set your table on
  too steep a hill.

- Do make sure you keep an eye
  on how high the tide may rise.

- Don't forget to be charmed
  by how incongruously Maximalist
  having a posh dinner under the
  stars actually is.

- Do remember to love
  every minute.
  Even if you've set up your feast
  in the middle of a highway
  roundabout.

MAXIMALISM AND FLORABUNDANCE

Minimalist floristry is hilarious. I know the Japanese floral concept of *ikebana* comes from a subtle, spiritual place and its traditions are thoughtfully created to inspire insight – but in an all-white living room in St. John's Wood, a designer vase with one budding twig and a droopy chrysanthemum will always look like a satire of itself.

In the wild, nature is exultant and will eventually triumph over all, even the anti-Maxers in their polished concrete Scandi-style coffins. It's that sense of nature's triumph that needs to be brought into the home, not some super-contrived posy of barky stems that looks more science fair exhibit than floral display. Mainstream style has forged a very odd idea of what nature actually *is* ever since Modernism raised its follically challenged head.

Funnily enough, William Morris and the well-meaning but ponderous Arts and Crafts designers of his day were so much more engaged with the glory of nature than any designer the twentieth century has to offer. Morris's printed repeats and stylized blooms all evoke a mouth-watering natural abundance that could only come from a place of passionate respect. A late Victorian middle-class drawing room was a hymn to the might and Maximalist excitement of living nature. The discordant colours, the lush leaf patterns and the unapologetic interplay of textures all conjure a thriving, rather untidy, Victorian garden.

Nature and natural are the two words that have been most overused by designers during the last two decades, but this version of nature has totally lost the will to photosynthesize. A nature where the natural materials at the heart of the design are, in fact, dead. Skeletal remains with no growing left in them. It's nature comprised of pebbles, arid colours, desiccated driftwood and a moribund bundle of twigs in the corner.

To a Maximalist mind, a mass-produced garland of improbable blossoms in garish shades of Chinese plastic, with a generous sprinkle of gluey glitter and integrated fairy lights, gets far closer to capturing nature's bounty.

Let us leave the high street Modernists behind and drill down into what makes a Maximalist floral display most mighty.

There is something about flowers in the home that reminds me of a Mongol horde. It's like the conquering hero decapitating nature and displaying it on a side board. Once the stem has been severed, we all know the head will wither, but in the days that remain to delight, there's doomed and decadent pleasure in its beauty. (Doomed and decadent are very Maximalist tropes.)

The traditional attraction of flowers in a vase was the combination of colour and scent. I've always felt there is a hidden chord that brings slight melancholy to each bouquet: the acceptance of entropy. There's beauty in every stage of the lifecycle of a vase full of flowers. Following the trajectory from budding anticipation through a glorious meridian and then to twisted decomposition takes the arrangement from exuberant Post-Impressionist still-life to Dutch Master *memento mori* within a week.

If the lifecycle of the flower is too tragic, is it right to go *faux*? Of course. Maximalism is the magnificent and assured confidence in your own aesthetic and if that aesthetic celebrates La Traviata-scale floral arrangements of out-of-season exotics, then by all means go for fauxliage. Personally, I find the perpetual state of perfection that cruelty-free flowers celebrate wearing after a while. There's a danger one will take everlasting blooms for granted. The excited contentment to be had from new flowers replacing a past-it posy is like clean bed linen, fresh-baked bread, the first cuckoo of spring and a long-awaited bowel movement all in one.

Although, I'm very much at home with the idea of having the best of both worlds. Keeping a stock of improbably perfect perpetual blooms to stud your arrangements of cut flowers makes the sort of Baroque floristry you see in period dramas quite possible. Boughs of blossom which, straight from the garden, give you 24 hours of gorgeousness before each petal spontaneously commits *ättestupa* all over the carpet.

Consider using dried elements as padding. Pussy willow goes on forever, BTW, or try compositions of photogenic fruit clustered around the vase to dial up the impact.

Plants at home have enjoyed a mainstream renaissance too. Thanks to the cultural revival of all things 1980s, tumbling waterfalls of indoor greenery inspired by malls, waiting rooms and the style-free sets of *The Golden Girls* have all become obsessions in Instaland.

Go big or go home with houseplants. More accurately, go big or get out of my home. Huge palms that look faintly man-eating have an in-built majestic Maximalism to them and there is a strong case for not even trying to keep these nervy, high-maintenance (and super-expensive) exotics alive. Prosthetic palms are definitely the way forward, more than anything because the real thing looks so unnatural in the first place. Committed Maximalists, so adept at owning each and every situation, might even celebrate the fact it's fake by spraying it gold or – better still – copper.

The final word in floristry goes to spring bulbs. My favourite. All the benefits of fragrance, joyous colour and a time-lapse lifecycle that brings a true sense of real living nature into the home. When they die, there's the bonus that they're not actually dead. The minute the flowers have wilted into a floppy blob, the bulb can be planted into the garden for next year.

I have an aesthetic predilection for making miniature (dare I say, bonsai) gardens within my Maximalist displays and using slightly surreal receptacles for the bulbs to thrive in. Soup tureens, tea cups or lichen-y urns brought in from the terrace are all excellent options. After the bulbs go in, a layer of moss hides the soil and budding twigs get pushed in, so as the bulbs bloom the heavy flowers have a naturalistic support.

These arrangements become charming vignettes, little close-ups of nature which can be further enriched with pebbles, bark picked up on dog walks or the discarded, brightly coloured shells of fledglings who've flown the nest.

That's real nature.

HAVE A VERY MERRY MAXIMALMAS

The point of Christmas is Maximalism. Since its beginning, the festival observed on the winter solstice has always been a jewel in the crown of humanity's celebrations. The solstice marks the scary moment when the sun disappears and creation holds its collective breath during the longest night, hoping it will return again come morning. And then return again the next day, and the next and next and next, so that crops may grow, fruit may ripen and the central heating may be turned off.

Such an important day has always deserved marking in style. Most early societies saw midwinter as the point when the stockpile of enticingly edible food was starting to get worryingly low. So a feck-off feast, a Maximalist blow out of all that was in the store cave was the only way to pass the longest night.

And so it was for millennia. The deities changed, but the festival was celebrated in very much the same way. Over-indulgence, tawdry decorations, carousing, far too much sherry, not enough trifle and a traditional family fight.

Which is all quite amusing for those worrying that Christmastide is losing its traditional values.

The less Christmas focuses on mangers, stars and shepherds tending flocks, the more traditional it actually is, and the closer our celebrations get to the way the solstice was marked by our ancestors. Although isn't it wonderful that casual human sacrifice on an oak stump has fallen by the wayside?

Having driven a tractor through the concept of the kindergarten nativity play, let us also decry any attempt those poor misguided anti-Maxers might make to turn Christmas tasteful. There is something hollow and chilly about a double-page spread in some style supplement featuring 'a hip, modern take on holiday decorating'. There is no place for brown paper, jute string, miniature galvanized pails or neon signage spelling out *ho ho ho* at the solstice. If your solstice is to be passed alone with an anorexic cat in a downtown bedsit surrounded by Minimalist euphemisms for 'jolly', then more fool you.

Midwinter is all about lights, sparkle, ersatz opulence and more more *more* of everything. Everyone needs one day a year when more more more is not just allowed, it's compulsory.

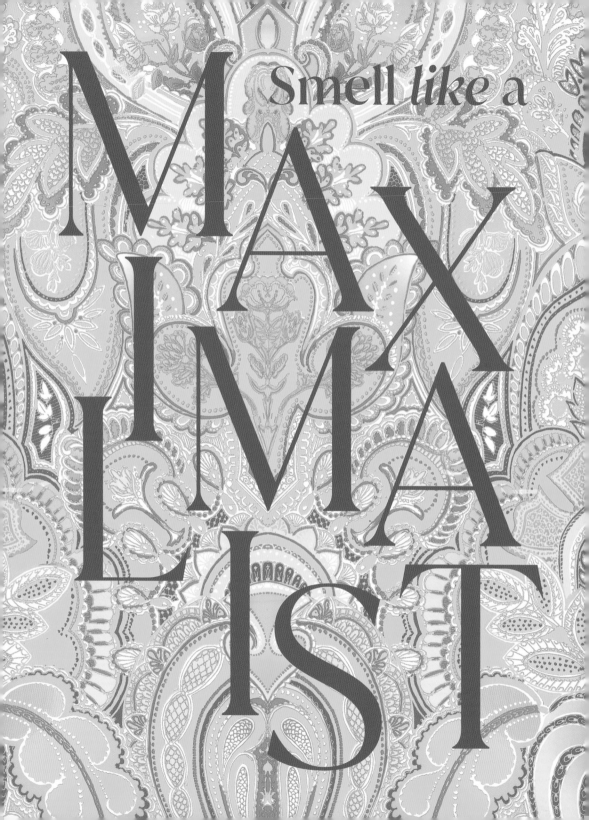

Smell *like a*

MAXIMALIST

Maximalists, being true sensualists, know that what the nose experiences in a room is every bit as important as what occupies the eyes. Smell goes deep into our psyches, and certain scents evoke specific mindsets, so playing the nose for the powerful and impressive organ it is remains an important element in a Maximalist *mise-en-scène*.

There's a whole palette of impromptu everyday smells that it's become fashionable to scientifically duplicate. Fresh laundry, cut grass, baking bread, baby's head, new car… This, friends, is Modernist meddling. These are indeed lovely smells, but what they're *not* is scents. Of course Maximalists adore babies' heads and oven-fresh loaves. It gives me great pleasure watching the gardener mow the lawn and the smell of the back seat of a brand new Bentley is lovely. But I'd swap them all for a sniff of frankincense.

In the spirit of sharing, which motivated *More More More* in the first place, allow me to introduce you to my collection of Maximalist smells that make the most scents…

FLORALS The best florals are real flowers or indeed plants. Bottled rose or essence of freesia often end up reminding one of the unwashed elderly who use perfume as olfactory camouflage (which hasn't been *entirely* effective). The best florabundant smell is, without doubt, the sultry chocolate-laced scent of the Stargazer lily. It's a not bad-looking flower either. For complexity and truly Maximalist delectation, however, I adore the earthy, herby, *vinho verde* smell of a warm greenhouse full of growing tomatoes.

LAVENDER The Romans gave lavender its name because they liked the way it made them smell after they'd been vigorously washed by one of their oiled-up slaves. It translates to *lavande*: to wash. Personally I think it's a crispy, slightly vinegary smell that catches in the back of the throat, but it is the only true antidote to cat wee, which is super useful for cat ladies.

PATCHOULI As a child of the 1970s, patchouli is a perpetual worry for me. It's so all-pervading and bodily, which is why it was overused during the pre-deodorant era of free love. I'm more than happy for a new take on patchouli, but it'll need to clean up its act first.

BERGAMOT Smelling citrusy, or indeed fruity of any sort, denotes a slightly mawkish take on life that most Maximalists should shun. But bergamot is definitely on the acceptable side of the fruit bowl. It's juicy and summery but it's also bitter and fabulously savoury, which gives one the opportunity to smell like the perfect gin and tonic.

PINE Best left to loos and Scandinavians.

FRANKINCENSE Most cultures worth being cultured have singled frankincense out as the smell of the divine. Spicy, sandy and buttery, like a savoury block of halva, the point of frankincense is that it *clings*. It'll hang on silken robes or vellum prayer books with a tenacity that barbecue smoke can only dream of. The ghost of frankincense, the residual phantom that haunts places of worship, makes it a powerfully Maximalist scent.

SANDALWOOD Sandalwood smells in technicolour. It's a rich mid-tone red, with a brownie-like hint of aubergine.

OUD Top of the Maximalist perfume pops, oud is the most mighty fragrance of all. Literally, as it's super-strong stuff. But here's the rub of it, it doesn't actually smell 100 percent nice. Nice smells are ordinary smells. Mainstream high street smells that have a popular ability to smell the same to as many people as possible. The way oud smells can vary between armpit, incense, sealing wax, groin, sweet decay or truffle, depending whom you ask. And, like truffle, it's actually not a very nice thing. Oud is not a fungus but a disease. It's the smell of agar wood that has inoperable gangrene. Maximalism is not, and never will be, about the nice side of life. Maximalism is the skull beneath the skin – it encourages you to see the same beauty in the bone as you see in the flesh. There's grounding relief to be found from a philosophy that celebrates the fact that dark and light coexist to show off the best in each other. So much more powerful than the hysterically misguided optimism of Modernism. Oud is the ultimate celebration of the rich dark alchemy of Maximalism that enshrines everyone's right to their own take on taste and the fact that what's good and bad are a matter of personal choice. I love oud, don't you?

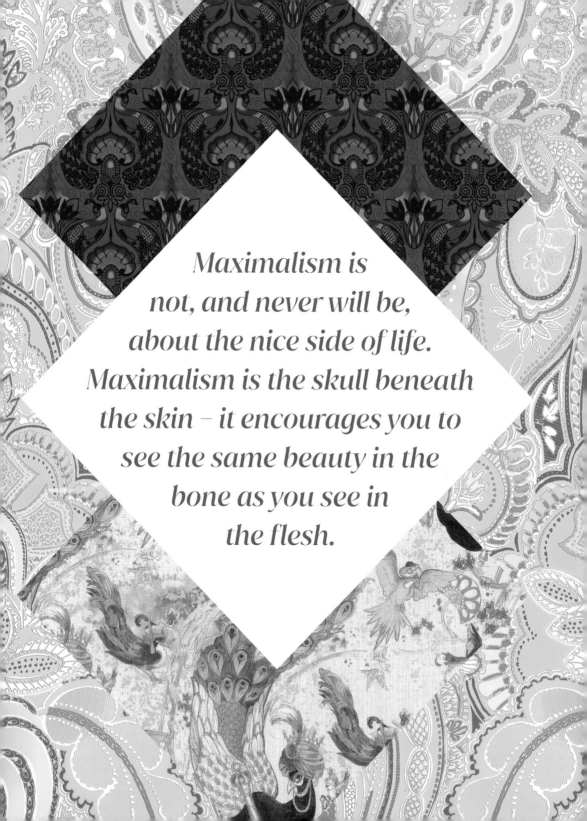

*Maximalism is
not, and never will be,
about the nice side of life.
Maximalism is the skull beneath
the skin – it encourages you to
see the same beauty in the
bone as you see in
the flesh.*

ONCE UPON A CHINGE – BEARDS THAT BETOKEN MAXIMALISM

I'm super-proud of how far gender politics have come and the fact that the noble tradition of beard-wearing is no longer solely in the male domain. Some of my most favourite beards belong to ladies, who are without doubt past mistresses at their maintenance and adornment.

Beards are a funny thing. They're in-out, in-out, shake-it-all-about, throughout the history of civilization.

As they flip-flop into and out of fashion, the statement they make about their hirsute owner is open to varying interpretations. By and large, historical periods of maximal *chinge* seem to coincide with key periods of great Maximalism.

Certainly the Assyrians would agree. Their culture elevated the ornamented beard to heights of oleaginous curlytude. If Assyrian sculpted bas-reliefs are anything to go by, Gilgamesh and friends must have cut the most magnificent dash. Enemies would have doubtless found themselves overtaken with fearful panic at the sight of serried ranks of weaponized Assyrian beards and attendant gnashing white teeth.

The Egyptians (who are, in my book, anti-Maxers) were not beard believers. They were super anti- both body and head hair in general (how Minge-malist). Confusingly, while not actual beard owners, they affected a bizarre fad for prosthetic beards tied to the chin with string. They looked like fat cigars with a slight curl to the end. These faux-goatees were made of plaited linen and became a regal accoutrement worn by all pharaohs. This was handy for the odd lady Pharaoh, like Hatshepsut, for whom biological bearding was out of the question.

The beard makes a most magnificent return to history's chins with Roman Emperor Hadrian. Hadrian was super Maximalist and probably the easiest to love of all the Roman Emperors because of his swanky-pants sense of style and extraordinarily Maximalist palace building. Don't ever write Hadrian off as merely 'the wall guy'. He brought to Romanity an aesthetic stylequake of sophisticated Greek-inspired culture that he knew would be best accessorized with a large and and luxuriantly lush beard. Up to that point, Emperors, clinging to transparent respectability and old-school Republican values, had eschewed the beard as an affectation best left to the jowls of potentates.

Over-excited Jesus-followers who were busy taking what was left of the Roman Empire and fixer-uppering it into the Roman Christian church were also anti-beard. Barbarian is literally translated into beard-user. They were also into the fabulously ridiculous tradition of tonsuring – shaving a perfectly decent hair-bearing man so he looked as if he'd suffered from male-pattern baldness.

Needless to say, no one would claim early Christianity as Maximalist. But Islam was growing apace, and in parallel, and they maintained the beard as an appropriate symbol of fierce dignity. Maximalist centres of excellence such as India and Persia spent long sunny days inventing all sorts of ways to incorporate beads, bows and bobbins into the voluptuous Marcel waves of courtly beards as black and shiny as raven wings.

The Renaissance brings the beard back. It was an era known for great sleeves, hats with curly ostrich feathers, codpieces and big bad beards, all built for feasting, jousting and laughing in the face of your enemy. This Renaissance beard-ism was painted magnificently by Hans Holbein, as modelled by Henry VIII, which made a beard the gold standard for Maximalist chins.

Your hair became a bumper sticker to advertise your politics during the English Civil War which, let's face it, was a war declared by anti-Maxers against a Maximalist elite, headed by the soon-to-be beheaded king. The van Dyck beard was named after court painter Anthony van Dyck (rather than the over-excited, singing chimney sweep Dick) and became a badge of Royalist pride. Despite the fact it always has a rather wriggly, straggly look to it, the big indicator of what side you would fight on remained the flowing Cavalier locks, which defined the decadently doomed Maximalists that stood up to Oliver Cromwell's anti-Maxer army.

In Russia, Peter the Great (actually Peter the Seriously Tall would be more accurate) came back from a tour of Europe with bad beard attitude. His homeboys saw beards as equivalent to particularly large trouser bulges so were appalled to find their Emperor attacking their chinny-chin-chins with a soapy razor and Minimalist zeal. Peter saw clean-shaven faces as an important step on the road to Modernity. They saw it as losing an old friend that kept them warm in the winter and provided snacks of ticks and lice in the summer…

Beard-ism returns during the age of super-sized Maximalism that appears in the Victorian period. Big beards = big attitudes + a lot of judginess. For these citizens, tumultuous waterfalls of grizzled hair falling from the lower half of the face made anyone a Moses or a Merlin. In America, this period sizzles into a vigorous glory far eclipsing Europe, and facial hair becomes fine art. Extraordinarily elaborate grooming routines turn facial hair into *My Little Pony* tails of contrivance and curly glamour. Even remote back-woods cow-folk fall on the creative potential of a beard and develop ways with moustache wax that could mirror the prodigious proportions of their longhorn cattle.

The original Modernists were beardless, while the halitosis-prone denizens of the Bauhaus were all fearful of chin hair's distinctly un-twentieth century Romanticism.

When someone started playing their instrument a tad awry, jazz, in all its contorted glory, was born, and the Jazz Age opens the door to a beard revival. Beards sprouted on the chins of the middle class with the same vigorousness as the wallpapered feature walls spread through suburban living rooms. The tide of the high street Maximalism that swept the 1960s and 1970s spawned an almost Cavalier swagger in male wardrobes. Beards were the perfect signifier of the dawn of glam rock, whose sequinned sunbeams were starting to break the middle income horizon.

As you can plainly see, Maximalism and beards have form. More accurately, beardaphobia has forever been a way of declaring oneself to be an anti-Maxer.

Everywhere you go, the young have embraced the noble traditions of face fuzz with a lusty enthusiasm. There's now a rash of high street beardatoriums to which the youth take their chins for a good stroking and a finishing flourish.

Which must fill us all with shining hope for a happy and distinctly un-Minimalist future for the beards that surround us.

The future
is bright.
The future
is bearded.
And where
there's a beard,
there's a
Maximalist.

ST. HELENA

*Avid collector
of Christianity's
tchotchkes*

The Roman Emperor's purse-first Mom is bustling round Jerusalem like a Floridian matron on a supermarket sweep, picking up as many mementos of Jesus as possible. She has an imperial-sized budget but needs local knowledge to fulfil her mission of harvesting anything and everything she can find that's got the brand stamp of Christianity.

It's not an easy job. Jerusalem is wrecked. Several revolts tried the Roman Empire's patience until the last straw caused the camel's spine to give up the ghost. The Roman army moved in under tough guy Emperor Titus, who crushes Judea to powder (after he's stripped anything of value).

It's easy to imagine Helena, scrabbling over the ruinous

detritus of Old Testament history, shielding her eyes from the sun and constantly checking her fanny pack, lest light-fingered urchins try to sneak out a gold coin or two. A gold coin that would have had her son, Constantine (the Great) on one side and her own, much younger, profile on the other. At this time, Helena would have been close to 80.

Later to become a patron saint of archaeologists, Helena was on a pilgrimage to the Holy Land, although she was finding it pretty complicated to find the five-star locations from the Jesus story. Constantine's predecessors had obfuscated much but, thanks to some Emperor's Mother-scale bossing, Helena hits the jackpot and finds Jesus's supposed burial site, the empty tomb of legend, under a Temple of Venus at Calvary.

Miracle of miracles, literally, when the temple is demolished and the sinful statues and carnal columns are burnt, there is indeed a rock-cut sepulchre which is – wait for it – empty.

Nearby, and rather conveniently, three ancient crosses are buried in a ditch. Then some nasty-looking nails show up, followed by a deluge of Jesus memorabilia that works its way to the surface and into Helena's commodious shopper.

But who was Helena? Saint Helena has three very distinct origin stories. The first has Helena growing up lowly, among cattle at the back of an inn, in the Greekified bits of the

Roman Empire. The second substitutes 'poor but humble cattle herder' with 'bar-room floozie'. Serving flagons with a wink and a whisper. Perfect for the character arc of a fallen woman who repents and ends up sainted. The third is pants-out-preposterous, but has always been highly prized by the Brits: this Helena is an Essex princess, daughter of Old King Cole (yes, that jolly old soul). Helena is already so Christian that local pagan wells cast out the devils that possess them when young Helena dips her bucket. Celtic Christianity always has the best stories.

Helena's next episode sees her meet and shack up with a Roman Centurion who was very much a man going places. One of these places was fatherhood – Constantius and Helena welcome a lusty-limbed son called Constantine.

The Roman Empire is huge and unwieldy, with several million miles of borders that are as bad-tempered and itchy as a vigorous bout of eczema. The current Emperor, Diocletian, is a civilized and vigorous administrator with a good eye for architecture and a reputation for creating more Christian martyrs than any Emperor before or since.

He hit on the genius idea of splitting the Roman Empire up into chunks, each under a demi-Emperor, one of whom was Constantius. Based in Britain, Constantius was a good choice to lead. He was charismatic and looked great in leather at the head of a Roman army as it smashed the ancient Scots into gibbering retreat. Inconveniently, just before he could pick up the Oscar for best battle scene in sandals, he died. His army was high on victory, Scotch whisky and the idea of the House of Constantius, so from their camp in York they proclaimed heir Constantine as sole Emperor.

After a lot of slashing, gouging and impaling, Constantine fights his way to Rome, removes any opposing Emperors and becomes the main man. Along the way he's meant to have seen a cross in the sky and thus the rest becomes RE.

Whatever Constantine's faith journey, mum Helena was definitely a bible-bashing Christian.

Whether this was from birth or a conversion after she escaped her father's grotty pub, her vision was to create the most magnificent places of worship she could, like a series of beautifully encrusted jewel-boxes, in which to show off her astonishing collection of Christian tchotchkes. Helena was thoroughly supported by Constantine who sent out decree upon decree to endorse any building project she thought fit. Helena's building spree led to a rash of lavish churches, some of which were the first purpose-built places of Christian worship.

She kicked off with St. Peter's in Rome, the most important pin drop outside the Holy Land, and churches and monasteries then popped up here, there and everywhere, each displaying the very latest in ecclesiastical architecture and some jaw-droppingly lovely mosaics.

But it's the Church of the Holy Sepulchre, built over Jesus's empty tomb in Jerusalem, that has Helena's Maximalist spirit on proud display. Nearly two thousand years later the original structure has been encased within increasingly ornate churches like Russian dolls, but you'll find a strong sense of this indomitable woman within.

RELISHING
MAXIMALISM

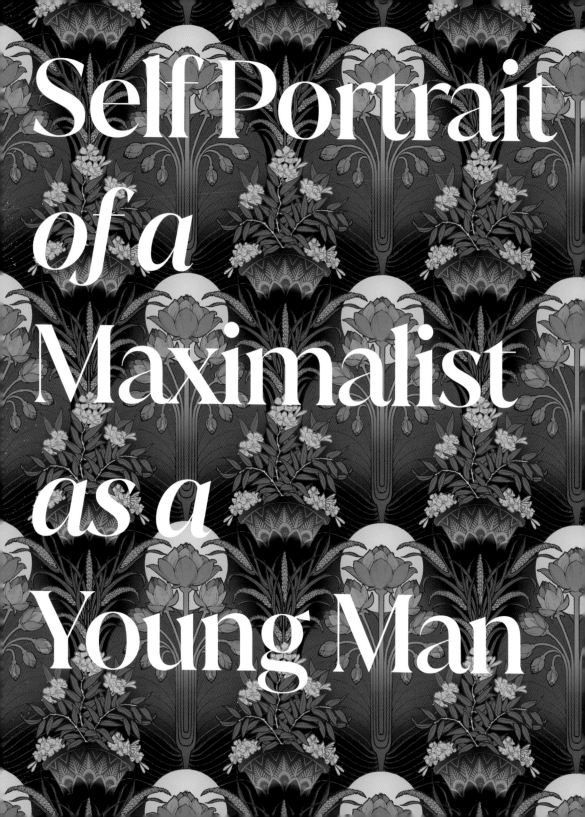

Self Portrait of a Maximalist as a Young Man

WRITING *MORE MORE MORE* HAS RATHER PROVED TO ME THAT MY MAXIMALISM IS VERY MUCH *MY* MAXIMALISM

There's something oddly skewed about the way that, on the one hand, I want it all to flow so very freely, and yet, on the other hand, I simply can't help but give it a nudge in the right direction.

I am, I've decided, a proponent of curated Maximalism. Maximalism that has been induced to go for a jog round the block and do a few star jumps before facing the world.

Weirdly, there's something a bit Modernist in me. I can often see in my work that strange doomed optimism of Modernists who somehow suppose that they can make the world better by making it simpler. I think I may very well suffer from a mild messiah complex that's convinced me I can make Maximalism better by making it tauter. Apologies x.

So where does this strange, conflicted aesthetic actually come from? Looking back, I'd love to steal a literary conceit and say that my childhood was overshadowed when I was stolen from my crib by Minimalists and raised in their Modernist ways. It's actually all far more prosaic.

I know my earliest memory is a memory because I've never seen photographs of my grandparents' house in Newport, South Wales. Soon after the trip that created the reminiscences I'm about to unpack for you, my grandparents moved to a large bungalow near Llandudno with a basement and loft extension, neither of which compromised its status as a bungalow, apparently. But I must have been three or four when the memories of their creepily crepuscular Victorian villa were so indelibly made.

 *Every room downstairs had at least one wall, and sometimes two, given over to the worshipful containment of books.*

The house rose like a brick cliff face from thickets of laurel and rhododendron that, I discovered as I played, were as hollow as diving bells. It was important that the house was high on the hill. Status in Newport was defined by altitude and my grandfather looked down on the docks from which he and his family had been sailing their ships since the 1840s (ish).

I never quite got to the bottom of what cargo he carried out east, but there was evidence all over the house that on the return trip he'd be weighed down with oriental exotica. Flitting from Singapore to Hong Kong and on to Nagasaki meant my grandparents' house groaned under the weight of bazaar-bought tchotchkes. There were an awful lot of ceramics – mostly Japanese Satsuma-ware with that strange, gold-leaf-saturated orangey-brown colour palette that has always struck me as melancholy. Grandfather started off converting some bits into lampbases, with others becoming open coffins for decomposing potpourri. But his retail addiction soon got the better of the list of cunning uses he contrived for these ostentatiously overdecorated objects, leaving the majority to be displayed as function-free ornaments encumbering most flat surfaces in the house.

As a child, I was the right height to be face-to-face with the deeply carved decoration of the many treacle-coloured chests congesting the house's narrow passages. There was always something gurning back at me with popping eyes and a tusky grimace. While I found so much of it overpowering, I do remember the fairy-light delicacy of the way the distant landscapes were carved. Intricate pagodas and lattice bridges with the most minute matchstick people going about their minute matchstick business.

Grand luxe Victoriana added another layer of undulating carving. I loved tracing the contorted shapes with my chubby fingers. And I remember so very clearly my mother's exasperated dismissal of it all as dust traps as I did. Which made me worry for the safety of my fingers.

And that's all to be expected because home in London could not have been more rigorously opposite.

The rooms were large but practically empty compared to the dark carved excess my grandparents had cocooned themselves in. Interestingly the house was high on a hill (I don't think my mother could escape the snobbery of altitude that easily) but instead of the Lowry-esque grey industrial prospect of Newport, the views we commanded were aerial vistas of the leafy parks and stolid suburban streets of south London stretching to the hazy horizon.

Built in the late 1930s with the occasional nod to the taste-free diet-aesthetic known as Stockbroker Tudorbethan, the house was large, square and saved from squatness by an unnecessarily steep roof pitch.

Occasional, rather panicked applications of architectural detail in a faint-hearted Arts and Crafts style were treated by my parents with reverence. But the odd beam or red-brick fireplace surround aside, all I remember are endless white walls between glossy white fitted bookshelves. Books furnish a room, my parents said, in a slightly self-satisfied tone. Every room downstairs had at least one wall, and sometimes two, given over to the worshipful containment of books.

Their taste in furniture spoke more eloquently than anything else of my mother's rebellion against the home that she grew up in. Unusually for the time, my parents bought antiques, to the consternation of their friends who were all hip-deep in Conran. These antiques were expected to be as polite and unadorned as possible, and to have an ability to take polish until they shone like conkers, while not denting the acres of don't-judge-me sage-green carpet with their brass castor feet.

So with all this politeness and dignified restraint the sudden intrusion of a sofa and armchairs fresh from John Lewis came as a shock. The concession that had been made to the gentility of my parents' sitting room was that the William Morris golden lily fabric that covered the new arrivals had been sourced in colours that were but anaemic shades of their former selves. Even in its chromatically reduced state, the unrepentant decorative muscularity of Morris's hothouse fantasy seemed indecent. Fabulously indecent.

Don't, for one moment, pity me my childhood. In all the usual origin stories I should have been aesthetically scarred by the forced understatement of the home I grew up in. All the while taunted by exposure to the overt Maximalism of my grandparents. But it wasn't like that at all. Yes, the house I lived in was plain to the point of a comfortable suburban Puritanism but the childhood was warm and secure despite the buffeting it later got from disease and my father's early death.

What it did do was heighten my visual appreciation for big design when it crossed my path. Hence the clear memories I keep of my grandparents' house. It was a bit like being kept in a state of aesthetic clinical control, like a visual Petri dish, uncontaminated and ready to rock. So when I discovered the 1970s and the style overload that era brought with it, I was as receptive and as easy to seed as agar gel.

Despite their strait-laced appearances, my surgeon father and teacher mother had a wide range of really very interesting friends. You could always spot my parents at a party: my mother in hat and gloves and my father in a suit and bow tie, while around them swirled a fashion bacchanalia of boho that was best bought from Harrods. Long-haired men in denim shirts with a shark's tooth on a chain around their indecently hairy neck. I don't think I ever saw my father's neck. Women flowed in envelopes of Op art printed silk, their hair falling in cataracts from paisley scarves worn as Alice bands. They were all architects, graphic designers, anaesthetists, society dentists or restaurateurs. I think they found my parents charming survivals of a bygone age, the 1950s transported to the 1970s.

The houses were large, either Victorian buttress rectory types or open-plan too-much-glass modern. And the furnishings oozed a high-ticket, too cool for school sophistication. Looking back on their asymmetric picture hangs, floor-to-ceiling Sanderson curtains, conversation pits, cantilevered chairs and all-white kitchens, it's like the sun shone brighter and for longer then. I've never forgotten that in the 1970s glamour smelt of cigarette smoke.

I've always been quite diagnostic about what I like and why I like it. So quickly I wanted to find out how these Venusbergs were created. An architect friend of the family took me to Osborne & Little, where I nearly passed out from the rarefied atmosphere pungent with Chelsea set design.

I discovered Biba. By then, this once-great retail totem of revivified Hollywood glamour was setting into a *Hollywood Boulevard* sunset of debt and litigation. But walking through the doors of the Kensington High Street *Wunderkammer* emporium, where you could buy everything from Biba baby clothes to Biba baked beans, still defines in my mind the intense theatrical pleasure that buying stuff can release on the endocrine system.

It was during a trip to buy handbags with my mother at Simpsons of Piccadilly that I fell head over heels in Maximalist love with the work of David Hicks. His design style became the quintessential definitive of 1970s international jet set elegance and in this 1930s Modernist department store he'd created a series of retail interiors of deep dark chocolatey allure.

He'd also just failed to become a TV makeover star when he'd blown the entirety of his £200 budget on putting a dado rail in a Birmingham front room. The show's presenter, incredulous to find nothing else had happened, no colourful reveal or *ta-dah* transformation, was curtly told by Mr. Hicks, as he drew deep from his ivory cigarette holder, that now Mrs. Housewife had a dado rail she could get on and pick the colours for herself.

The growth hormone that took my Maximalism to the next level came from the cinema of the late 1970s and early 1980s. Punk had evolved into an extraordinarily Baroque hybrid style that revelled in its traditions of shock and anti-bourgeois aggression but combined it with levels

I suppose that
the library of style
detail that clutters
up my imagination
is truly the seat of
my Maximalism...

of historically inspired art directing not seen since, well, the Baroque. It was heaven. Derek Jarman's *Tempest*, Peter Greenaway's *Draughtsman's Contract* and, later on, his version of the *Tempest*, plus Joseph Losey's *Don Giovanni* were all cinematic experiences I still count as über-influencers on my Maximalism.

And in a way, the design neutrality of my day-to-day life helped in the osmotic absorption of what I saw and, most importantly, how it was made.

At art school I flung open my as-yet underfurnished mind palace and allowed the empty bookshelves of my imagination to be filled by art history. From Bronzino to Beardsley I found I was instinctively drawn to the naughty side of art. Much to the horror of my tutors who'd been schooled in the English tradition of still-life compositions in shades of burnt toast, strong tea and Marmite.

After art school: the big wide world. During all of this there was no Road to Damascus moment when I fell from my horse, blinded by the effulgent radiance of Maximalism. Looking back, every day in every way my outlook became more and more Maximalist. Ratcheting up bit by bit. Even when I was asked by a client to provide design in a Modernist idiom. Heavens, I even did Minimalism occasionally. But I'm proud to say my Minimalism was so Minimalist it was actually Maximalist in its Minimalism. But I found designing in a Modernist style easily absorbed, easily forgotten and thoroughly unnourishing.

I suppose that the library of style detail that clutters up my imagination is truly the seat of my Maximalism. There's a cabinet of seriously curious curiosities between my ears that I constantly call on to provide the fuel for the ever-burning boiler that steam-powers my imagination. It's simple: the more data, the better the result.

But there's another deeper event that steers my Maximalism and, rather surprisingly, it's restraint. I need framework, bone structure, intellect on which to hang the glorious panoply of kick-ass Maximalism. For me – and this really is just a me thing – I can't do Maximalism that's got no backbone.

And funnily enough, even after all these years, I'm now even more aware of the fact that beneath all you see in front of you, behind the Cavalier curls, beats a Roundhead heart. A Roundhead sensibility I can't help but thank my proto-Minimalist upbringing for.

VENICE – MAXIMALISM'S CAPITAL CITY

For a city that soaks up words, there's one word never spoken about Venice, and that is *practical*.

That's the point of its knee-wobbling loveliness. Nothing in Venice was conceived to be easy to use, easy to access or easy to operate. Everything is beautifully, almost spitefully, inconvenient.

Il faut souffrir pour être belle.

It's that very spiky inconvenience that caused Venice to come about in the first place.

Welcome to the 450s. Romanity is crumbling beneath the smelly feet of invading hairy tribes with names that mostly end in 'goth'.

The highly civilized central heating engineers, double-glazing salesmen, mosaicists, column carvers and toga-wearing double entry bureaucrats of north-east Italy embrace the inevitable. As one, they abandon the convenient grids of Roman cities and hide in the salty marshes of the desolate Venetian lagoon.

They seek refuge where islets of solid mud slouch sulkily just below heavy sulphurous mists and spiky reed beds that camouflage land and sea alike. Profoundly deep channels alternate with super shallow rivulets in random, impossible to fathom (literally) undulations.

The minute you think you've got the hang of it all, the tide changes and the land and seascape shifts again.

Once they worked out that the clustered muddy blobs in the centre of the lagoon were only accessible to those who knew the way through an ever-changing maze of man-eating mud, they started to build themselves a new city. For these refugees from Romanity, civilization was muscle memory.

But the new city our proto-Venetians embarked upon couldn't be a city of squares and Roman-straight roads. It had to be a city that rose out of the natural world around it. For a start, there's no way all that mud would provide a stable enough foundation for building, so large tree trunks were thumped straight down into the ooze to create a crazy beaver dam of over a million timber pilings. They're still there, 1,700 years later.

When you fly to Venice, always sit on the right hand side of the plane. Looking down, you'll notice myriad irregular puzzle pieces of bronze-coloured brick buildings, each surrounded by its own canal. Each canal is connected to its also randomly shaped neighbours by humpbacked bridges. These individual pieces of the Venice jigsaw are fascinating. They began as individual communities, established by a family unit or two on one of the original muddy blobs (sometimes you can still make out their rough shape). Over time, buildings start to fringe the edges of the islet to create an open space in the middle. These became squares with wellheads at their centres. A church then designates the area as its own parish and an informal market around the well provides a communal economy. Meanwhile, should you want to visit or shop, the bridge or flat-bottomed ferry boat will take you to the surrounding islets.

And thus, the world's most special city is born to a mudscape where no city should ever really be.

The surrealism of seeing buildings – big, tall buildings – thrust through the pellucid mists is shocking enough, but these buildings are like no other. This isn't Kansas anymore, Toto, this is an Oz that Ozymandias would be proud to call home.

At the time, the rest of Europe is busy constructing buildings for defence. Heavy, thick walls, tiny windows, concealed trapdoors through which molten lead or (far worse) poo can be dropped on enemies' heads. In Venice, towers rise and domes inflate. Exotic lace-fine carvings frame repeating patterns of tall windows and loggias flanked by coloured marble columns. Flat facades become ornately patterned playing cards, standing side by side and lining the reflective canals that double the depth of their ornamental geometry. Each different but every one uses the same vocabulary of decorative motifs.

The Venetian lagoon is one giant booby-trapped moat. Totally and treacherously impregnable to anyone who doesn't know it but thoroughly navigable if you happen to be a Venetian who knows it like the back of their Venetian hand. It meant that the architecture of Venice could evolve to do one thing and one thing only: look absolutely spectacularly fabulous.

Tauntingly fabulous, mouth-wateringly fuckulent but, like all fairy cities, just out of reach. It needed no defences – no portcullises or fort-studded curtain walls – as it had the carnivorous lagoon to protect it.

These flat-faced structures, highly and impactfully decorated (many were originally painted with huge figurative murals just to add some pizzazz) are pure surface. The wooden piles and shifting mud would never support a stolid stone Norman keep. However, the delicate grace of a one-brick-thick Venetian fairy castle, hammocked on either side by the walls of its neighbours, worked perfectly. Venetian builders became specialists in building featherlight buildings, like houses made of playing cards.

These stage-set frontages often taper backwards into long wedge-shaped buildings, allowing the whole row of houses to follow the natural curve of the flanking canal. By embracing non-rectilinear, non-classical geometry, a Venetian building is designed as a symbiotic partner to the nature that surrounds it. As the mud settles and the ancient wooden piles moan and groan beneath, Venetian buildings often sag. One window might droop like a stroke survivor's eye. Venetians will use an additional piece of cornice or balcony as visual realignment, basically painting on a new eyebrow to straighten out the building's face.

Venice is spectacularly showy in its triumph. It's incomparable in its victory over all enemies (it really wasn't properly invaded until the Nazis) and its magnificent ascendence over the bitter salt marshes that give it a home. And yet, Venice didn't just survive, Venice started to thrive. From the get-go it was a community, a Republic, with elected administrators and non-hereditary leaders.

Venetian society did stratify, but everybody held close the belief they were all in the same boat. Which they were: a ship of state. The very lagoon that protected the city's back also offered deep-water channels that could debouch a veritable navy of traders straight into the Adriatic and on to Constantinople, that shiny super-mall of luxury shopping.

These channels now bring mega-cruise ships right to the city's heart and the most surreal of all Surrealist sights is a twenty-storey-high floating mall with a theme park slide, seen behind the ornate skyline of an ancient city, where design of such monumentally twentieth-century plasticity would never be allowed a permanent home.

Quickly Venice became the Amazon Prime of the early Middle Ages. The rich exotica of the Orient filled its shops and markets, luring gawpers from the lumpen north (invitation only) to salivate over the inconceivably shiny shizzle that was making Venice super rich.

It wasn't just the merchandise that caused jaws to drop. Style became one of Venice's biggest imports. The quick Venetian eye hoovered up details from wherever their ships sailed and the exotic, the oriental, the fanciful and the fairytale all inspired innovative and particularly Venetian ways of decorating where you lived or what you wore.

Look closely and you'll see genuinely Arab arabesques incorporated into the Maximalist architectural mix of ancient Roman, Egyptian and Greek column capitals and corbels. There are those highly coloured discs of marble within carved stone frames that were regularly sprinkled over Venetian palazzi like blind portholes. They're actually slices of ancient column, cut like salami and integrated into the very Venetian rhythm of the building's bling. It's all there for display, for effect. None of it has a practical use at all, which makes Venice a Maximalist Mecca.

There's a strangely successful realpolitik to Venetian impracticality. There's nothing King Canute about Venetian design. The citizens constantly refined their Maximalism into style solutions that suited their particular climate.

Plaster isn't great in the damp lagoon air, so the art of fresco (murals painted in egg tempera on wet plaster) is abandoned. Instead they start painting with oil-based colours on oversized stretched canvass. It creates a much richer and more atmospheric painting style, immediately recognisable as Venetian.

Rather than Michelangelo-esque big and heavy marble, the best Venetian sculpture is wooden. Thanks to the huge boat-building factories that created a fully operational warship in a day (they did it once, to show off to Henry III of France) there were thousands of skilled wood carvers.

It was noted that large areas of marble flooring will crack as the buildings settle on their piles. So the Venetians revisited the ancient Roman technique of scattering tightly packed randomly distributed marble chips into polished concrete. Terrazzo provides a thousand and one minute expansion joints, which allows the floor to do all the moving it wants without unsightly fissures.

Big holes in the wall (i.e. windows) are a marvellous way of reducing the weight of a building but will be draughty when the wind whips off the Dolomites. Luckily, the state-sponsored glass factories on Murano (housed on their own island to minimize fire risk) learned to provide enormous screens of bottle-bottom glass roundels, held together in a tracery of lead. Technology moves fast and panes of glass get bigger and clearer, allowing whole arches to be glazed in one seamless piece.

Venice invented itself, and like all self-made entities, Venice knew how to display itself perfectly. It was, and still is, all about luxury. No one can do Venice on the cheap. Don't try. If you can't afford it, don't go.

But the art of separating visitors from their money has evolved into an experience of such sophisticated finesse, a real *commedia dell'arte* of elegant extortion. I'm always tempted to give the first version of a restaurant bill in Venice a round of applause before pointing out the handful of plutocratically expensive errors in the adding-up.

From the outset, Venice weaponized design. It invested in the best scenographers to create a city where every giddyingly beautiful detail seduces the visitor into a state of aesthetic intoxication.

Napoleon called St. Mark's Square 'the finest drawing room in Europe'. It still is. But like all old fashionistas, this architectural marvel still keeps one eye on the catwalk. It's never going to totally rebrand and go Modernist (although the Italian Futurists did suggest it before World War I) but this Grande Dame does pep up the family jewels with a few Modern additions. Venetian architect Carlo Scarpa (the only Modernist to truly enjoy opulence) made a few updates to the squarescape, which shine like flashy gold teeth in a full-beam smile of Renaissance white.

Let's face it, the finest of fine arts in Venetian design is deception. Making a ceiling look further away by painting it with an infinite sky and surrounding it with counterfeit architecture. Painting papier-mâché to look like Oriental lacquer. Creating wood that looks like gold. Making paper look like marble or glass that mimics crystal. Making a maid look like a marchioness, a courtesan look like a queen. Or even making a Legoland of bricks, faced in stolen marble, standing on an ancient raft of pick-up sticks, look like the most beautiful city in the world. Which it is.

This is why Venice is catnip for Maximalists.

BUMPING UGLY – A MAXIMALIST TRIUMPH

As we've already agreed, kitsch is the sriracha sauce that brings taste to a new level, enlivening the beige and even giving the vanilla some *va va boom*. Maximalists, being Maximalists, are adept at taking kitsch to entirely new heights of style heaven when they fearlessly turn up the bad taste dial to goddamn ugly.

The way it works is that ugly is allowed to occupy such an extreme state of style consciousness that you are compelled to focus on its aesthetic power, rather than the associations or the baggage it comes with... wow.

Basically stop seeing something as 'ugly' and start seeing it as 'not beautiful' instead.

This is the point where Maximalism comes into focus. The criteria that others use to judge the beautiful, ugly, good and bad are no longer relevant. Instead, the unchained originality expressed through the authorship of a room creates its own intoxicating charisma.

Let's meet Diana Vreeland, fashionista royalty. Literally, absolutely, incomparably the most super stylish woman of the 1950s, 1960s and some of the 1970s. A Grande Dame of such grandeur she was actually fabulously good at not standing on grande at all.

Diana was the antithesis of the cutesy, button-nosed, freckle-faced beauty that America designated as the paradigm of mid-century attractiveness. But then Diana wasn't one of the Borsi-elegant, whiplash-thin, racehorse-faced, super-model mannequins favoured by European couture Führers either.

Diana couldn't be shoehorned into anybody else's straitjacket of beauty, which is something she used throughout her life as a method of propelling her own self-created Diana-ness right to the very top.

Diana became the summit, the pinnacle, the pyramidion of the sheer-sided fashion pyramid erected to celebrate glossy magazine super-style – despite the fact she was, to all intents and purposes, really rather *ugly*.

There were all sorts of stylist tropes that could have been called into play to mitigate Diana's looks. Heavens, a fringe would have gone a long way to take the edge off. But Diana was unashamedly, unrepentantly and joyously *bien dans sa peau*. She windlassed her lacquer-black hair straight back off from her biscuit porcelain forehead and painted the off-centre geometry of her lips in unmissable vermillion.

Extraordinary. And extraordinarily powerful.

We're used to the eccentricities of style mavens like Dame Anna Wintour or the rigid fashion carapace of the late Karl Lagerfeld, but by and large their style choices weren't deliberately or aggressively unflattering. Unlike Diana's.

But what made Diana *Diana* was her repudiation of the ordinary definitions of ugly. She elevated it to something else, something much more exciting. It was anti-beauty.

The sorcery was impeccable. Diana's anti-beauty always arrived born aloft on a body enrobed in such exquisite and traditionally understood beauty. As a whole, Diana was a perfect bittersweet cocktail. The anti-beauty of Diana's head making the conventional beauty of her clotheshorse couture body so very much more intense.

This hymn to DV is actually nothing more than foreplay. I can tell your excitement has achieved the perfect pitch that will allow you to join me in the most blissful penetration of one of the twentieth-century's most powerful Maximalist interiors. There were Vreeland frenemies who were quick to suggest that the decoration of Diana's sitting room had more than a little of the downstairs to it.

You would have walked into a miasma of red. Not something polite and well behaved like dining-room red or tomato-soup red but incendiary, fire-truck red. Diana once drawled 'All my life I've been in search of the perfect red'. Personally I'd give the talon-rouge-red lacquer of her ceiling a solid 8.5/10 in the perfect red Olympics.

Diana's brief to Billy Baldwin, interior designer to Manhattan's style set, had been to create a sitting room that looked like a garden in hell. Billy duly let loose an infernoflage of devilish decorating, that in its teasing sophistication, conjured up a space of the most excitingly unconventional chic. How very Diana.

Giant Mughal plant motifs in blackish indigo (a super-clever pairing with all that vermillion) crawl up the walls, looking like they'd take you straight to a giant's castle or eat you up in two big gulps. Inspired by observation windows in mental asylums, the wall behind the man-eating sofa was made from a large piece of mirror within a theatrical proscenium of rigidly pleated swags in the same pattern.

Opium den overpowering. And yet incredibly invigorating. Diana loved commenting that 'contentment is for cows'. Giving the vigorous wall pattern a 3D dynamic, small gilded brackets with little half-moon shelves were dotted here and there to counterfeit the randomness of nature. Each displayed an Oriental artefact or lacquer tchotchke, specifically chosen for their anti-beauty. An ever-changing cast of chairs clashed in perpetual conflict with each other, constantly refusing to offer up a single aesthetic reason as to why they should ever be thought of as part of the same design scheme. A glorious lack of order was matched in the dislocated collection of warring cushions, each with a different diabolical pattern in yet another shade of red. Inevitably – since this was both hell and a garden – bamboo cropped up a lot. An enormous stuffed buffalo head was hung high on the wall and reigned with toffee-nosed refinement over the operatic excess.

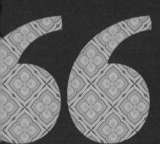 *Diana admitted, 'in my life exaggeration is everything'. There's no getting round it, it looked like revenge decorating.*

Diana admitted, 'in my life exaggeration is everything'. There's no getting round it, it looked like revenge decorating. Revenge porn with tassels on. To a certain extent it was – revenge against a world that crisply prescribed what beauty was and what it was to be beautiful.

Beneath the eye-catching theatrics, there was a steely intellect at work. Diana was one of the first American Maximalists, inspired by Madeleine Castaing in Paris, to use animal print as a neutral. Yes, that most racy, wild and untamed of decorative design repeats became, in the context of Diana's infernal sittingscape, a rice pattern of carbohydrate stolidity.

However, the biggest story was the eternal tale of heaven and hell. What you don't see from photographs is that all of this high-octane anti-taste came as a climax to an open plan, L-shaped space of refined architectural restraint that was drenched (literally) in nail-varnish red. Any claustrophobia one might have felt under the venomous boughs of undulating pattern is banished by the temple serenity of the red room that adjoins it. Clever.

And it was clever, too, that this tastemaker, with her iconic anti-beauty, used Maximalism to create a haven for herself from all that the world called ugly, which made the perfect background for Diana Vreeland's distinctive glamour.

The garden room in hell threw the I Ching sticks of aesthetics up in the air and the way they landed changed style forever. Before DV, ugly happened by accident or from a lack of skill, but she single-handedly rewrote the rulebook of taste, undermining its authority forever.

There's a clang of caution that needs to be sounded at this point. Playing chicken with taste, having a Mexican standoff with the runaway rollercoaster of style like Diana, takes Jedi decorating skills. You need fathomless reservoirs of steel-plated self-esteem and great, great skill to pull it off, but the key element to Diana Vreeland's style, which made it work, was polish.

The woman was as smooth, as shiny and as supremely elegant as one of Fred Astaire's dancing shoes.

KARL LAGERFELD

Maximal Minimalist

These days the lovely Kaiser Karl is currently identifying as 'dead'. But, as we've all noticed, this fashionista supreme being has always been full of surprises and super-good at using tech and medical science for his own glamorous purposes. Karl Lagerfeld did Maximalism in a way no one had dared before or since.

His steel-trap mind and surgically sharp eye swept all before him like he was a barcode reader with a ponytail, scanning every last binary bar detail and sucking inspiration until his brain became as swollen as a blood-engorged tick. Not only was he super clever, he was apparently super funny, with an abrasive wit which he'd use like the rough side of a cat's tongue, smoothing ruffled feathers as soon as they were riled by his whiplash sense of humour.

But the big thing about Karl is his lack of signature style. Now I'm sure there are front row catwalk acolytes who'll click disapproval and try to draw my attention to a particular sleeve detail or seam that's quintessential Karl. But in his milieu, the world of late twentieth-century fashion,

picking a Karl from a rail of Saint Laurent, Versace, Lacroix, Ralph Lauren or Jean Paul Gaultier wouldn't be easy. Although, of course, the joke is picking out Lagerfeld himself from a police line-up of all the aforementioned would be super straightforward.

It's interesting that the essence of Karl had sci-fi shape changing as its most useful X-Man ability. In fact, Lagerfeld's greatest achievement was as an editor and curator of fashion brands that had become almost inert after too long at the top. He was exactly what the House of Chanel needed to re-engineer their stultifying

bouclé box jackets edged in rickrack, which had become fashion-brand straightjackets. His reinvention was all the more clever because of its good-humoured coercion of Chanel style into something amusingly irreverent. The obvious thing to do would have been to punk it up. Karl was much more subtle.

He waved the same wand over Fendi and Chloé. He used the huge success it brought him to stoke the shopping habit that puts him squarely at the top of the twentieth-century's Maximalist tree.

His living quarters went through more quick changes than the Amazonian models shrieking like

parrots as they hurriedly swapped looks backstage at a KL fashion show. In fact, towards the end, he didn't bother making a home over – he'd just buy new. There was a palatial apartment that, apparently, he never actually got it together to see for himself, despite the fact he superintended its lengthy and haute-couture-level fit-out by fax. Don't you miss fax? It was so Maximalist.

Karl did Rococo grand luxe in the country. Isn't it funny that fashion führers seem to be overly fond of museum-like rural retreats where they can let rip with a particularly ornate historical style? Gigantic *nids d'amour* in which panto passions can be naughtily played out among the topiary. Yves Saint Laurent went all Proustian in his Normandy château, while Roberto Cavalli hit his palazzo with the Napoleonic stick. For a style obsessive like Karl, Rococo, which has an implied Maximalist excess to start with, got cranked up to a level of hysterical shell-based schmancy even Mozart might have found giddying.

In town, he'd choose from a variety of different decorating styles, depending predominantly on which town the home happened to be in.

When he bought in Monaco, he went Memphis. This strangely addictive design movement helped define the early 1980s with its Italian panache and sherberty ice cream parlour patterns. Memphis schemes always look like scaled-up dollhouse interiors. The candy crush colours and number-inspired shapes are always presented beneath a layer of brightly coloured sprinkles that, these days, look just a little bit too mall for comfort. But back then choosing sugar-rush Memphis for a home in the capital city of eurotrash was style genius.

But Karl Lagerfeld is one of my Maximalist super icons for one reason and one reason only: he was fabulously good at Minimalism. Karl was one of the first designers to harness Minimalism's laboratory looks to sell fashion with several totally unnecessary noughts added to the price tag. By putting his own KL label schmatta in white concrete polished spaces, stripped of everything apart from aggressive Italian lighting tracks and a floor-to-ceiling piece of mirror, he demonstrated a fabulously buccaneering Maximalism. He knew that the last place anyone would expect to find flighty and essentially unnecessary fashion

It's the perfect moment of design clarity where the literal bests of both worlds come together.

would be in a pseudo-scientific context. It was like his clothes were some kind of life-enhancing or life-extending experiment. Weird science indeed. And wonderfully clever. In a world where designer boutiques had chandeliers and velvet ropes, the sheer perversity of using anti-beauty to sell beauty sets Herr Karl very much apart.

For Karl himself, Karl created a carapace of monochromatic inflexibility. In fact, nothing about Lagerfeld's personal wardrobe was designed to bend and it all always looked like it must have chafed terribly. Maybe Karl needed chafing just to feel alive – Chopin always claimed in his fabulously dandified way that his personal style always had to hurt.

And so it's to Kaiser Karl, the true vanquisher of Minimalism, that we give the victor's laurels. In his astoundingly grand Paris home, just outside super-swanky Neuilly, our Karl created the most extraordinary interiors, all white with eye-catching structural accents of black that can only be described in terms of Maximalist Minimalism. They are chock-full of stuff, but everything is white (or perhaps black), and everything is ordered with the sort of detailed appraisal one only normally gets from double-entry book keeping. The control is extraordinary, so extraordinary it's masterful, so masterful it's god-like. It's the perfect moment of design clarity where the literal bests of both worlds come together to create holy grail interiors.

And as for Karl himself, well, I feel sure he'll be back shortly. There's still so much for him to do.

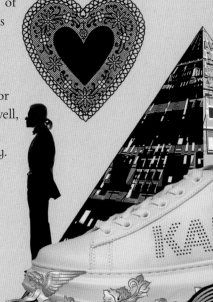

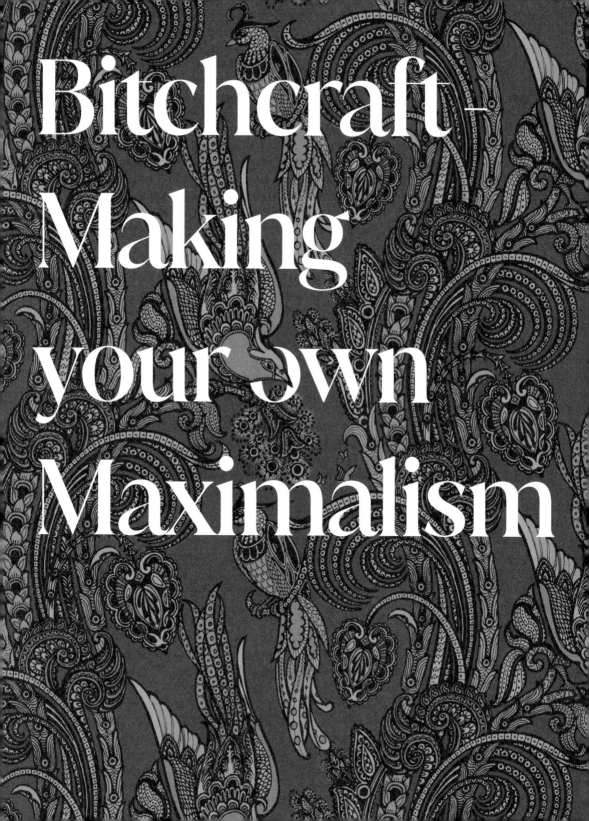

Bitchcraft – Making your own Maximalism

The impermeable divide between the 'pink jobs' and the 'blue jobs', which prescribed who did what in the twentieth-century home, wasn't as historically fixed as you might think. Victorian patriarchs actually became quite giddy with the excitement of picking out carpet colours and wallpaper borders, while the lady of the house (despite being almost card-carryingly disabled, thanks to her outlandishly upholstered gownage) adored undertaking makeover projects involving sticking, gilding and even some dignified whittling.

The point was *not* to score points in the battle of the sexes, but to come together under the jolly aegis of homecraft to create a loving and loved space in which to raise a family. Or unusual ferns, miniature show dogs or – heavens – maybe even a flea circus. The object of the exercise was to show flair and originality (but not *too* much, mind) so that the varied inhabitants felt reflected in their surroundings.

The modern age was tough on home-crafted craft. The mass-produced and the man-made were much preferred by the overbearing, giant-headed men in shiny suits, who were universally believed (mostly by themselves) to know much, much more about what was going to be good for you than you did. And they had long decided that anything charming, quirky or hand-wrought was wrong.

That said, craft with a capital C could be bought from the giant-head-approved craft council outlets, but this was professionally made Craft, created by Craft specialists. Besides, you had to watch having too much of it at home, since a surfeit of macramé might inspire the neighbours to think you beatnik.

Post World War II you could, of course, DIY. In fact you were *encouraged* to DIY. But the point of the DIY was to Do It so it looked like somebody else, somebody properly trained, had actually done it for You. Don't go having your own ideas, whatever you do.

This is the point in history where home enhancement tasks were inflexibly apportioned between the pink team or the blue team. Ladies would never bleed a radiator. Gentlemen might be allowed to do something as frivolous as wallpapering, but only while sporting shirt, tucked-in tie and (optional) furled umbrella.

Decoration is the first indicator of culture and culture is the cornerstone of civilization (*do feel free to have that tattooed*).

And as we've seen, homecraft carried *way* too much pink with it to ever be allowed into the modern home. Craft is surplus to production. A thing is made to be useful, practical and durable (which is a blue job). If it falls into female hands this simple, noble object then receives a thorough pinking which besmirches it with unnecessary, distracting and unmanly decoration. Ruffles, fluffles, ribbons and lace.

Modernism, and particularly Minimalism, used rationality as the rallying cry for the witch hunt they conceived to cancel the culture of craft. And in its stead, they created the frigid cult of the designer object. The name of the maker, the crafter of said object, became a throwaway and unremarkable disposable detail.

The view from our fabulously appointed Maximalist eyrie allows us, fellow travellers, to see with far greater clarity than twentieth-century anti-Maxers. The view we have of the culture of craft is a view that shows it to be the culture of belief.

Our shared ancestress, Jenny from the Rock (meet her on page 10), used what she could make with her own opposable thumbs (something of a recent innovation) as a way to help her contend with the deeply confusing world around her. There were a number of objects without which her life, and the life of the hairy, gnarly litter hanging from her breasts, would become super-difficult. Flint scrapers for separating animal skin from flesh, clay coil pots for water, baskets for berries, pelts worn for warmth: all of these things were made to be useful, practical, durable – but for Jenny they were more than just that. They were precious, they were life-saving, they were magical. Our Jenny just couldn't stop herself from celebrating that magic with a few marks on the pot's rim or a change in the colour of the basket's weave. Suddenly these magical objects were *her* magical objects because she had decorated them with marks that were *her* marks.

Decoration is the first indicator of culture and culture is the cornerstone of civilization (do feel free to have that tattooed).

Nobody made marks like Jenny's and as the survivors from her various litters made it to womanhood, they too started making pots and baskets for themselves, with new marks, ornamented rims and new patterns integrated into the weave. I'd love to think that alongside the marks made by Jenny's daughters, approximations of Jenny's marks survived, becoming part of a decorative narrative passed from mother to daughter. The new side-by-side with the old.

The sharp-thinking among you will have quickly worked out that these marks, with their shared meanings and diagrammatic expressiveness, developed into characters and words and therefore marked the moment that peoplekind start their much over-celebrated ascent. Cheers Jenny.

Fingering the fast-forward button, post-prehistoric communities didn't ever see craft as we see craft. Making wasn't a leisure-time hobby for them, it was a necessity. There's something rather lovely in the idea of make-at-home consumerism. If you fancy a swish handbag like your bestie's, make it out of twigs and vines. Nespresso machine? There's a brook over there and you'll find flints to light a fire on that rock. Obviously you'll be waiting 2,000 years for the coffee plus another 500 for the pods, but it's a start.

Everything you needed, you made. If you were particularly productive and made too many socks, you swapped your excess with neighbours. Socks bartered for with panties, perhaps.

The act of making is indivisible from the act of ornamenting. While particular patterns could be shared within larger groups (there are only so many ways of weaving, after all), particular motifs developed specific meanings to smaller clusters of people. If apples are a major player in your village's five-a-day quota, then stylized apple trees are a decorative shoo-in. Meanwhile, down the road, the dragon that a neighbouring hamlet whole-heartedly believed lived atop the nearby mountain could be expressed as a decorative running stitch. Ornament made the craft into something much more special and - dare it be said - spiritual.

Actually, the same is true today. Maximalists don't take craft lightly. It's not a leisure activity, a way of unwinding after a salaryman's day at the office. Craft to Maximalists sits triumphantly within its own historical tradition as an extraordinarily emotive and powerful element of homecraft that requires immense, hushed respect. Craft, for a Maximalist, is not about making something as a cheap alternative to buying. Craft enshrines the creative ability to personalize an object, which in Maximalist hands is akin to a superpower. Who doesn't love a monogrammed antimacassar or a spindle-turned candlestick that transforms into your grandmother's profile when viewed from a certain angle?

Maximalists throughout history (and remember, before the twentieth century Minimalism wasn't a design style; it was poverty) have used craft to make votive offerings to the household gods. They celebrated history and worshipped ancestors who had gone before by embellishing the objects that had protected them, sustained them, nourished them or kept them warm for generations. By adding their own monogram or symbol to an ever-growing composition, they showed their part in the communal story. A hymn to the beautiful legacy of connection.

So it's easy to see why a movement like twentieth-century Modernism – for whom history is a dark and troubling place full of wildness, fairies and irrational notions such as love – hated homemade. Homemade home craft is a dangerous portal through to a Narnia of meaning and emotion.

And here's where it gets super sticky for the Modernist camp. Homecraft is the historical preserve of that creature they feared the most: the all-powerful matriarch. Modernist man's arch-nemesis. It's no accident that so much of the twentieth century's so-called comedy revolved around the mother-in-law joke. Comedians were mostly men.

Women were priestesses long before men took over as the priests and created bureaucratic pantheons of deities and divided divinity on sectarian lines. The matriarch priestess used the simplicity of everyday abundance to worship their particular hearth and their home. These days it's smaller rituals, perhaps more like superstitions, that are squeezed between the chores, the tasks and the responsibilities with – of course – the career at the top of the list. But the *puja* still gets whispered on the way to pick the kids up from football practice and the incantation for protection is silently intoned every time the front door gets pulled shut and the alarm is set.

And it's in the objects created to embellish the home that the eternal flame still burns brightest, whether they are embroidered, moulded, carved, cast or baked.

SOMETHING FOR THE LADIES – MINIMALISM AND MISOGYNY

We should all be terribly pleased that modern Maximalism has no irritating gender bias. If it has feminine moments, that's because we *all* have feminine moments. If there's something a bit butch in a corner, so much the better. Who hasn't got a butch corner?

Maximalism truly is the stylistic church whose big-sleeved arms are open to all. There isn't an entrance exam or an arcane initiation ritual to undertake. Getting started with Maximalism can be instantaneous. The story that Maximalism tells is the particular story of the Maximalist who lives in that home. It's a story without judgement, without inherited morality and, crucially, without any of those hideously predictable preconceptions of class or gender. Yuck.

It's joyous to know there's a happy ending but, before we get too comfy, I'd like to crunch through the thorax of the twentieth century as it lies decomposing on the autopsy table of taste and revisit just how crushingly sexist Modernism actually was.

It's all too easy to say Modernism looks male. But not male in an Italian-waiter-hairy-chest-tight-trouser-macho or indeed masculine like tall, dark and handsome Bridgerton butch. No, this is male in the steely-grey gaze of the implacable, incorruptible, charmless über-bureaucrat way. The one that won't let you on the flight 48 seconds after boarding finished. The one that won't let you have a mortgage. The one in the hospital room who switches off the machine that goes bleep because… well, just because.

This is purely anecdotal, but the mention of Modernism or Minimalism elicits two separate responses that divide the genders, more or less, down the middle. Ladykind roll their eyes in faintly exasperated amusement at the hubris required to force a vital family home into a Modernist mould. While, in the man mind, visions of perfectly stacked, stored and filed *stuff* dance a seductive dance. A bit like the garage of their dreams, where sparkling chrome tools make patterns of impeccable geometry on white-painted cinder block walls and an acreage of gloss-black garage floor has nothing to do but reflect neon tube lights overhead. Garage porn, indeed.

I admit this is sheer conversational superstition but I want you to know I intend to totally own this generalization while being fully aware it would never stand up in court.

All the things that the social history of aesthetics enshrined as male characteristics bristled in the Modernist vision. Straight lines and right angles are the very maker's mark of man-made civilization. Likewise, the vertical, the erect and the sculpturally heroic all become testosterone-infused tropes of Modernism. Then there's technology and engineering… the closest real blokes are allowed to get to creativity, apparently. They both become clunkily integrated to make the Modernist machine-for-living-in surpass its mechanical potential. Hell, even the way the building was held together became part of the display, as an essential ingredient of the 'haven't I been a clever boy' bragging rights.

The language of design was replaced with machine-shop speak. Flow, function, storage, structure, zoning, interconnection: all words with no pretence at lovely. Hinges were more important than art. Switches and sockets became focal points and objects of desire in their own right. How a cupboard door opened subsumed any thought of what the door looked like.

This was all spitefully deliberate as we've seen, having met the designosaurs of the Bauhaus orthodoxy earlier. They were all egging each other on in a hysterical, weaponized campaign to build a new Modern world order. The Bauhaus were desperate for a social reboot to free the globe from the stifling Maximalism of the bourgeoisie. (Boo hiss.)

The Bauhaus were interesting because they actively encouraged female followers. Grandmaster Gropius himself was adamant that their joyless Modernism should be sexually integrated, available to bore male and female alike. Although, here's where Bauhaus gets busted… The female Bauhaus-erteers weren't building architecture or designing furniture. At Gropius's command, women were there to weave rugs and print pelmets. This new shiny Modernism expected women (despite their mannish haircuts) not to progress beyond the traditional female skills of home crafting at all.

It's worth revisiting the Modernist revulsion for the bourgeoisie, to see exactly what it was about the middle-class home that turned Gropius's aesthetic stomach. It was too comfy, too cozy, too sentimental, too romantic,

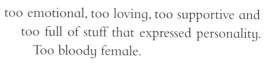

too emotional, too loving, too supportive and too full of stuff that expressed personality. Too bloody female.

The warm comforting smell of stew, the photographs of happy memories, the distracting hand-wrought and crafted decorations that looked far too much like superstitious offerings to ancient fairy folk… All that got in the way of a rigorous intellectual (read: male) appreciation of the building's heroically man-made structure.

As if that wasn't unpleasant enough, there was pattern. Plenty of pattern. Layers of distracting shapes and colours that evoked fairytales, sunsets, landscapes and – worst of all – nature. Modernism hates nature. The pre-modern bourgeois boudoir was a veritable Eden of nature-inspired pattern making and, if possible, nature itself. Plants on étagères and flowers in vases created unrepentant indoor hedgerows.

Walter Gropius's Modernism wasn't merely sexist, it was misogynistic.

The history of the twentieth-century home is a fascinating and scary tale of patronizing somebody called Mrs. Housewife. Mid-century media created this domestic plenipotentiary as an everyman (sexist). She was to be the fall guy (super-sexist) recipient of disembodied plummy-voiced mansplanations of how the modern home made her domestic lot more bearable. Listen hard. You'll hear a desperation behind these announcers' pronouncements, which hints at a fear that all of this man-made Modernity was, in fact, easily discreditable snake oil. Which it was. That's why the Formica was so highly coloured. It was all to distract the easily caught feminine eye.

Today high-street Modernism still perpetuates the male myth that being in control of where you live is far more important than actually *enjoying* it. Homes need to be driven like machines. Homes also need to be a paradigm of modern, man-made materials that will never grow old and never need cleaning. Those materials will also save the planet by being a slick alternative to peskily slow-growing natural materials.

Ever-watchful, you're supposed to keep a close, weaselly eye on the succubus attraction of interior comfort. Cushions can conceal steely mantraps, curtains block out the light, carpets are too soft underfoot and any ornamentation, let alone any *actual* ornaments, would constitute the height of dust-trap decadence.

Meanwhile, the ultimate attribute of the modern male – as they're happy to beardsplain in simple terms – is *business*, and their total mastery of commerce dictates that homes become featureless, homogenized products that are easy to sell and easy to buy, with little effort required in appraisal. Provided you have blinds rather than curtains, gleaming acres of shiny floor instead of carpet and serried ranks of storage in which to imprison your possessions.

Maximalism has no rules. Maximalism has no must-haves. Maximalism doesn't fit trend forecasts or follow fashion but it's no accident that most Maximalists list curtains, carpets and ornaments as key ingredients in their own Maximalist mix. F U, Mr. Modernist.

There's a big chunk of comfort decorating in Maximalism. Flavourful, nourishing, warming and, yes, calorific. But I think that's more than forgivable after the brutal eating-disorder diet Modern homes were forced to endure for a hundred years. Comfort is love, support and a cool hand on a hot forehead alongside a whisper: *it'll all be all right*. It's the sort of love you only get from a mother.

Maximalism is mothering. Maybe Modernists don't like their Mothers? Poor things.

VEGAS –
THE MODERN ERA'S VENICE

Casino is Venetian. It was slick street talk (actually, *canal* talk) to describe a *casa*, a house, in which gambling was conducted amid all the seductive, creamy luxury the 1750s could spread before you.

Before then, betting was a barroom thing. Beery, beefy, blokey. But the Venetians, masters of the art of elegantly separating you from your coin purse, came up with the idea of laying on an immersive and voluptuous environment in which to gamble. They gave players the finest booze, served in Murano crystal. Mountainous all-you-can-eat buffets of picture-perfect *pasticcera*. A welcoming wink from the hostesses with death-drop cleavage and – if you were lucky – Mozart might be playing a residency.

Venice, in a place of too much water. Vegas, in the place of none. And for both, the Maximalist excess they offer comes with an added side slice of *contra mundum,* where the deadly environments that surround them only serve to heighten the hysterical luxury within.

Both use sex to sell. Venice, being Venice, offered visitors a beautifully printed copperplate catalogue with a flowery descriptive paragraph, a price list and a few helpful hints and tips. Vegas has phone booths festooned with calling cards like forbidden fruit waiting to be plucked by anyone wanting a sweet juicy treat. Or there's the internet…

Both use Maximalism as a crucial ingredient.

Vegas's ascendancy starts in 1931, when the US state of Nevada decides to buck prevailing morality and legalize gambling, as well as relaxing the divorce laws.

'The sun will come out, Gomorrah…'

By the late 1940s, the city begins its journey to the centre of Maximalism. Largely untouched by the economic privations of the European war and entirely uninterested in Old World ideas of 'good taste', Vegas shook with a wholly American stylequake.

Interestingly, most of the grim designosaurs who had created the Bauhaus were, at the time, available for architectural hire and living in the US… But the last thing Vegas wanted was *mnah mnah* Modernism.

Instead, the city created an entirely new aesthetic for itself, best described as nuclear. *Literally*, nuclear. The nuclear test zone in the Nevada desert was close enough for visitors to watch, as gaily coloured mushroom clouds rose majestically to fuse with the gorgeous hues of the golden hour sunset. Vegas even called itself the Nuclear City. Catchy. Like cancer.

And where Venice used the delicacy of the Rococo, 1950s Vegas designed for itself a livery of soft squares, splats, kidney shapes and Sputniks, all wrought, not in gilded carving or delicately chased ormolu, but from super-slick, man-made, ICI-generated sheet plastic. Call it blokecoco.

The influence of John Lautner, the go-to celebrity architect for the American cocktail set and the Rat Pack, casts a long shadow over 1950s Vegas. Organic Modernist met the Jetsons. Space Age spaces, jacked up scale, huge vistas, excitingly fractured by full-height screens and dense pockets of indoor tropical planting, all welcomed gamblers to a Bakelite bacchanalia. As more hotels came to Vegas and more casinos launched, an escalating style war started, with different brands offering alternative takes on what 'American luxury' looked like.

Hollywood Regency was made for Vegas. To show itself at its best, it needed enough space for an acreage of shiny floor and enough height to hang mega-sized burlesque draperies with tassels as tall as a toddler. It sold a fairytale fantasy of *mittel* European grandeur (but without too many of those difficult-to-dust twiddly bits) remixed on a Brobdingnagian scale. In its earnest showiness it transformed Sleeping Beauty's enchanted ballroom into an all-night milk bar.

Soon, *style* oozed into *theme*. Rather than simply sprinkle their hangar-sized interiors with injection-moulded *enfilades* of ersatz, in order to evoke an abstract air of fine living, the casinos went full-throttle for literal.

Excalibur, Caesars Palace, Mandalay Bay, the Venetian, Treasure Island, Luxor, Paris and New York, New York. The world spread out at the players' feet, like an all-night Vegas buffet.

The city's super-charged Maximalist era is ushered in by Steve Wynn, who opened the Bellagio with the extraordinarily tidy idea of embedding players into a world of pumped-up, mega-high-ticket luxury as they gambled. All this would be yours – should the slots pay out big-time. It wasn't just sports cars and Louis Vuitton stores, Wynn also pioneered a vogue for campy high culture, opening art galleries to show the bogan would-be-billionaires what Post-Impressionist paintings look like.

Maximalism's too-cozy relationship with not quite whiter-than-white morality is all too gleefully condemned by the anti-Maxers.

Looking back at how the Baroque was weaponized by the Roman Catholic Church as a way to seduce souls, Moderns see Maximalism and the all-too-delicious role it plays in Vegas as a Trojan-horse design experience, glistening on the outside, but chock-full of perdition on the inside.

And I'm not going to apologize for that. Maximalism is all about the glamour. If you look up the word 'glamour' in old Scottish prayer books, it's always used to describe the overwhelming sensuality of evil. But evil is a choice. And the choice is up to you, to decide what you believe is good, what you believe is bad, what you believe is light and what you believe is dark.

I do, however, appreciate that it's easy for me because I'm immune to Vegas. I really don't get excited enough about money to *want* to gamble. I'll meander through all the furore, the flashing lights, the whoops of delight, the waitresses on roller skates, the seniors on oxygen, the ostentation, the grandiloquence, the sheer aesthetic bombast and see it for what it is. Design unleashed, Maximalism unmuzzled, the affirmation that money can't buy good taste – but it can buy an awful lot of densely patterned carpets.

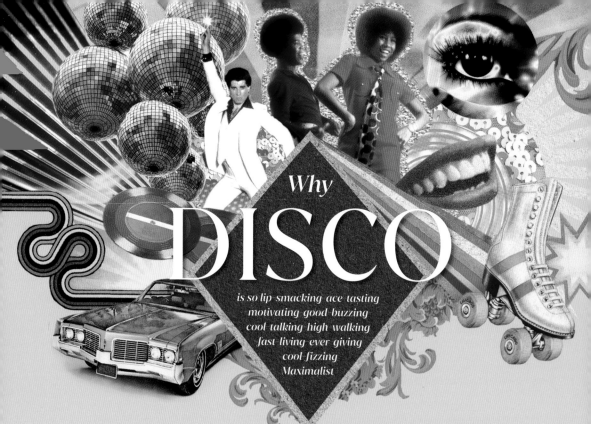

DISCO

is so lip-smacking-ace-tasting
motivating-good-buzzing
cool-talking-high-walking
fast-living-ever-giving
cool-fizzing
Maximalist

Disco is all about the voluptuous, sensuous sense of throwing everything you've got into having a great time. There's nothing pared-back, understated or beige about disco. Hearing a disco beat makes you smile and that's what Maximalism does too.

Maximalism puts a smile on your room's face. It flirts and jokes with you. Like Maximalism, disco isn't about *need*, it's about *want*. No one *needed* the bass, the synth, the wah-wah strings — but once you'd heard it, you knew it was just what you'd always wanted. At its inception, disco was the dancefloor antidote for a popscape wizened by neurotoxin prog rock, heavy metal, hippyish folk and occasionally likeable glam rock. It bounced into the mid-1970s with a sexy sass that swept away all of that, thanks to the sheer size of its symphonic confidence.

Disco is Maximalist to its very core. It gathers you up and welcomes you into its naughty lair, generously be-ribboning you with infinite musical references. It's like everything's been tipped into the disco bucket. Everything is classy, crafted, smoothed and honed to be the best it can get. Disco is slinkily sophisticated.

And it's sexy. Super sexy. Cherry lip-gloss, everybody's delighted to see you sexy.

The best disco records are super clever – that earworm beat is only the start. Many of the top disco producers had thorough classical training, which they plundered to help furnish their soundscapes. Let's face it, Tchaikovsky's 1812 Overture is a disco hit waiting to happen. Melody, counterpoint, *adagio*, *arpeggio* and plenty of *parmigiano* – disco never minded being cheesy.

Above all, the surging, soaring strings were underpinned by a relentless heartbeat bass line.

Like the Baroque period, with which it shares so much, disco escapes the frame. It wasn't just the music; disco is an embodiment of an era when tech joined the creative. The impact that an amplified sound-system and choreographed lighting had on disco's success is unforgettable.

Disco also had the best look. Etymologically speaking, mid-1970s disco style has its roots in the extravagant golden era of Hollywood.

It inspired disco designers to scale the heights of a powerfully glamorous aesthetic. Signature style included flawless skin, big hair, emphatically super-shiny lips, satin, sequins, marabou feathers and shoulder pads. We'll get to what the girls wore later.

The ubiquitous flares and pointy lapels of the decade stemmed from the zoot suits of the 1940s, while graphics, printed patterns and disco interiors flirted with lustrous gee-gaws from the dressing-up box of late Art Deco.

The sound itself often reflects the 1940s too, with the syncopated sophistication of Big Band swing, as well as cheeky references to the Latin glamour of nights out at The Colony Club or the Copacabana…

If I was only allowed one Maximalist thing to take with me to enforced and chilly exile, it'd be disco. Just because it's got so very much in it.

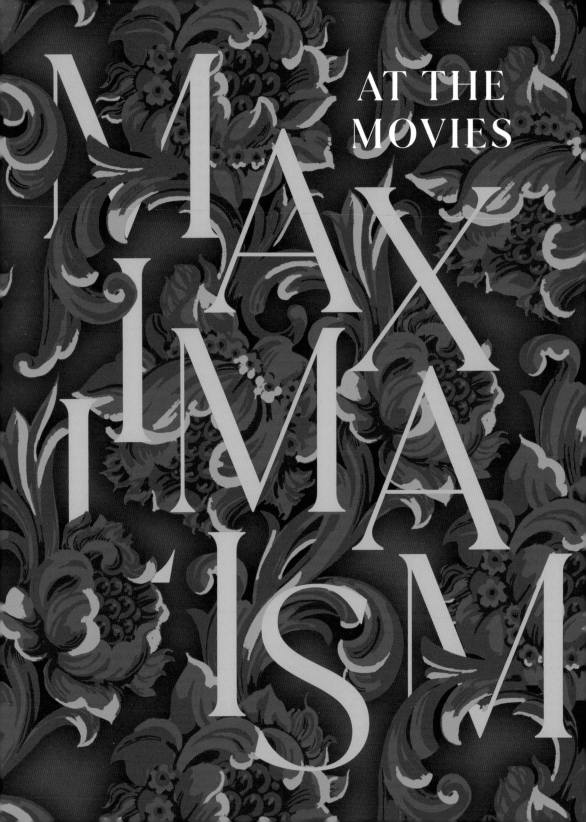

AT THE
MOVIES

MAXIMALISM

By a long shot (actually, by a backlit, dolly-track, long shot) Maximalism's best-ever iteration on the silvery screen goes to… drum roll, as I open the golden envelope… the Bond films.

Yes, Great Britain's only *really* sexy sex symbol is, without doubt, cinema's most Maximalist franchise.

As we've now seen, to be a successful Maximalist, there has to be a suavity in the excess. There's nothing more embarrassingly clunky than self-conscious superfluity. Each and every Bond film manages to generate a cinematic extreme that thrills but that then immediately shrugs its shoulders, turns its back and lights a fag. So bloody cool.

The films have been going as long as me. Based on books written in the 1950s, every film from each of the five decades perfectly pinpoints the particularly Maximalist sweet spot that defined the era. Like Maximalist-seeking missiles.

In the 1960s, Bond films were taut and purveyed a misogynistic elegance that was sophisticated and careless in its violence. The clothes were spare but luxurious. Interiors, inspired by John Lautner's sputnik Modernist aesthetic, were a kinky combination of over-designed Minimalism and improbably priceless antiques. With lots of ferns in polished brass planters. Oh, and shark tanks.

Meanwhile, your ears hit the wall-of-sound backing track like a pair of crash test dummies.

By the 1970s, Bond discovered pantomime and a lot of 'he's behind you' audience participation, which made the inevitable violence somehow bloodier. Bond himself became a member at Club 54 and, in direct contravention of his MI6 origins and SAS training, got a pair of *who flares wins* trousers and a matching silk shirt/tie/pocket square combo. Inevitably, disco hit the mix, bringing another level of Maximalism to all those orange explosions. The villains, equally urbane, occupied surreal lairs inside ruinous Hong Kong junks or Space Age ski chalets, cantilevered atop vertiginous snowy outcrops.

Bond girls in the 1980s were allowed more depth. Not much more – but they could be Russian spies in their own right, provided, that is, that their lips stayed yacht-varnish-sticky and their fringes erect, even after taking off an enormous fox-fur hat. Bond hilariously embraced the safari suit as an

Maximalism is so truly powerful, that even when it's just one man in the middle of a huge screen, he's still Bond: the ultimate Maximalist.

acceptable tropical choice and was even seen with brass snaffles on his loafers. The Bond interiors of the 1980s teamed lashings of taupe suede with some daringly sleek brushed aluminium, reminiscent of the Ford Cortina.

Without an old-fashioned villain to battle, in the 1990s Bond found himself confronting all sorts of big eco-crises caused by malevolent business moguls. It was the era of stadium rock supergroups, so the most Maximalist thing about the soundtrack was how much the band cost. Crazy studio-built sets were replaced by crazy real locations, like the Eden Project or crazy-large real Russia. And in a fashion first, Bond started shopping for his look on the High Street with franchises hoping you'd be inspired to do the same.

After a palate-cleansing break, Bond came back in the Noughties, every bit the violent conflicted loner Ian Fleming conjured onto the pages of the original books. But with none of the glamour. More specifically, Bond was surrounded by glamour, hip deep in it, but he consistently shrugged it off. There's such Maximalist cool in his refusal to be impressed, although one can't help wishing he'd move beyond the 'Dad at the school gates' leisure look, even if the default dress code Tom Ford tuxes and gender-reveal bathing trunks gave audiences a sartorial refresh. Bond girls become dark, fraught and rather draining, while the music, under the fabulous Maximalist baton of David Arnold, becomes the best yet.

The most recent Bonds get even bigger. In a few, even the suits get better. The decision was taken to hang Bond's twenty-first century outings on a perilously stretchy narrative thread that deepened the gene pool of characters. Which is just as well, because the typical Bond eye candy – the swanky hotel lobbies and tropical cocktail lounges – are all gone. Stripped away with a Minimalist aplomb that's sheer Maximalism, leaving a very fighty fellow, often bloody and dusty, shooting baddies with super-big music in the background and orange explosions dimming the sun. And that's it. The Maximalism is so truly powerful that even when it's just one man in the middle of a huge screen, he's still Bond: the ultimate Maximalist (despite the fact he's slightly scruffy, rather dog-eared and a little bit mantique).

THE HIDDEN CHORD
OF MAXIMALISM

More More More hasn't been about *decorating* like a Maximalist because, as I keep saying with honeyed firmness, that is up to you.

But I have been holding back on a piece of decorator's knowledge that I'm now going to share. I think you've progressed far enough to know how to use this interior truth for the good of humankind.

Meet the lovely Dorothy Draper, queen of America's Hollywood Regency decorating scene, who gave the 1940s and 1950s some of its finest and most fun hotel lobbies. She saw the way that twentieth-century Modernism was going and guffawed (she was a *great* guffawer). DD knew that what people *really* wanted wasn't mid-century Modern but mid-century *Maximalism*. In her interiors she pioneered super-sized Disney Georgiana with metre-wide candy stripes, eagles the size of ostriches, palm leaf prints in 50 shades of chlorophyll and circus tent swag-and-tail pelmets. But underpinning it all was… a classic black and white chequerboard floor.

And that is the philosopher's stone of Maximalist decorating: a black and white floor. If you do a Google swoop of sexy Maximalist interiors, make a note of how spaces that set your taste buds a-watering have black and white alternating floor tiles, a black and white rug or a zebra skin on the floor.

There's some optical science to back this up. Our brains can be tediously rational about what they see. They take their responsibility for making sure we don't walk into walls and trip over stuff *terribly* seriously. Sometimes a magnificent and distracting display of high-calorie Maximalism can send our poor cerebellums into something of a spin of over-stimulated excitement.

Black and white, the ultimate negative, provides the mind with a grab bar to cling to, whilst everything settles down a bit. A black and white floor can *literally* earth all that fabulous Maximalist energy. A black and white chequerboard floor gives the brain a high-vis grid in which to place the relative distances and relationships of the fabulously confusing visual mélange that Maximalism creates. It means the brain can breathe a sigh of relief and get on with braining.

MODERN MAXIMALISM –
A DESIGN AUDIT

When super-posh Mayfair night club Annabel's reopened after a £55m refurbishment, everyone was gobsmacked. What was once a Sloane safe space with a lot of politically dodgy, days-of-the-Raj print chintz was now decked out like a tart's boudoir. And a tart who was certainly not out of the social top drawer. It was as if a museum of bad taste and interior design cliches had been gloriously and unrepentantly gussied up into a blancmange of high-kicking snogtastic naughtiness. Heavens, there were even golden swan taps in the ladies' lavatory (the very acme of anti-beauty and the most easily read symbol of more money than class or taste in the history of aesthetics).

Needless to say it was, and remains, a magnificent success.

This was 2018, and although Martin Brudnizki's fresh on the market Maximalism seemed to spring fully formed from nowhere, with hindsight Modernism had been losing its mojo since the early Noughties. There were several signs that middle-age spread was enveloping the once lean lifestyle. As history teaches again and again, youthful revolutions always get decadent by the time they start growing love handles.

Meanwhile Scandinavian-ism had definitely fallen off its oiled ash perch. All that blonde wood and nightmare acoustics had driven design towards finding inspiration in a style that had more to it than skinny-ass bone structure and unpronounceable range names that used ö and ø far too often for comfort.

History helped, offering up for inspiration the American incarnation of mid-century Modern. A school that had taken a deep draught from the wellspring of contemporary Italian design to create – *ta-dah* – Hollywood Regency. Much of the shape, styling, tailoring and detailing was Modernist, but the colours and finishes pulsated with an Italianate luxury that the wives of mid-century American oily-garchs could not get enough of. As a style, it earned its (Regency) stripes thanks to a love of super-sized motifs, loosely inspired by Georgian or maybe Louis Quelque Chose interior architecture.

It was a look Madonna loved, and very soon rap stars, reality stars and LA boutique hotels started casting aside the sepulchral simplicity of Minimalism, welcoming instead Disney-princess crown mouldings picked out in white gold leaf, Chinoiserie, Gin-oiserie, black lacquer panelling and carpets woven with gigantic palm fronds. At the crest of this revived design wave (wearing leopard-print board shorts) was Chelsea's party boy and interior designer deluxe Nicky Haslam. Credit where credit's due: Nicky had never done Modernism. In fact, he had been throwing Baroque bombs and rolling Rococo hand-grenades at his Minimalist rivals for years. He also really knew how to do posh so well, he could do it backwards. Haslam's Hollywood Regency was more like Regency Hollywood.

Less celebrated than Nicky, Ashley Hicks has been diligently refining a craft-based proto-Maximalism that would be the starting point of any contemporary *Wunderkammer*. Hicks's encyclopaedic knowledge of style history informs design that always has at least one limb in the Mannerist past, if not several other extremities as well.

There was a tangible sense of anticipation. The waves were withdrawing from the Modernist shoreline at great speed. The air was heavy, the gulls were silent and then the tsunami was spotted on a darkening horizon.

If there was going to be a fight back against meddling Modernism, there needed to be a design-led vanguard with the right kind of aesthetic authority. Cue the exhumation of William Morris. After Big Bill expired, the Morris style never really died, it just went into suspended animation in plasticized tote bags, under the clinical care of the National Trust.

It took the inspired and youthful style intervention of House of Hackney to re-sanguinate this Brit brand *par excellence*, plumping up its cheeks and turning its design dial up to 11 to make it hip, rather than hip-replacement.

In fact, what Javvy Royle and Frieda Gormley were looking for from their quirky East London-based design brand wasn't really a resuscitated Victorianism, but a revival of the Romantic soft hippy styles of 1970s homes, overlaid with a fashionista-approved colour confidence, all fried up in plenty of kitsch. At its core they enshrined an unshakeable commitment to anti-taste, which quickly got the style sphere salivating.

Harnessing the cult of the influencer and Instagram, the success of their punk rock attitude relied on the use of weapons-grade pattern trebucheted at

Minimalism's now-vulnerable citadel walls. The House of Hackney aesthetic looks sensational at 1080 px by 1080 px. Minimalism simply couldn't withstand the digital onslaught, which is hilarious, bearing in mind Modernism's supposed mastery of technology.

It helped that House of Hackney hit the catwalks at the same time, giving Millennials their first experience of feeling William Morris next to their skin. It felt good, it felt kinky, it felt like they were wearing granny's cast-offs. Which is funny because granny felt exactly the same way when she first slipped into Morris in the late 1960s.

This is when granny becomes a good word.

To accommodate the fact that style journalism had gone digital, design headlines had to become scroll-finger-friendly. What would have formerly been floridly expressed, exquisitely paginated and type-set in a wonderful font, now had to be said in as few characters as possible and genetically modified to grab the immediate attention of an ADHD scrollship. Hence grannycore, cottagecore and cluttercore. One supposes the core bit comes from hardcore, perhaps.

These Millennial-propelled lifestyle labels all share an aggressive anti-Modernity with a love for through-the-looking-glass narcotic nostalgia. For the adherents of these fairytale styles, it's as if the ormolu clock has stopped in your fictional granny's sitting room, suspended in a warm toffee-toned amber. The electric filaments glow orange behind fake plastic coals in an ornament-bestrewn fireplace, nylon lace antimacassars protect the arms and backs of florabundant chintz sofas, and patterns gossip with each other as they undulate over carpets, rugs, walls and curtains. It's a place of tremendous emotion, great love and protection. Three things no one ever said about a Minimalist room, no matter how lovely the granny who lived in it was.

Now, what's so unusual in all of this is the fundamental lack of any serious über-retail brand one could ever call Modern Maximalist. Twentieth-century Modernism formed great commercial alliances with high street retailers and multiple flat-pack merchants, making it the vanilla behemoth we now decry.

But because Maximalism is so dang personal, it's almost impossible to range it, in a conventional sense.

There's a Maximal-list of design houses like House of Hackney, Abigail Ahern, Wendy Morrison, Emma J Shipley and Jonathan Adler, but the retail engine room of Modern Maximalism comes from pre-loved. Yup, Maximalism is coming up second hand rose-y. Thrift stores, charity shops and vintage boutiques are all Maximalist safe spaces, but the biggest player is the internet. And Millennials, who are fabulously responsible and so much kinder than their forebears and forebearesses, love how gentle their shopping sprees can be if their consumerism results in minimal consumption. They are, it seems, delighted when their shiny new purchases are your old, tired throw-outs.

Thrift stores, charity shops and vintage boutiques are all Maximalist safe spaces.

Likewise, craft is massive. Making, reconditioning, reupholstering, hand embellishing, cross-stitching, edge crimping, egg glazing, knitting, crocheting and taxidermy… We've already met the power of craft, and for Millennials craft has become a Hogwarts-inspired spell with which to crank the hands of time back a few decades to an era they believe to be a time of warmth and safety. Plus you get great stuff that's unlike anything that anybody else has got. Or wants.

But, Millennials aside, let's now out Maximalism as the glorious umbrella term under which grannycore, cottagecore, cluttercore, fairycore (yes, really) and all the others shelter. Maximalism, unlike nearly all the design styles that precede it, does not attach itself, limpet-like, to one specific social class, gender, age bracket, demographic, income group, sexual preference or star sign. It also doesn't have rules (other than mine, obvs) or a dress code (although no smasual, please, I *beg* of you).

If I were pushed and had to concoct a typical Modern Maximalist space as a teaching aid, to be used with great skill and understanding in a sequestered clinic for repentant Minimalists, what would it look like? Would it actually be possible with this totally subjective style? I'd need to consider Maximalism's inevitable rebound-aesthetic, which inspires Maximalists to do the very opposite of Minimalist Modernism. The cross-hairs of which settle with pin-sharp focus on pattern. Pattern: the great dissembler, the camouflager, the paper-overer of cracks, the gaudily ornamented succubus that drains righteous Modernist masculinity of its mojo. Pattern is one of the greatest indicators of Modern Maximalism. As is a vigorous disregard of provenance and a joyful disdain of the Presbyterian doctrine of restraint. Modern Maximalists have started to look hungrily up at the ceiling as a largely unused Maximalist canvas.

History plays an important role in a Maximalist psycho-drama. Objects, patterns or colours that can port your aesthetic imagination to other eras were all strictly verboten during the Minimalist ascendancy. Today's Maximalists are indulging themselves with a thirsty appreciation of the old, the second-hand and the retro, showing a gusto to be expected from those who've been formerly parched. The same is true of colour. Social media developed a passing fancy for dark blue walls several years ago – a passing fancy that simply didn't pass. Instead, dark blue paint became identified as the patient zero of the current chromatophilic glamdemic that's painting the world's walls every shade of gorgeous. It's hue-bris of magnificent intensity.

If I had to pick a current exponent, a Maximalisto on whom I would rely to create a Maximalist space of the kind of power we'd need to inspire contrition in our fallen Minimalists, it would be Luke Edward Hall.

It helps that he's a Millennial and, obviously, distantly related to Harry Potter. Hall's work pulls together so much of what Maximalism loves, but he underscores it with a jolly coercion that inspires all the elements to still play together as a team. Like a firm but friendly school prefect. Of all the professional Maximalists for hire, he's the one that's not in any way fazed by Maximalism's bourgeois suburban-ism. In his hands, the exotic tropes, the gilded pineapples and the flamingos become less aggressively kitsch and instead explore a design lineage that takes them back far further than Annabel's or Auntie Rita's tiki-bar cart, to their true origins in the opulence-is-all decorating styles of Regency salons.

Your

AUNTIE RITA

Keeper of the flame

I say your Auntie Rita, but actually, we've all got an Auntie Rita. Auntie Rita is an archetype, a paradigm, and you'll find her everywhere, no matter which corner of humanity you call home.

Auntie Rita is the Auntie that doesn't ever quite fit the family dynamic. Thank goodness. She's the one that turns up at family dos wearing French perfume that's a wee bit too strong and a blouse with buttons that are a wee bit too undone. Auntie Ritas always have the biggest hair, the shiniest nails and the loudest, lustiest laugh. Auntie Rita is the most fun.

If your mum is the Auntie Rita of the family, that's a whole different conversation. I would imagine

you're now squirming with embarrassment, feeling super self-conscious that mum has – yet again – found herself in the spotlight.

But that's the thing about Auntie Rita. All too often she's taken for granted, derided and judged unfairly. In families where nurture rules, Auntie Rita is an unwelcome force of nature. She's the harbinger of high days and holidays and signifies the moment that rules relax, collars get loosened and rugs get rolled back so the dancing can start.

By necessity, those yawning caverns of time to be endured between fun moments with Auntie Rita are about the constraints of responsibility. And where does the responsibility come from? Your family. They're the ones telling you to sit up straight at the table, to not hog the sofa, to brush your hair and tuck your shirt in. But when Rita's around? Rules dissolve. Very much to the disapproval of the rest of the family. In fact, Auntie Rita's rule-breaking becomes yet another waypoint on her Via Dolorosa of the supposed sins the rest of your family condemn her for.

But Rita's rule-breaking is what makes Rita the icon of Maximalism that we all love and adore. Ritas live in homes where personality hangs as heavy in the air as the scent they use with such fabulous liberality. Auntie Ritas love scent marking. They smell, therefore they are. And their homes are mini-triumphs of emotional Maximalism. OK, there's always a lot of feeling in a Maximalist lair, but Ritas make spaces that weave love, lust and sentiment into their very fabric. This is why the rest of the family, particularly those on the polite side, find time at Rita's so tough.

If Rita bought something for the mantelpiece, she bought it because she absolutely loved it. Everyone else is buying things for the mantelpiece because it would look nice. The gulf between love and like could be measured in knick-knacks. Rita's style is the prevailing style of the glamourati, but shrunk to fit and reconfigured for mass production. Classic Auntie Rita decorating vacuums up all the influences from the Hollywood Hills homes of the A list. A community who, let's face it, never shrink from turning the design volume up beyond 11.

When I was growing up, Auntie Ritas had all fallen in love with the soft glow of old rose, which they teamed with red carpet and white-painted, wrought iron occasional furniture that had the dim DNA of an unspecified Louis hidden in their curlicues. Telephone furniture was a

Big Thing – specific pieces designed on which to recline, while having a good gossip. The thing that struck me was that Auntie Rita rooms were friendly rooms because they were so full of faces looking back at you. Auntie Rita art was emotively figurative: a plump-lipped ragazzo with a shiny tear or a heavily chested girl of non-specific ethnology glowing like last night's embers in shades of purple. Polite families (like mine) had maps or landscapes or gentle-hued abstracts. Nothing to catch your eye or engage your attention. But Auntie Rita rooms had faces on

things that didn't normally have faces. Lamp-bases with fringed shades which sprouted from swaying figurines or busts of what Rita referred to as 'dusky maidens'.

Exotic provenance was important to Rita. She may or may not have actually travelled herself (rumours in the family were rife, ripe and risqué) but in her head she was always drawn to the glamour of other worlds and the allure of other cultures. Rita harboured romantic fantasies which were terribly off-colour, as far as the rest of the family were concerned. Rita rooms had plenty of pattern too.

Pneumatic roses were a favourite, as were flock facsimiles of damask repeats with unapologetic abandon and more animal print than an audition for *The Lion King*. Rita used the printed pelts of apex predators with a commitment to, and respect for, the untamed power of the animals themselves.

Auntie Rita loves to take a walk on the wild side.

And the absolute apogee of Auntie Rita-dom had to be a bar cart. Super luxe Auntie Ritas might have actually had a bar. Brick was a favourite, with a few Spanish motifs or Ye Olde English horse brasses. But everywhere you found an Auntie Rita bar, you'd find a pineapple. And it's with the pineapple that the cult of Auntie Rita moves up and beyond kitsch, into a space of far greater aesthetic subtlety.

Unknowingly, Rita was invoking a decorative tradition that goes at least as far as the courts of Louis XIV and Charles II. Resplendent pineapples, whether carved, painted or embroidered, were used as an elegant symbol of hospitality and welcome. Hospitality and welcome? That's Auntie Rita all over.

Despite the shudders of disapproval that Auntie Rita engendered from the tut-tutting, strait-laced side of the family, she did her own thing and ploughed her own style furrow.

Let's face it, Rita was the absolute embodiment of all that the Modernist theorists and Bauhaus designosaurs reacted against. Emotional in her reactions, sentimental in her tastes, bourgeois in her outlook and way, way, way too fabulously female. Just like one of those heavily flavoured, voluptuously sweet and dangerously narcotic cocktails she loved, Rita had the frighteningly elemental power to seduce. While the Modernists and the Modern world did all they could to tame this magnificent shield-maiden of Maximalism, Rita held it all at bay. She kept the flame burning and the tchotchke sanctuary safe until the day dawned when it was OK to have pie-crust edging on your cushions and multicoloured Murano glassware on your sideboard.

That dawn has dawned. That day is now. Your Auntie Rita is Maximalism's Icon of all Icons.

She'd be very proud.

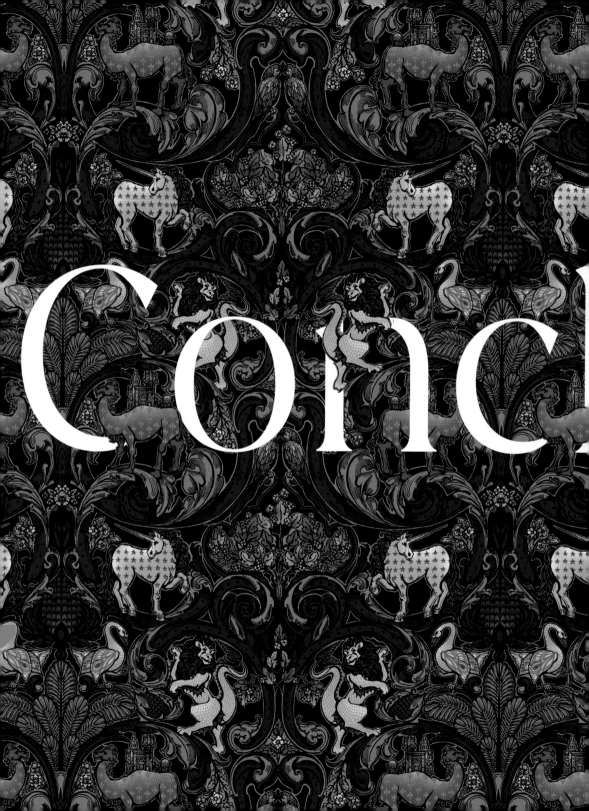

So, apologies if *More More More* has felt like a perpetual diss on Modernist Minimalists. Extremely ungentlemanly of me. After all, it's a big, brave world of design out there and everyone should come to their own conclusions on what their style is. Modernism and Minimalism, which is what happens when Modernism comes into super-sharp focus, are a lot less understanding than that. We, as generous and elegantly evolved Maximalists, forgive them nonetheless.

One of the things I'm most proud of is Maximalism's conciliatory ability to wipe the slate clean and move on from the inherent sexism of the twentieth-century Modernists. Their mistrust of the darkly feminine arts of homemaking, the celebratory display of family totems, home-made craft and tchotchkes with lovely personal stories to tell, made their uncompromising aesthetic unfriendly. And it's thanks to our iconic Auntie Rita, who refused to bend with the Modernist wind, that the glowing torch of Maximalism stayed alight, effulgent within a pink pleated silk shade edged in bobble fringe. For all its talk of democracy, Modernism was frightfully snobbish. The bourgeoisie got it in the neck, which is amusing, since from where I'm sitting I see a world now that is more bourgeois than ever before. More people have a vote, a home, a job, a TV, a pension and a voice. And yet they aren't living in Le Corbusier-approved concrete 'villages in the air'. In fact, the Bauhaus flavour of the future – white-Lycra-clad, man-made purity, in ordered-drone societies and mechanized cities – never arrived. Instead, the future in which we now live is formed by the past, just with a few tech tweaks and a whole heap of much needed sociological integration. The future we live in now is less *Metropolis* and much more *Blade Runner*.

Maximalism is so fabulously right for us, right now. It works for who we are and what we want from our living spaces. Its fabulous flames have been fanned by the digital age, which in itself is so captivating. I love the idea of lo-fi living being so explosively promoted by wi-fi technology. Maximalism's greatest arbiters are the Instagrammers who are sharing their way of doing things. Instantly, it means this design philosophy has incredibly compelling democratic credentials. Maximalism is interior design's first-ever street style. Its most creative proponents aren't designers, but homeowners. Maximalism's shop window isn't a glossy magazine, but the open-all-hours glowing screen of Instagram.

As planetary crisis casts a gloomy shadow across dinner-party chatter and water-cooler gossip, it's inevitable that taste starts to mistrust any design that feels as if it has an irresponsible appetite for raw materials and planet-unfriendly consumption. Thus, Maximalism becomes even more attractive. Reuse, recycle, shop with circularity. Pass one thing on to make room for the new. These aesthetic fundamentals are at the creative heart of Maximalism's design philosophy.

Meanwhile, the clunky hubris of the Modern age's faith in its own technology and man-made science has been exposed for the emperor's new clothes it always was. Actually, nature will always trump nurture, entropy will always defeat technology and growing old gracefully will always be the best way to age. Maximalism takes decay and disorder and uses them as piquant accents in its tumbling, rambling and joyously naturalistic aesthetic. I do feel sorry for Modernists. They must view with horror what they see as a retrograde *volte-face* from future forward to decadent nostalgia… But that misunderstands how design works. Besides, originality isn't a light bulb that's suddenly switched on above a designer's head. All creativity comes from somewhere. The creator's job is to put together their own unique recipe from influences and past experiences and make a creation that has its own never-before-tasted flavour. We are now simply moving into a phase of design where more of the recipe comes from the past. It happens. It doesn't make it less creative or actually less original. Just different. It worked for the Renaissance, after all.

And the final word on Maximalism? Well, it has to be all down to the effect Maximalism has on you. It's an effect that you decide upon. Maximalism accepts the dark, the wrong, the bad, the anti-beauty that modern aesthetic philosophies condemn. It accepts them just so long as you accept them. Just as long as you are happy to own them. Owning is a very powerful word these days. In our digital, text-speak world, 'to own' means to be proud of, to stand by something. Maximalism is all about owning. Owning the stuff that surrounds you, the stuff that gives you pleasure. Maximalism is the art of curating the museum of you.

Should you need inspiration for that butt tattoo you've always wanted, might I suggest:

Maximalism celebrates owning the stuff that celebrates you.

INDEX

PICTURE CREDITS

ABOUT THE ILLUSTRATOR

Martin O'Neill is a uniquely versatile graphic artist who creates mixed-media collages for a range of international clients. His distinctive style evolves from a subtle alchemy of collage and textural elements drawn from his vast archive of self-generated and collected ephemera. His work can be seen across publishing, advertising, film and interiors and has won critical acclaim at the Sundance Film Festival.

ABOUT
THE AUTHOR

LAURENCE LLEWELYN-BOWEN is the O.G. of Maximalism.

In this incarnation since 1965, LLB qualified with a master's degree in Painting before spending a few highly productive years in industry. His classically rigorous Fine Art training informed a highly original aesthetic expressed in a panoply of much applauded public and private design commissions once he set up his own design consultancy in 1990. Always high profile, his work quickly attracted attention and in 1996 the BBC launched *Changing Rooms* in which LLB starred. Overnight, the show became an international sensation. It trebucheted LLB into a global media career that continues to grow alongside his incredibly successful company, whose design projects and branded product ranges always reflect the LLB Maximalist philosophy.

For more information about the gorgeous LLB patterns used throughout *More More More*, visit: **LLB.co.uk**

Penguin
Random
House

Senior Acquisitions Editor Stephanie Milner
Senior Designer Louise Brigenshaw
Project Editors Kiron Gill, Amy Slack
Editor Lucy Philpott
Art Editors Simran Lakhiani, Aanchal Singal, Mohd Zishan
Senior Managing Art Editor Arunesh Talapatra
Production Manager Pankaj Sharma
Jackets Coordinator Jasmin Lennie
Senior Production Editor Tony Phipps
Senior Production Controller Luca Bazzoli
Managing Editor Ruth O'Rourke
Managing Art Editor Marianne Markham
Art Director Maxine Pedliham
Publishing Director Katie Cowan

Text Development Alexandra Fullerton
Copy Editor Sara Goldsmith
Proofreaders John Friend, Elizabeth Dowsett
Indexer Elizabeth Dowsett
Art Direction and Design Studio Nic&Lou
Picture Researcher Emily Hedges
Photographer Ruth Jenkinson
Illustrator Martin O'Neill

First published in Great Britain in 2022 by
Dorling Kindersley Limited
DK, One Embassy Gardens, 8 Viaduct Gardens,
London, SW11 7BW

The authorised representative in the EEA is
Dorling Kindersley Verlag GmbH.
Arnulfstr. 124, 80636 Munich, Germany

Copyright © 2022 Dorling Kindersley Limited
A Penguin Random House Company
10 9 8 7 6 5 4 3 2 1
001–333386–Sep/2022

Artwork copyright © 2022 Martin O'Neill
All patterns © 2022 Laurence Llewelyn-Bowen
Text copyright © 2022 Laurence Llewelyn-Bowen
Laurence Llewelyn-Bowen has asserted his
right to be identified as the author of this work.

A CIP catalogue record for this book
is available from the British Library.
ISBN: 978-0-2415-9045-4

Printed and bound in Italy

For the curious
www.dk.com

MIX
Paper | Supporting
responsible forestry
FSC™ C018179

This book was made with Forest
Stewardship Council™ certified
paper – one small step in DK's
commitment to a sustainable future.
For more information go to
www.dk.com/our-green-pledge